ABOUT THIS MAN CALLED ALI

The Purple Life of an Arab Artist

About this Man Called Ali

Called Ali

The Purple Life of an Arab Artist

AMAL GHANDOUR

ELAND

First published by Eland in 2009
61 Exmouth Market, London EC1R 4QL

Copyright © Amal Ghandour 2009

ISBN   978 1 906011 32 1

Jacket photograph:
Ali between two masters © Diala al Jabri
Text set in Great Britain by Antony Gray
Printed in England by the MPG Books Group

FOR ALI

Contents

	Acknowledgments	ix
	Family Tree	xii–xiii
	Prologue	xv
One	*The Ottoman Widow and Her Nephew*	1
Two	*I am the Last Descendant of Salah al Din*	24
Three	*One Day You Shall Be Queen*	63
Four	*Faded Levis, Biba . . . Mouloukhieh, UAR*	83
Five	*Ah, Ya Hamada O, King of My Heart!*	111
Six	*Don't You Dare Call My Works Paintings*	139
	Epilogue by Diala al Jabri	172
	Glossary	181
	Bibliography	199
	Notes to the Text	209
	Index	237

Acknowledgments

The path of *About This Man Called Ali* to readers has not been an easy one – and perhaps understandably so. An obscure artist, an obscure writer and, worse still, a place and a time fraught with obscurities are not the stuff of great sells. And yet, from that very early thought, which made the book live, it has been infinitely more blessed by friends than it has been cursed by impediments.

I know that had it not been for the passionate advocacy of Hanan al Shaykh *About This Man Called Ali* may well have remained a dream. I know that if it were not for Raghida and Fadi, sister, brother and great friends, I may well have had enough doubts and second thoughts to abandon the effort. I know that if it were not for Sami, the fiercest of critics and yet the gentlest of human beings, I may well have been far too confident of the memoir's chances and too unaware of its weaknesses. I know that Joye, whose advice about narrative is as invaluable as it is about life, made the last few years mercifully less lonely.

Inevitably, however, researching Ali and reconstituting him on the page could not have been done without the generosity and openness of his many friends. I am grateful to all of them, but I am especially indebted to Rula Atallah Ghandour and Antonia Gaunt, an extraordinary woman who left life and us far too early. To the late Ronald Cohen, another very dear man, François Larche and Frank Drake I am also ever so obliged.

I would like to express my sincere thanks to Diala al Jabri for trusting me with Ali and his story. She and I have at times differed in our interpretations of events or emotions or memories but, I suppose, such are the hazards of writing about lives that have been passionately lived and people whose essence insists on many possible explanations.

Finally, I owe an enormous debt of gratitude to my editor Rose Baring in whose very capable hands *About This Man Called Ali* came into its own much like an eager apprentice grows in the care of a great mentor.

Publisher's Acknowledgements

All the black and white illustrations, except where stated, are used courtesy of Diala al Jabri. The same is true of Ali's works shown in the colour plate sections.

We would like to thank Michel Esta for his photographs of *Shajarat al Durr* and *Aqaba Boat*, Frank Drake for his photograph of *Sketch of Parthenon Frieze* and last but not least Jan Kassay, who photographed the rest of Ali's works shown in this book.

The written word has taught me to listen
to the human voice, much as the great
unchanging statues have taught me
to appreciate bodily motions.

Marguerite Yourcenar
Memoirs of Hadrian

Family tree

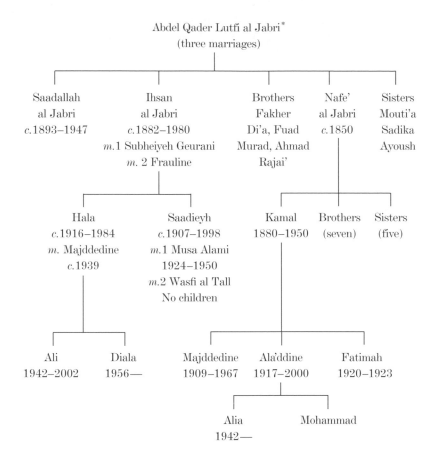

Abdel Qader Lutfi al Jabri*
(three marriages)

Saadallah al Jabri	Ihsan al Jabri	Brothers Fakher	Nafe' al Jabri	Sisters Mouti'a

Saadallah
al Jabri
c.1893–1947

Ihsan
al Jabri
c.1882–1980
m.1 Subheiyeh Geurani
m. 2 Frauline

Brothers
Fakher
Di'a, Fuad
Murad, Ahmad
Rajai'

Nafe'
al Jabri
c.1850

Sisters
Mouti'a
Sadika
Ayoush

Hala
c.1916–1984
m. Majddedine
c.1939

Saadieyh
c.1907–1998
m.1 Musa Alami
1924–1950
m.2 Wasfi al Tall
No children

Kamal
1880–1950

Brothers
(seven)

Sisters
(five)

Ali
1942–2002

Diala
1956—

Majddedine
1909–1967

Ala'ddine
1917–2000

Fatimah
1920–1923

Alia
1942—

Mohammad

---

* Saadallah, Ihsan, Fakher and Fuad were from the same mother.
Three main sources were used: The Jabri family tree, Alia Alai'ddine al Jabri and
Khaldun Kikhia.

Al Jabri family tree

The al Jabri family tree is reproduced courtesy of Hanifa al Jabri

Prologue

Because of the friend in the man, because of the poet in the artist,
because of the eyewitness in the painter, because of the pauper in
the aristocrat, because of his addiction to this land and everything
tragic about it, because of those eyes that could see beauty in the
most ordinary and breathe every manner of colour into the staid,
because of his humanity that seduced the brother in every stranger,
because of those spirits within him that sparred only to make love
again, because of his loud genius and his obscure name, because
of the rich life he lived and the death he should not have died, I
decided to write this book about Ali.

An agonisingly sensitive man hailing from a venerable Syrian
family, for whom the twentieth century was distressingly harsher
than its precursors, Ali was bound to feel the tempo of his history
with much pain and passion. That he was a lover of the written
word and the painted image, that he was such a master of both,
made his insights and experiences and visions all the more inspired
and breathtaking.

Ali died a revered artist to those who knew his work, many in
Jordan, fewer in the Arab world, still fewer elsewhere. He died
virtually unknown because he wanted it so. There was nothing he
loathed more than the exchange of paintings for money. He sold
what he sold because he had to live.

When he passed away, I knew that his was a story too compelling not to tell. Elusive to even those closest to him, Ali sent

enough our way that told of lives and thoughts and talents and dreams and days and moments, all worth exploring, all worth knowing. What he had to say with ink, acrylic and pastel about his own roaming existential pleasures and struggles, about his family, about his Arab terrain, flows in streams of perspectives and interpretations. This book strings together some of these, trying to make this fragmented man more whole, to shake off the dust of time that has made his story barely intelligible.

I did love Ali, and grew to love him even more while researching and writing this book. Parts of him were so utterly imperfect, the entirety of him exquisite. There are those among his friends and family who probably feel I could have been more discreet about certain raw family memories. There are those who probably feel I should have been more delicate about his sexuality, less explicit. I have thought long about this and felt what a shame it would have been for me to deny this man his marvellous identity in death the way circumstance denied it him in life. For decades, Ali went here and there in search of roots, yearning for them, all the while cursing them. Ever since his twenties (and perhaps even earlier, for that I was not able to determine) he celebrated his sexuality and embraced it. I thought, to this peripatetic man and that constant in him, I want to give anchor.

Amal Ghandour

CHAPTER ONE

The Ottoman Widow and Her Nephew

If in that Syrian garden, ages slain,
You sleep, and know not you are dead in vain,
Nor even in dreams behold how dark and bright
Ascends in smoke and fire by day and night
The hate you died to quench and could but fan,
Sleep well and see no morning, son of man.

But if, the grave rent and the stone rolled by,
At the right hand of majesty on high
You sit, and sitting so remember yet
Your tears, your agony and bloody sweat,
Your cross and passion and the life you gave,
Bow hither out of heaven and see and save.

A. E. Housman, 'Easter Hymn'

'She left me a crown of briers.' That about summed it up for Ali – devastating words uttered in a whispery flat tone that carried the full weight of his desperation. Saadieyh al Jabri al Tall, at ninety-one, had abandoned life and him with it. Thirty years of promise – promise of family, promise of security, of love, of meaning – had come to this: 'a dish of thorns.'[1]

Hardly a month after he wept at her death, 'hateful black thoughts and . . . chilling revelations'[2] began to tumble out of her secret bequests. Dear, darling Saadieyh, as Ali used to call her, seemed to have chewed over all her options and decided to leave him nothing, except that small plot of land near her blessed house, the house she had said she would bequeath him. This is Ali's house, she always repeated to her friends.[3] That she withheld from him, in the full throes of dementia, the one gift he coveted most would torture Ali, like so many inexplicable Jabri slights.

*   *   *

On the ninth day of June 1998, three days after she passed away, Ali wrote in his diary, 'In the name of God the Merciful . . . Dear, darling aunty, you've gone.' By February 2002, he will have made many, many references to 'Saadieyh's clammy harassments from beyond the grave'.[4]

The glory of Saadieyh! Immaculacy with a human name. Hair like a soft, perfectly fitting turban, dark eyebrows over hazel eyes, a slim nose, parted teeth between half-full lips, a mild, easily attractive face, sun spots here and there, and fineness so obvious to the beholder it swiftly introduced itself before withdrawing gently to its place.

How could such physical grace share space with so much unkindness?

Who would have thought, back in 1968 when this aunt became saviour to this nephew, that things would turn out this way? Back then, it seemed like such a tidy family affair: a loving, rich, powerful aunt embraces a suddenly fatherless, penniless, unnervingly vulnerable twenty-six-year-old nephew. Ali finds himself a patron, and Saadieyh, childless, gets to play mother, since mummy Hala, well, Hala was never really quite there. End of story!

As with most wishful thinking, theirs never made it out into the real world. Too much pain and sadness intruded. Small tragedies and big latched on to these two Jabris and their closest kin, like those cliché-soaked grape vines of wrath. For decades on end, Saadieyh, her sister Hala, Ali, and his sister Diala mourned sudden deaths, stumbled over piling inheritance problems, and cried over land lost and property taken away. For them everything started out so right and ended up terribly, terribly wrong. In soap-operatic mode, this Syrian aristocratic family, aeons old, through nasty events and wrong turns, became scattered across the Arab world and fell easy prey to even the mildest of foul plays. Perhaps

Ali and his aunt Saadieyh in the Aqsa Mosque in Jerusalem.
Early 1960s

their perch was so absurdly high that feckless fate, in vengeance, had to make their fall unbearably steep.

Towards her end, as Saadieyh finally gave way to decrepitude, Ali could probably trace the decay of this exhausted family in the wrinkles on her face and recognise half a century of dispossession in her fading mind. For a man who toiled to preserve so much of history's heritage, it must have been the saddest of ironies that history would choose to spare almost nothing of his, cruelly eating away at noble pedigree and corroding its pomp and substance. That the fortunes (and fortune) of his Jabris should surrender, over the course of fifty years, to the rough winds wrecking everything Arab and become symbolic of a whole people's descent into irrelevance was appalling to Ali. A family's ruin more by rash, indulgent choice than accident seemed to him the unkindest of legacies to impart to a son.

He was such a delicate human being this Ali al Jabri, son of Majddedine, son of Kamal, son of Nafe', son of Abdel Qader. All his life he struggled under every Jabri burden and in vain pined for scraps of its trophies. All his life he chased after free days only to pay dearly for each one that came his way. He could commit to canvas the sublime and reap nothing for it. He was such an extraordinary talent and yet so indefinable. He tiptoed on the edge of life, indulging very disquieting appetites, all while dreading their temper. He hungered for change the same way he craved stasis, and saw the very hilarious even in the throes of heartache. He romanced so many cultures and wrapped thick Western fibre around Arab veins. 'There was not one practical bone in his body,'[5] but the mind inhaled life around him like a marauding drug addict.

Why would dear, darling Saadieyh, who had seen all this in him, who had known all that was special about him, refuse him that long-promised parting gift of love and mercy?

*   *   *

Habibti [my darling] aunty, please forgive this delay in . . .

Dearest Aunty, I hope you will understand and forgive me for delaying my departure stop My natural feelings make me want to be with you to share your grief and to support you stop but I feel nervous about creating . . . (I don't know whether . . . [6]

December 19 in Ali's 1971 diary is filled with these draft telegrams to Saadieyh. He was practising what for him was the very difficult art of condolence. Ensconced in London, Ali had yet to make it to the side of his aunt, now the grieving widow of a slain man. On November 28, Wasfi al Tall, her husband and Jordan's prime minister, had collapsed in a storm of bullets at Cairo's Sheraton. Black September, a Palestinian group named after the Jordanian regime's bludgeoning of Palestinian guerrillas in the autumn of 1970, carried out the hit. To most Jordanians he died a martyr, to many Palestinians a villain, a traitor to their cause. He was one of the masterminds of 'Black September', and the architect of its final offensive against the Palestine Liberation Organisation (PLO) the summer after.[7] In that macabre war dance between Hussein's Jordan and Yasser Arafat's PLO – in that bloody collision between a Hashemite king's quest for quiet borders with Israel and uncontested authority within them, and a swaggering liberation movement's determination to inflame them and flout him – Wasfi was a fearless anti-PLO agitator. When Hussein wavered, Wasfi stood his ground. When official Arab rhetoric was ritually applauding Arafat and his men as freedom fighters, Wasfi was unhesitatingly referring to them as 'professional criminals'.[8] Long before others were calling Arafat names, Wasfi was shouting them from the rooftops. The son of a Jordanian poet and a Kurdish mother, Wasfi was perhaps his country's most astute politician. Of all the King's men, he was the most charismatic and, doubtless, the most creative.[9]

Exactly one year before the assassination, Ali had written to Wasfi and Saadieyh to congratulate them on the premiership and complain about everything under the sun. In it, he presciently lamented to the dead man walking the thwarted humanity of his future assassins: 'I wish to God the Arabs would join the human race . . . It's just sometimes evil seems to come from the very people who think their cause is just.'[10] Not particularly generous words by Ali, but they were not entirely devoid of wisdom. Throughout history, vengeful bloodletting had bruised the face of every other beautiful cause, disfiguring magnificent features and twisting a glorious spirit into something repulsive. On that November morning, Wasfi was the latest casualty of genuine victims playing pitiless victimisers. 'Justice had been done, one of the hangmen of the Palestinian people had been executed.'[11] With that, Salah Khalaf, the man allegedly responsible for the assassination and one of the PLO's chiefs, justified this abuse of his people's legitimate grievance.

'Are you happy now, Arabs – sons of dogs,'[12] Saadieyh shouted, after she and Fadwa Salah, the wife of the Jordanian foreign minister, rushed down to the hotel lobby and saw Wasfi's body. Later, in a more stoic moment, she whispered to Fadwa, 'We Jabris know how to bear our sorrow with dignity.'[13]

*   *   *

Saadieyh's woe was terminal. When Ali finally reached Amman in December 1971, her anguish was all he could see.

> Late at night. Trees tossing in the wind, inky blackness lashed by storm. Rajia in bed, Wafaa's mother serene in her chair, auntie absolutely desolate and beyond consolation, closed in on her herself. Suddenly, the king [Hussein] arrives, is ushered into the upstairs study in a few seconds. Scuffle barely perceptible from the bedroom. Then the sound of auntie weeping before the monarch in whose service (or rather for whose country and people) Wasfi was slain. I take in a fresh Kleenex box for her, bow slightly and salute the king and leave them to their closed interview wrapped in the night. Water had seeped in through the large sliding windows. Jamil, the apathetic servant droopy with bronchial inflammations, swathed in his checkered head gear, has been drowsily swabbing the study . . . My hopes rise in prayer in noxious anticipation that this royal visitation will give some solace to her heart and prepare her more peacefully for the mercies of sleep.[14]

Saadieyh and Waşfi al Tall in Aqaba. 1960s

Wasfi's death descended upon Ali like a permanent chill. He
adored Wasfi, the last sentry at the gate, the last man of the family,
the only bridge between a much better Jabri past and safe harbour.
Daddy. Wasfi had doted on Diala and loved Ali, often softening
Saadieyh's sudden displeasures and absorbing her erratic huffs
and puffs.[15] There was no one left now. Heart failure had taken
Ali's father, Majddedine, in 1967, and a chronic case of narcissism
had kept Ihsan, Saadieyh and Hala's father, from them long
before. As for Alai'ddine, Majddedine's younger brother, all one
hears from accusations here and explanations there is the clash of
alleged good intentions with supposed wicked designs.

Everything changed after Wasfi. From that year on, when Ali
was twenty-nine and Saadieyh sixty-four, Ali began to teeter on
the edge of her largesse by turns wide and slim, expanding with
maternal moods and shrinking with feline whim. Whatever she
gave him never seemed enough and whatever he offered in return
always seemed too little. 'An Ottoman woman,' became his
favourite description of her, with all the caprice, all the
imperiousness, all the sadistic fickleness of her ancestors. He had
to play too many roles now – nephew, companion, 'aide-de-camp
who does the phone calls, arrangements, taxis, reservations, dates,
schedules, shopping, deliveries . . . ',[16] dinner escort. And she was
turning from mere aunt to the living answer to all the things that
troubled him: money, shelter, anchor, safety, what to do, where to
go, how to be. On June 19, 1973, as he sat waiting for his return
flight to London at Amman's old airport, Ali recounted to his diary
the tragi-comic mess their relationship was fast becoming:

Left the house (radiant sunshine, flowers, garden blossoms) in a
turmoil of upset feelings, contrite regret, anger, mortification,
sense of injustice, & the hopelessness of embroiled family duels,
bad blood dans la famille from generation to generation – the
difficulties of access, the barriers between cultural attitudes.
Last night had to pack after arriving from the heat of Aqaba,
tan already flaking off, towards long exile from the sun. Aunty
invited to dinner to some sheikh's house, she can't stand to get

King Hussein ibn Talal and Wasfi al Tall in Aqaba. Late 1960s

Wasfi, Ali and Diala. Early 1960s

back to her home in the hills all dark empty and widow-bereft,
no Wasfi to greet her and make her feel secure. Ayesha, the
beautiful dark, blonde little girl of Abu Mohammad the gardener,
comes to sleep in her bedchamber to provide comfort of human
company – guests like me next door don't count. Well, I couldn't
accompany her out, had to get my stuff packed, etc. The last
straw I guess, after having not driven back with her in the un-
comfortably servant-stuffed Mercedes all those long hot dazed
hours on the desert road. Off she went. I packed. Nina Simone
on TV singing a distant blackness (Arab soul a different kettle
of fish altogether). Aunty comes back, changes into nighty. No
hot water. I go down to fix small supper. 'What are you doing?'
She calls down in horribly unbending severity of tone. 'Who left
the icebox open?!!!' etc, etc. I carry my plate back up to find
her bedroom door closed against my face. 'May your happiness
increase,' I mutter as I walk past, the classic ironic phrase of
Arab 'thanks a million'. She hears it and pursues me to my room
where, stunned, I find myself under a barrage of accusations,
lies, condemnations, rejections, curses, blood curdling grudges,
phrases stored up from what I'd casually said here and there,
stored up in the armory of grudges, transformed into a perverted
unrecognisability of alien hostility. We shrieked at each other.
She calls down curses on my head and all her other imagined
dependents and relatives not providing enough fawning gratitude. 'Tu es un ingrate!' Accusations and counter-accusations
fly back and forth, I keep teetering between a terrible fury and
the continuing wish to keep balanced and cool but, no hope, she
says too many things that wound me to the quick, her long
accumulated store of injured pride, till finally I can't take it, the
negation of it all is too overwhelming. I start beating myself on
the head in an uncontrollable frenzy of humiliation and grief.
'Get out of this room,' I blaze at her, making a sudden dart
forwards at which the poor Dame completely wigs out and starts
screaming the classic hideous high-pitched, night-piercing
screech of spinsters and lonely old female murderees. She flees
down the corridor sans robe de chambre, down the stairs, yelling

that she's frightened of me, she doesn't even know me, has no relationship with me, I am nothing to her, she knows not what or who I am, she wishes to be rid of me forever (if only it were that easy), charges down into the downstairs salons, locks the door against me as if I'm coming after her with a knife, threatens to call up her household attendants. I have this grim flash of her turning me over to the police or something. The whole nightmare blackness of the Arab world comes swooshing down on me with its ubiquitous plunge of darkly feathered wings, the velvet evil of ignorance, barbarism, and human exhaustion. I sit at a respectable distance on the marble stairs in white crumpled pajamas and Wasfi's silk dressing gown pleading with her for a return to logic and sobriety. I appeal to all her instincts of loyalty and familiar ties but the poor beldame has flipped too far into her pitchy terrors and can no longer venture out into bedtime re-establishment of trust. 'Go upstairs and lock your door,' she yells at me from behind bolted doors. Ever so weary I drag myself obediently back up, temper spent, feeling only sorrow at such futile misunderstandings – all because I have apparently neglected to pay her enough attention while we were at the sea. Some truth to it, since vanity for sunshine and beach exposure overcame my capacity for patiently abiding her confusions with engineers, plumbers, cooks, and tribal guests. Totally lacking, the openness of trust. Back in the room I roll a [consolation] spliff to calm me down, can't read, can't sleep, can't touch that little mess of food. Light out and door banging in draught. Awake this morning for my flight, no breakfast, aunty downstairs, the time for departure arrives, bags carried down plus clutch of useless pretty things, dried foliage from the native soil. Can't touch the pretty little breakfast laid out perhaps in a slight spirit of apology (?), 2 cafés au lait instead and for Persephone-symbolic reasons rather than any appetite, three glistening green olives from their Mediterranean dish. Wrapped their stones in a Kleenex to leave my dish unused. We're late. Muhsin, the noble Bedouin officer, waits outside in strong sunlight by much-avoided silver sedan. We step out at last, I in cream suit I came in and blue and white striped shirt, poor aunt in black embroidered caftan – how ageing these long oriental-hostess robes of widowhood have become as her adopted style of weeds. finally the time, the moment, for which I have been waiting since our dreadful separation last night arrives. Whatever the rights or wrongs I don't wish her to be angry, nor to add fuel to her already tragic circumstances . . . Never mind the money. If it pleases my fate, may I never have a penny; these material dependencies small sustenances of last resort morale must cease (must accept a totally autonomous world stripped of all aid or comfort whatsoever – man needs to support himself entirely solo in this shipwrecked world.) I take her hand and bow deeply and kiss it, touch it to my forehead, Arab traditional gesture enacting respect for elders and one's parents . . . people who guide us briefly before they go accomplished with a slight bumping clumsiness of execution (it's not a gesture from a world I am accustomed to) but I bend myself to it with wholehearted sincerity to entreat her restoration and pardon, without words. Into the car, through golden fields, to the airport where I wait.[17]

For the rest of their lives, this fury and regret suffused an entanglement made up of all the elements of suffocating love. But the signs of trouble were all over the place long before Wasfi died. Since the last of his Bristol University days in the late 1960s – which he would not have finished had it not been for Saadieyh's cash – Ali understood her expectations of him and saw the lie that would inevitably eat into their affections. He knew his part well, he knew all his lines, in this charade between him and Saadieyh, 'whose pride and joy is the false image of me, whose respect for learning and getting ahead in the world and making a success – full marriage, and begetting lots of healthy offspring, etc, etc, who sees me alternately as future ambassador, university professor, good taste guide, etc, etc'. So long as the plot remained the same and the roles were faithfully played, Saadieyh could always be relied upon to extricate him from his habitual penurious state and re-launch him in his 'natural place among the butterfly colony of the race . . . '[18]

Had Wasfi lived, Ali might – just might – have gotten away with it. The 'beldame' would have been too busy, too satisfied, to fret about him. But with Wasfi dead, every favour carried with it a price tag. Against every dollar, the usual litany of pleas and appeals had to be sounded. The code words, the concessions, the accolades, the expressions of loyalty to her and Arabhood itself, pack every surviving letter of Ali's to Saadieyh. Read a few and you will have read them all.

London, February 6, 1970:

I thank you with all my heart, my dear Saadieyh, and hope that God will give me the opportunity, and Allah Yishhad (God is my witness) that one day, when I am firmly on my feet, that I will show you my profound gratitude, not only because of your financial care, but because of the morale boost you give me . . . and the example you set through your generosity . . . I will not forget my country, my family and the magnificent culture in which I was born.

Two years later from London, on November 1, 1972:

There is a bill outstanding for the deposit on the little flat in Curzon street . . . about 19 sterling pounds, so at last I will pay this . . . Last month also another 20 sterling pounds came from you, which I thought was sent especially for this bill, but I was so penniless that I spent it on my own debts instead . . . Anyway dearest Saadieyh, I don't want you to spend any more money on me. I'm a grown man now and have to stand on my own two feet . . .

One year later from London, on January 19, 1973:

You and me – we are the same, except that you are more established, respected and well known, and you have your own house. I have no one but you in this entire world. I think that we two have only each other . . .

One year later from London, on March 28, 1974:

There has to be a solution to this problem . . . Diala needs to go to university and Hala should stay in Kuwait. How can this be done? You know that for the moment I am planted in the West . . . I don't want Hala . . . to be all alone. I have always wanted to be a good son . . . You are my only family . . . I will never ever leave you, as you write in your letters. You should never think that I am going to turn my back on the Middle East . . .

Almost a year later from London, on January 10, 1975:

The money you sent me paid for my rent but not my bank debts . . .

A little over a month later, on February 28, 1975:

. . . I am hoping that I will finally be able to send [Hala and Diala] some money . . .

Sometime in 1978, months after he moved to Cairo:

On the day of my journey . . . I cried every time I saw someone . . . I am so taken with the people and this city . . . but I know as well that you are the only one who understands me and who would allow me to finish my work here[19]

But Ali's rhetoric, year on year, had become so stale, his endearments so repetitive, his needs so incessant, his requests so patently self-serving, that they simply did not work on Saadieyh any more. In ripostes that blended glee with dismay, she stroked his needs and stoked his fears, eagerly feeding naked hunger for comfort while shunning every other overture for love. 'Get off my shoulders, you are killing me,'[20] she often hissed in his ears, only moments before or minutes after she sang to him, 'Ali, *mon cher.*' On and on this yin and yang went. It was as if he and Saadieyh were all alone in this world – him and her, two Jabris of a kind. Round and round they twirled, recklessly dancing over smothered aspirations and brittle dreams. From afar, to a tortured soul like Diala's, they seemed such a happy nephew and aunt, ticking the lovely days away. Up close, it was a sorry sight; a few scenes of bliss and laughter, many more of choking rage.

There was space for Hala and Diala in this melodrama: in Ali's diary entries, brief and too far between; in some of his letters to Saadieyh repeating puzzlements and heartfelt '*que faire*'; in telegrams between Saadieyh and Hala, fatigued from harsh accusations and bloated with blame – always about money, always about the bequests of the dead. Each sat in their little corner, picking at the scars of old wounds while inflicting new ones. As Ali and Saadieyh jostled with each other, Hala wrestled in Kuwait with Majddedine's partners and collected growing mounds of legal papers. To the two of them, she was obsessed, disturbed. To her, they were meek, foolish. And in the midst of all this stood Diala in Kuwait, in her late teens, coping with motherly tirades, clutching some fun-sounding London letters from her brother and receiving the occasional kind gesture from her aunt.

Nothing changed with the passage of years. Not one of these four individuals turned the page. Each nursed their pain into a full-blown frenzy and used it like a chisel to cut into the hearts of the others. For years, Hala refused to see Ali, blaming him for not being enough of a man, enough of a son. For years, Saadieyh screamed about the burdens of financially supporting them, while the other three complained about the scraps thrown their way. For years, Hala tore into Saadieyh for squandering every oppor-tunity for a reversal of fortunes. For years, Diala faulted Saadieyh and Ali for living the 'Dolce Vita life'[21] while she and her mother wasted away in Kuwait. 'Any pussyfooting around you see from anyone on this issue is bull. That's where my youth went, that's where Hala's youth went . . . she needed taxi fare from me . . . the woman who used to give sapphires as gifts.'[22]

So thin-skinned against even the most usual of belittlements, Ali simply could not comprehend why everybody wanted so much of him when he was capable of giving only so little. 'You see these,' he held out his painterly hands to his sister years later, after one of their violent rows about past wrongs, 'this is all I can do,'[23] he finished in resignation. For all those flights, for his absence, for

all those unintended injuries, he could only offer her cryptic con-
fessions on his private page: 'Diala left today . . . The heartbreak,
the empty flat, her words, her flowers, her brief happiness, now
gone to face terrible days alone while I'm in comfort and oblivion!
. . . Meanwhile, the clothes she washed and hung and folded for
me . . . What did I ever do for her?'[24]

Why would a family made so small by bad circumstance and
misfortune hack at the binding ties of kin and slide, eyes wide
open, towards such despair? Why would people who could feel
love for one another succumb to so much rancour? Why do the
moments of tenderness hang on for dear life in their flashbacks
and letters and diary entries? Hala's words to Saadieyh in 1974
about Ali as a 'compassionate and loving man',[25] his own fleeting
descriptions of his mother's beauty and wit, are teasers, lines beseeching you to come to them in a sea of prose that keeps pushing
you in the opposite direction. Saadieyh's letters to Diala that
begin with '*ma chère enfant*', and Diala's to her, writing of new
jobs, of bigger salaries, of journalism courses, of life seemingly on
the mend, fare no better.[26] Only in Ali's voluminous missives to
Diala do love and humour survive intact; like roads battered by a
deluge of bad memories, they take you into lives too beaten down
by the grim days to cuddle the good ones.

'A set of pretty helpless individuals, I'd say. Very old blood . . .
and very bad drainage. How else can I explain it to someone who
has never experienced being part of a family falling apart.'[27] That
more than suffices for Diala, the last of the line. To her, ages ago in
1975, Ali offered this take: 'Any account of our common heritage,
Darling Seester, is like a Chinese labyrinth, filled with the bones of
uncompleted riddles and non-terminated sentence structures that
died for lack of air!! . . . '[28]

*   *   *

1998. Summer. June. Saadieyh is dead. Twenty years Ali has
been in 'exile'.* Now what? Where now? This Jordan Ali sleeps in,

---

*   Ali continuously refers to this status in his diaries and letters to friends in

heaves and sighs; like him, it is too tired, too broke. With barely a moment's thought, it waves away expectations and ignores so much love. All for naught, these paintings and hard work to shield the old stone from concrete and resuscitate the green in the midst of grey. This country of withering palms and sleepy Jordan valleys, of cosy Amman hills and ancient neighbourhoods with a likeness only in faded photographs, is no sanctuary after all.

After Saadieyh's death, he kept carping on to his friends and sister Diala that 'all is lost now' – omissions everywhere, damned hectic days that refused to slow their pace into a gentle walk, a trickle of words in journals once chock-full of colour and poetry. Rut. Ali was in a rut, stuck at fifty-seven in an 'Arab milieu that's finally destructive; desultory; chloroforming; amnesiac'.[29]

And those Jabris, that past, this family, 'dust in the mouth' all; tears and collapsed castles in the air and spent fortunes and dead heroes and bizarre mothers and contemptuous widows and hard uncles and bitter sisters. Nothing, nothing at all, but that name, Jabri. 'I am Ali al Jabri. That is who I am.' He would always pronounce it thus – *Ali DDjaabri* – and stop there, keeping secret all those faces and stories that decorate soft memories and hang over hard recollections.

There was nowhere to be for Ali in this kingdom. There was nowhere for him to go. It seemed to him such a waste of a journey after all these years of grind. It all started out with so much love for things as they were, such yearning for modernity to soften its changing ways. He was a painter constantly on the prowl for discarded native textures, inanimate or made of vibrant human clay. There is not a thing in any of his paintings which he did not live and did not know. 'I used to see him strolling in our markets, carrying a large sketchbook and gently contemplating passersby, or peering into the small shops, the old houses, the sellers, the people,' George Sayyegh recalled in his critique of Ali's exhibition

London. The first time he uses it in his Jordan Diaries is on July 23, 1980. He writes: 'July . . . 3 years 7 months exile.' It had been that long since he left London for Cairo, in 1977.

at Jordan's National Gallery in 1983. ' . . . A man in search of
man, of the meaning of life, in the heartbeats of the streets. One
day, he was in Ma'an holding his notebook and that pure gaze
which asks life about life as if inquiring about the secrets of
things.'[30]

Jordan, at once adored and loathed, had finally folded itself into a
dead end. Much like the weariness that wafts through Cavafy's *The*
City, even after the revisions of a poet finally reconciled with his
Alexandria,[31] Ali's ennui fanned despondence over his own country.

You said: 'I'll go to another country, go to another shore,
find another city better than this one.
Whatever I try to do is fated to turn out wrong
and my heart lies buried like something dead.
How long can I let my mind moulder in this place?
Wherever I turn, wherever I look,
I see the black ruins of my life, here,
where I've spent so many years, wasted them, destroyed
                                        them totally.'
You won't find a new country, won't find another shore.
This city will always pursue you.
You'll walk the same streets, grow old
In the same neighbourhoods, turn gray in these same houses.
You'll always end up in this city. Don't hope for things elsewhere:
There's no ship for you, there's no road.
Now that you've wasted your life here, in this small corner,
You've destroyed it everywhere in the world.

Life in Jordan had become 'a Borgesian torture only an extreme
masochist would follow with such relentlessly immaterial logic'.[32]
He was 'shuffling from room to overstuffed ageing white room . . .
book-papers, files, portfolios, detritus from former creations like a
Schwitters Merzbau assemblage', and writing about 'the diminish-
ments of appetite, the desuetude of worldly involvements . . . and
just the daily grind of a banal un-celebrated life in a very provincial
town of the Arab world'. Amman itself, always a bit of a stranger,

had become alien, uninviting, ugly. 'We live on the edge in terms of what the daily nervous circuit can apprehend, as we absorb atrocity on atrocity just across the border while over here (even under my very flat – the hottest spot in Amman!) . . . babes in bare-tummy leopard skin halter-ensembles do valet parking with their nokias . . . 2 different cultures co-exist: the Islamic poor and the licentious rich and I seem to partake of both in my willed semi-exiguousness and make-shift existence.'[33]

True, Ali was always a nag, confusing real grievances with imagined ones and crying over both with equal zeal. But that was Ali. To him there was nothing contrived about this crash. Whisky at midday was a daily reprieve, cheap wine in the evenings a sure thing. You could easily have called him beautiful once – blond hair, eleven inches on top of five feet, a strict waistline, a Roman head, blue, blue eyes, a straight moustache over straight lips. The teeth, a minor concession to imperfection, hit the wrong note, parted and weak and mildly dreadful. Now, not half-way bad, he looked a very tired, worn-out impression of his younger self.

There were times he tried to recall every friend and write the name of every dear one. Name after name after name dots his journals, reminding him of compassion and its warm embrace. He drew heart shapes next to Antonia, wrote thoughts about Diney, dates above John, impressions for Ronnie. Every few pages he asked 'Ou es tu, François?' a question he never stopped asking after François left for Luxor in 1987 to head the French archaeo-logical mission at Karnak Temple. There were blessings for Hazem and Fadi and Essa and Widad and Nuha and Rula, scribbles about Raghida and Nawal. These jottings were not new to Ali – his diaries were always replete with the stuff of daily living and its characters – but they were suddenly urgent, frantic, as if he was trying to freeze-frame a fading life.

Ma'an, Petra and Aqaba, his three old, grumpy, much-loved aunts, in thoughts and dreams, came to him every other morning and lingered until the wee hours of the night. Every time he repaid the visit, the mementos of yore grew pale and the bitter images of today stayed.

Ma'an – that way station on T. E. Lawrence's route to 'his' victory – was 'bereft after all these years of total ignorance, neglect, philistinism & destruction from every sector of high rule & local admin, with me as the happy responsible 1! Sole guardian of its irreplaceable cultural features! How wonderful to end up with nothing and how does that make me feel.'[34]

Petra had 'collapsed to no better than the Bedouin's kiosks of hot Miranda! Junk from everywhere but Jordan[35] . . . Hip Hop Petra . . . full of mixers and the sites are upside down. The itch is for the fixers and the money is pouring down . . . the hotels they keep rising all wonky and askew with a godamn license . . .'[36] Now he can enjoy 'breakfast on a terrace with the aroma of sewage floating around . . .'[37] he wrote to his friend Ronnie in 1998.

And old, old, sweet Aqaba: this one's demise he had prophesied ages ago.

> The people and the place are being bulldozed right out of the picture, dumped into mid-50s type Nasser era authoritarianist mass housing units out on the edge of the desert. Their watery shoreline dwellings once splendidly oriented to a traditional way of life pulverised to make way for the new regime of modernised standardisation. Police, corruption, graft, perjury, the marauding secret agents wrapped up facelessly in their kaffiyehs [traditional head gear] a real cockroach nest of vipers' collective of false practice and personal gain for the powerful at the expense of the weak.[38]

*   *   *

Today, in a drawer, sits a hand-painted proposal to Aqel Biltaji, Aqaba Regional Authority's one-time director, to preserve Hafayer, Aqaba's palm shorefront. It was presented in 2001. On two private walls hang lifelike, grainy renditions of Aqaba's rundown back-streets and two of Petra's carved Nabataean stones shimmering with the spectacular colours bestowed by one very bright spring day. Had the Aqaba paintings been life-size, *trompe l'oeil* would have found you a heartbeat away from the sun-soaked alleyways.

These were Ali's last brush strokes. For a man who insisted he was a preservationist, a man for whom the title of painter seemed offensive in Amman (yes, let's give them art that matches their panties)[39] it did not escape his notice that the only preservation of his that lasted was where he was at his most brilliant: on canvas. In this, he saw no consolation at all, only miserable failure. A mournful fixation on 'dislocation, disturbance, disruption, disculturation, dissolution, disappearance . . . '[40] pervaded his last commentaries and finally stamped his last major work. For 'Disorientation', a multifarious project that brought together many of the Arab world's artists under the roof of Berlin's House of World Cultures in February 2003, Ali's posthumous contribution was room-size enlargements of his photographs of the massive, high-tension electricity poles that line the new Amman-Aqaba highway and follow 'that topography of jagged ravines (their now traceless memories of the Arab Revolt campaigns of 1918) to the city-enclave on the Red Sea shore'. For him, there was no depiction more apt than this of Jordan's 'degenerative urbanism'.[41] Possibly even of his own.

*　　*　　*

'Is it sunny today?'

This was Ali's computer password hint – his wry way of coping with an existence that, in 2002, was becoming literally much darker. The onslaught of concrete and dust on him and the sun was making his apartment and work studio unlivable. The sandblasting of his building was in full swing and construction activity on an adjacent plot was reaching a near frenzy. His windows, taped up by day, gasped for breath by night. Those sunrays that brought him back to life at the dawn of each morning, the glow that illuminated his stunning manipulations of light and shadow, had dimmed into the faintest of hues. It was time to move.

'Who will take care of me when I die?'[42] he kept asking his close friends in that final year. He was only sixty.

*　　*　　*

Something was definitely wrong. It was not unlike him to disappear, but this silence was total, eerie. Incessant messages on his answering machine went unanswered. At a dinner party at Hazem's only three days before Ali was discovered, Essa murmured, 'Allah yustor. Ma ykunu Dabahou?'[43] (God protect us! Have they slaughtered him?)

When I entered his apartment, I felt it was almost scripted. A few days before Hazem had sent me an e-mail that Diala is very worried about Ali and was wondering if we knew where he was. I remembered him mentioning wanting to visit François in Egypt. I thought he was in Luxor already. I had a nine a.m. appointment with the dentist that morning. When I arrived in the office, Diana, my secretary, rushed into my office to tell me that Diala had just called her a minute before and told her that she found Ali dead in his apartment. I rushed to the apartment with Ziad [the driver]. When we reached the building's garage, Diala was sitting in her car in total shock. I took the keys from her and went up. I opened the door. There were tiny splashes of blood on the wall, a trickle on the floor. In the L-shaped living room, Ali was on the floor, between the coffee table and the couch. There was a huge puddle of blood around his head. His body was black, his stomach was protruding. He was in his penny loafers, light blue tee-shirt, and white jeans. I could not tell how he was killed. Next to him was the small side table with a glass of whisky and a beer bottle; the white couch was drenched with blood. He lay there in a perfect position, palms facing up. It did not look like there was a struggle. I walked around the house. There were footprints of blood. The bedroom was a mess, the bathtub was bloody.[44]

This is how Fadi found him on December 3, 2002. He finally understood what Ali was always trying to tell him. He wanted the certainty of a decent death as desperately as he craved a decent life. That pervasive fear of aloneness and abandonment was as much for the here and now as it was for the hereafter.

The coroner's report indicates several knife cuts to the side of the torso and a few around the upper wrist. There were seven slits to the throat, the last apparently to sever the neck. The murderer did not succeed. The report estimates the day of death to be November 28, the same day Wasfi died. 'A ritual killing?'[45] Allan, one of Ali's closest friends since the 1970s, asked after hearing the details of the crime scene. Maybe. That is the time-honoured way sheep are slaughtered in this part of the world. Body straight, in a perfect position, palms facing up! A gesture of contrition by a believer to help Ali receive his God? Perhaps. We may never know. The police identified the killer, but he slipped out of the country before they could arrest him.

Ali lies in his beloved Petra extinguished by too much thirst for this earth's soiled underbelly. Years ago in Cairo, on one of his less happy days there, he asked himself, 'Is it me who hunts for the dark gutter's silver lining finding only the fascination of the unobtainable . . . ?'[46]

Ali and Petra overlapping, 1995. Courtesy of Rami Sajdi

CHAPTER TWO

I am the Last Descendant of Salah al Din

We rule like princes over nothing.
Our history dissolves like foam.
I warn you. 'Go away.'
Mud engulfs us like a net.
We drown in it.
Slime
Covers our eyelids.
It scarves
Our necks like silk

Adonis
Remembering the First Century

On a Friday, sometime in early February 1971, during a drive to the Ghor (the Jordan Valley), Ali, prompted by the old road his father had helped build, let slip this marvellous nugget of biography describing Majddedine and Hala's life in the 1940s:

My father, heir to immense lands in North of Syria, newly married to his cousin, my mother, both freshly hatched from elite American colleges and post grad degrees[47] being given the inevitable tribal conditioning treatment by authoritarian Victorian-Edwardian type family structure 'Do this Do that' dictates accompanying the running of lands along traditional lines of Oriental aristocratic oligarchy. Well he wouldn't toe the submissive line that was part and parcel of the silver spoon heritage and my mother was too much the early 40s Bonwit Teller liberated woman to put up with Aleppo society and its demands that the female should sit mentally veiled at least between 4 walls . . . producing endless male heirs – so they up

and pulled out moved south to what was then semi-British
protectorate in Trans Jordan – ruled by the Hashemite dynasty
along proximity to Palestine proper. Israel still a distant Zionist
aspiration – the extermination camps of Europe not yet un-
leashed on the naïve conscience of post-war West . . . Anyway my
mother was pregnant with my older brother (if only he had lived
what a different course one's life would have taken . . .) the boy
died in infancy and soon I was on the way, despite my mother's
already crystallising horrors of childbirth and all that
morphological mess or do I mean natural biology? No doubt
even after Vassar the destructive repressions of Islamic woman-
hood continue to obtain . . . they lived in Amman in a rather
pretty little villa made of stone with a balcony on which in an old
photo I once saw my mother posed young and beautiful in a floor
length flower strewn at home dress with Russ the long lamented
still-adored German Shepherd bitch who used to baby sit my
crib. I was a heavy baby it seems and when time of arrival drew
near my mother who had been taking pre-natal treatment in
Jerusalem, where they frequently drove on week-ends – it was
'smarter, more cosmopolitan,' a mixed society of Palestinian
landed gentry (like my aunt – mother's sister – and her first
husband Musa Alami immensely rich old family, my aunt
mistress of three sumptuous houses in Palestine, one particularly
lush place in Jericho, land with orange-bearing trees and palms
murmuringly stirring over high arabesque garden walls) +
erudite European Jews, Anglo Americans, professors and civil
servants, Abba Eban[48] at those dimly recalled dinner parties and
luncheons under the pines of old rustic restaurants near
Jerusalem . . . Against this background of hybrid transplants and
fresh moments astir, within the timeless landscape of olive trees
and ancient Arab villages winding round the soft contours of the
Holy Land, Jerusalem itself still the bazaar hubbub of the old
city where Jesus had trod – there I was born and a fair haired
baby was I . . . Now that I sit here writing this with my hair
decreasing daily, circles permanently under eyes, the com-
plexion marked by sallow dullness of anxiety, sweaty in the

armpits, nearly thirty years later already brief instance of a microcosm but how much suffering and experience the human individual must taste between these two stages.[49]

An unusual confession this, never again confided to the page – at least none as yet discovered. It exudes that unmistakable scent of overfed nostalgia that makes utopias out of puffed-up remembrances and brushes against the painful turf of 'if only' ('the futile pathos of ironic hypothesis',[50] Ali called it), that emotional space that could only have reminded him of shattering losses trailing catastrophic ones and laying waste to centuries of a good life.

*   *   *

'I am the last descendant of Saladin.'[51] The past could not get better than that, could it? What Ali had in mind when he concocted this fictitious part of his lineage for his friend Beth Regardz during his Stanford years in the early sixties cannot be known. If he truly believed it, then he suffered from an acute case of youthful gullibility. If he did not, then we have before us an early example of his delightful tongue-in-cheek fabrications.

No matter. With or without Saladin, the Jabris gave Ali plenty to crow about. Mind you, that he chose to spread his peacock feathers in the first place shows an unusual openness about family never displayed in his later years: in adulthood Ali made none of these boastful declarations or harmless bits of fun to his friends, only hints and muffled allusions. When he talked, it was usually something to the tune of 'we are who we are'.[52] When he was feeling generous, he would give away the 'vast lands and riding in daddy's silver car to check on our many villages'.[53] That's about it, really. The family was never brought out for proper intro-ductions. Ali, when it came to him and them, was a lousy story-teller. He 'had no conclusions, no beginnings . . . not a single complete story',[54] only fascinating small pieces of something obviously much larger.

Alia al Jabri, Ali's paternal cousin, has a wall-size family tree

Hala al Jabri and Ali. 1943

Hala in the Phenicia Hotel, Beirut. Mid 1960s.

with branches so many and names so small that it is virtually impossible to trace Ali's ancestry beyond the few recognisable recent names. This tree, unlike most others from its region, grew, it would seem, from the name of a woman, the daughter of Jabir Halabi, an Ottoman judge.[55] From there start decades upon decades of a rather satisfied and satisfying family life. By 1760, the Jabris had become one of Aleppo's one hundred and four notable families, one of its Ashrafs (descendants of the Prophet Mohammad, although whether they got there through marriage or financial persuasion is not known),[56] among its most prominent Ulemmas (religious scholars) and judges, and one of its wealthiest houses. 'Saying someone was a Kawakibi or a Jabiri, for instance, placed him in a renowned line of learned men.'[57] Theirs was a sprawling household that sat atop numerous villages and large swathes of land. They lived in the city's privileged quarters of Masabin, Frafira, Aynayn, Suwayqa Ali.[58] A goulash of Arab, Turkish and Circassian blood, they married into established Ottoman names, sent their sons to Istanbul's schools and then dispatched them to its corridors of power. For them, suffering was probably no more than a hiccup rudely intruding on perpetual heavenly favour. If there were downs along with the ups – and most probably there were – they do not appear to have been many. If there were punishing days along with the blessed ones – and most probably there were – the former would seem to have been few. As with most big families, among them were the very rich and the not-so-lucky. While the former basked in money and political influence, the latter enjoyed at least the pleasure of the name. These were the Jabris of *Halab* (Aleppo) and this is how they marched through recent centuries and contentedly entered the last.

Bliss! Or so it seemed to Ali. The chronicle of the Jabris is so breezy you can almost hear the rustle of the leaves and feel that subtle air of deep comfort stroke your face – yesteryears so ridiculously over romanticised they mould perfect lives out of a perfect past. Placed against the frightening prospect of a harsh present, these stories acquired the epic sound of a magnificent tale gone wrong. If not careful, the voice would slip into a husky droll at the mention of Jabri grandeur and that bit of Arab history that accompanied it – Ali's voice sometimes did, Diala's still does. And why not? This piece of the earth has always been a sucker for grand words and grand people. When recalling Arab or Muslim glories, the narrator is almost always overwhelmed by the mythical, as the factual retires to the near margins of his ode. Ask Duraid Lahham, that sharpshooting humorist from Syria, about this Arab helplessness before the ringing word and he will remind you of that telling line from his 1970s play *Day'it Tishrine* (The Village of October): 'I'll recite you a couple of poems that will bring us back Andalusia.' Listen to *Sa Narji'ou Yawman* (One Day We Shall Return), the ballad of Lebanon's crooner Fairouz, and suddenly you're sitting in the middle of those famous Palestinian orange groves (bayarat) lost long ago, because of war and fear, to another people, other aspirations.

The Jabris. Their drama is jam-packed with so many momentous events, so many sumptuous larger-than-life characters, so much heartbreak, the least Ali's life deserves is a dramatic opening.

*   *   *

In the beginning, there was an *Arab awakening*[59] – possibly. There was a dying Ottoman breed and a suckling mishmash of Arab creeds. There were French meddlers and British pedlars slicing and dicing a basket-full of nations, a whole bunch of borders, scores of people. There was Lawrence of Arabia snatching empty victories from colossal defeats. There was Palestine slipping fast from age-old loves and taking up with new ones. There were mighty men and their wives meandering through Levantine mansions and their leafy gardens, members of a close-knit tribe, masters of the land, beneficiaries of its bounty. There were faint stirrings in the towns and quiet sorrow in the countryside. There were slaves in everything but name. There was youth and its infinite possibilities. There was daring sexuality and its ambiguities. There was this East to that West, a delicious concubine, a fiery lover.

And then there was Ali, one foot here, one foot there and the rest scattered everywhere in between.

In youth, he was a thing of beauty. At first sight, two intimate
friends announced him: grace, which carried measured steps, and
sensuality, which kept every movement company. When he kissed
you, he bowed and gave you the high edge of his cheek before
lifting it away softly. Like his mother Hala, when he danced, he
entranced. Every life he swam in he sank into, and every time he
walked out on one, he left with feet dragging and a long, lingering
look back. He was a bundle of nerves and spoke with a thousand
voices. The likes of him could be found in that book or this place,
but when the whole was chanced upon the effect was the same and
forever: a sort of bemused love for a human being who embraced
within him ungraspable others but threw your way only parts of
one. He split, as mercury does, into pieces at a moment's whim.
He slipped into and out of your life the way he glided into and out
of conversations. He travelled between different worlds, relishing
each on its own, as if protecting it from contamination by the
others, and those who occupied centre stage in one were strangers
to the rest. You could creep from yours into theirs if you really
wanted to, but he would not have been the one to invite you there.
Only after his death did François finally chat with Hazem, Antonia
hear of Raghida, Essa of John. That is how he was everywhere. If
it was a piece of him you wanted, and 'everyone, everyone, wanted
a piece of Ali',[60] he gave you only that; the rest was his to savour.

Shame! Reminiscences about Ali read like fabulous stories in
miniature, short and half-blind by the weight of years and the
lightness of cryptic recollections. They take you on whirlwind trips
to that truckers' café on the other side of the docks at Bristol, to
night disappearances in Leigh Woods, to *mano-a-mano* scenes in
a dark London house bustling with ephemeral love, to the un-
bearable heat and the beauty of blackness in Ladbroke Grove, to
surreptitious friendships in dismal Egyptian Damanhour, to the
sudden departures from Amman's tidy neighbourhood of
Shmeisani to God knows where. Only a trickle of these came from
him, in chance whispers or rare film-like replays. If it were not for
those letters fat with the dazzling snapshots of life around him and
the characters that made it happy and miserable, or the elaborate

diary entries that take you through the tick tocks of his days, there would be so little to write about this most elusive of Alis.

Wherever he went, he found exactly what he was looking for: the flip side of the life he had just left behind. That is why against the sombre Nile apartment of his grandfather, Ihsan, stood his other Cairo:

> . . . A seethe in millions out on the hustle – super tough city that makes London seem a lost dream of pastoral innocence – at Ramses station dark brown soldiers bed down for the night on the pavement beneath metal overpass. The nightly bivouac of the indigent – Cairo sleeps anywhere, on sidewalks, mouths open parked upright in a car, small boys on worn parapets by the Nile, as I pass by silently in my ineffectual moonlit clothing, the vigilant voyeur, the hopeless observer recording a world of blistered lusciousness wondering where it should all go . . . [61]

That is why Cairo's City of the Dead offered the urgent physical entanglements of masculine silhouettes by night and gems for a painter's eye by day:

> Hustle, Hustle, Hustle . . . one o'clock . . . a taxi to the City of The Dead in search of pals and dope but a wrong stairway got me straight into gang of miscreants . . . followed me to threaten menace . . . wrench my wrist, grab watch and demand bread. Oh, God not that one again. Thank God I was not too far deep and got away . . . smack into two soldiers hungrily waiting for it . . . on a darkened plain by a tin statue of a defunct poet staring into oblivion . . . more money changed hands, though this time more equally and here I sit in the night café watching the same sharp excavational mind go by in all sorts of luscious shapes. Hustle! . . . [62]

A vast ancient precinct whose traditions stretch back to pre-pharonic times, sub-city of tombs, memorials and marabou's shrines, where the living haunt the noonday shadows of the shallow sands, where dogs lie basking between immemorial entablatures, Islamic blazons carved and fretted, the ancient

forgotten piles rising to earth mounds; (flies, garbage, ordure for
punctuation between the vocabulary of worn stone and crumbling
masonry) – sandy the pathways wind scrabble, rooftops, vast
domes open to the clerestory winds, Koranic verses against a
faintly breathing sky, the odd shy palm bursting its freshness
between zigzags of bricks and mortar . . . [63]

That is why Aqaba, when the sun set, shed the innocence of
Saadieyh's beach house next to the Royal Palace and donned the
more Baudelairian masks of life:

The Alcazar where 4 transsexuals in full rig out, swelling tits,
Las Vegas Chorine high heels . . . blond clouds of cheap Scan-
dinavian talc & even see-thru long dresses . . . the macabre aspect
as Aqaba Islam meets European sulfur with ever brandished
cocks ready to fill even surgically plasticised hotel . . . extremely
disturbing: the dichotomy now impinging on my consciousness
between ideal impersonal beauty referring to Platonic systems of
time & place versus the bizarre satire of human comedy at its
most grotesque and funky – how to reconcile the underneath
night-cloaked reality, the . . . slime, with the higher reaches of
nature under daylight, sunshine, truth? All false? An Arab
mixture of Jean Genet, Goya, Gauguin, hopeless paradise.[64]

'The beauty of Ali – parallel universes.'[65]

*   *   *

'I don't know. I just have this feeling that when he looked in the
mirror late at night, alone, he saw Lawrence.'[66] It is intriguing
that this thought by Hazem should echo in his reflections and
those of so many others on Ali. The man never dwelled on T. E.
Lawrence. He did not write about him; he rarely even talked about
him. What conjures up that name at the mention of this Ali?
    Could it be the colours gold and blue, a conspiracy of spirits, a
shared susceptibility to the desert and its 'virile heat'?[67] Could it
be their fascination with digs for buried relics, with Aqaba, from
Ottoman outpost to Jordanian signpost, with Ma'an in transit

Ali working in Aqaba on the Arab Revolt series. 1979–80

from warrior town to impoverished township? Could it be their uneasy reverence for Hashemite princes? Could it be that both segued from city to desert, mesmerised by 'the sweep of open places, the taste of wide winds, the sunlight . . .'?[68] Could it be that both brought to sensuous frieze the dark Semite, that for them physical pain and manhood were lovers, inflicting fear and sexual pleasure in equal measure? Could it be the voyeurism that attaches itself to those who know they do not belong or could never quite decide whether they wanted to? On good days they are giddy with the novelty of their native colours; rubbed the wrong way, they quickly fall into the condescending habits of mortified strangers.

There are not even hints in Ali's journals, only a few quotations from *The Seven Pillars of Wisdom* capturing some of Lawrence's pontifications about Arabs: 'They are a certain people despising doubt, our modern crown of thorns. They do not understand our metaphysical difficulties, our self-questioning. They all know truth and untruth, belief and unbelief . . . Their imaginations are

keen but not creative . . . no art . . . '[69] But then Ali never gave
much space to his favourite people. Nothing on Marguerite
Yourcenar.[70] Nothing on Lawrence Durrell.[71] There are a few
words about David Roberts' watercolour of Karnak, Egypt, a
lonely reference to Orientalist painting: 'Blimey! What a hand,
what an eye . . . the perfect integration of mystery and explicitness
– the perfect legibility of classicism with the breathing nuances and
suggestivities of Romanticism. Ruins and objects from the past
seem to demand this combination of contradictory visions . . . '[72]
This combination may explain all that is spellbinding in Ali's
paintings of the Ibn Tulun mosque, the cityscape of Fez, Sanaa's
brown facades – meticulous representations all, caressed by the
breath of a shy romanticism.

There is hardly anything on Mies Van der Rohe. Cavafy? Only
one interesting clip in Ali's 1974 London diary, alongside mention
of E. M. Forster's *Alexandria: A History and a Guide* and C. M.
Bowra's *The Creative Experiment*: 'Cavafy . . . Choice pleasure of
the pagan's way of life (Mediterranean Hellenism) versus taboos
and respectability of post 400AD monotheism (Christianity, Islam)
. . . Cavafy's anguish at the usurpation of paganism . . . tolerant
and eclectic by nature rather than militantly narrow in his
allegiances.'[73] These excerpts read like sneak previews of taunts
and doubts that would flog this hedonist's antipathy to godly
rectitudes and Jabrian dictates for the rest of his life.

What of Lawrence? Well, what of him and Ali? His bookshelves
hold many books by and about Lawrence: several copies of *The
Seven Pillars of Wisdom*, a copy of the *Mint*, the exhibition
catalogue of the National Portrait Gallery's *T. E. Lawrence*,
Richard Perceval Graves' *Lawrence of Arabia and His World*. We
know that Ali borrowed Jeremy Wilson's biography of Lawrence
from Hazem. In fact, he had many books on Orientalism,
including Edward Said's, and a dozen or so on British
Orientalists: Palgrave, Stark, Lane, Burton, Doughty, Bell.

'I can tell you that one of Ali's favourite books was *The Seven
Pillars*, but I would not go very far with it. He just thought the
man lived a very interesting life. And don't forget Ali's Arab

Revolt series. That is how he fell in love with the desert.'[74] Diala could be right. On the night of January 14, 1979, Ali was decamped in Wadi Rumm, the Valley of Rumm in the south of Jordan, researching the Arab Revolt for his paintings. That evening he wrote to Antonia that he was 'reading Lawrence now (the 7 pillars). It seems miraculous how he could recapture it so vividly in recollection, the lie of the land, the rough grain of wild relationships.' There is complicity here, but Ali says nothing about Lawrence and the Revolt itself.

For his research, Ali retraced Lawrence in the southern desert. He went everywhere and spent weeks and nights in Lawrence's old haunts. He slept in Rumm, he stayed at the residence of Audeh Abu Taeyh's (Anthony Quinn to us) children, and for months walked the streets of Ma'an and Aqaba. The result is a dreamy medley of brush work and portraiture on four canvases that bring together Hashemite grandfathers and grandsons with history and terrain. The overture is the Hashemite dream itself: Sharif Hussein ibn Ali, author of the 1916 Revolt, nestled between the Kaa'ba in Mecca and the Dome of the Rock in Jerusalem's Haram al Sharif, the two symbols of his family's claims, the two pillars of his envisioned Arab kingdom. Then enter Arab forces striding towards the palm trees of Aqaba and the red sea, trailed, in the third scene, by Abdullah ibn al Hussein, the son of the Sharif, posing for the camera on the extreme edge of Audeh's sword as he ushers in modern Jordan and its own Hussein. And there, in the most wistful, and last, of the chapters, the Byzantine Mosaics of Madaba, Nabataean gods, the shrine of Ja'afar al Tayyar and Karak's crusader castle are the treasured fragments of history over which the picture of a very young King Hussein appears to keep vigil.[75] At the tail-end of the picture, in calligraphic mode, 'Glory to our Master, the Sultan and King', perches as an ode to majesty. The face of King Talal, the son of Abdullah and King Hussein's father, removed by the British in 1952 and long ignored as a political blip, occupies very comfortable space. A kind gesture, perhaps, towards a maligned man. But Feisal, Prince Feisal, great man of the Revolt, Lawrence's

pick – as the Englishman never stopped boasting – is nowhere to
be found. There are camels and horses and men and tents but no
Feisal, only very faint mention of the name hovering above the
camel herds.

This was Ali's unusual, possibly even cheeky interpretation of
the Arab Revolt, rich with symbolism and empty of blood. As if he
wanted to say this is what remains after all the politics, all
the heroics, all the battles have been played on life's stage: the
testimonies to history and the precious progeny of nature in need
of a safe place to stay. He did fleetingly dabble with the idea of
'a flattering high art Van Dyke-type-Royal-patronage pictures
showing the history of the Hashemite dynasty (nicely done with
humour, that is)',[76] but the minute he set foot in the desert,
nature, the mother of all kings and their queens, won. The majesty
of Rumm, Ali's 'superb . . . Arab grand canyon',[77] where
Lawrence recalled how his own 'caravan grew self-conscious, and
fell dead quiet, afraid and ashamed to flaunt its smallness in the
presence of the stupendous hills',[78] had the final say. It 'sucked me
in,' Ali raved to Antonia, 'as if there were a preordained
connection . . . I connected with something eternal, unchanging:
pastoralism, burying my face in the sweet fragrance of a delicious
clean young Camel of the open wilds; and Krayem, the son of the
sheikh, with his feverish black eyes, gaunt cheekbones, a burning
Savonarola of the steppes . . .'[79]

There is wit and daring in these paintings. Not too many glorious
revolts have been painted without close-ups of their heroes
watching over, God-like, the rage of epic battles and the onrush of
a prophesied destiny. And not too many 'royal' painters would have
thought of reducing a visual celebration of a Hashemite 'triumph'
to a party of postcard-like pictographs? 'Sort of like Indian
Bollywood posters,'[80] John says of the series. Ali would have
probably been amused by his dear friend's take. Sixty years or so
after Lawrence's work, here was another with a gentler message, a
quieter ego, a different ending. There is in the canvases a devotion
to magnificent country similar to Lawrence's, but there is no
visible interest in the *Pillars* or its politics. Ali, it would seem,

did not buy him or it. If his storyline is a deliberate riposte to the Lawrencian tale, then it embraces its love of landscape, conspicuously leaving out the rest of its preoccupations.

The series must have perplexed Queen Noor and her Hussein of Jordan, for whom she commissioned the paintings on the occasion of his forty-fifth birthday, in 1980. To Ali, she, from the start, seemed indifferent. Soon after he received the royal assignment, he mused to himself that 'never was so much effort put into artwork so disinterestedly commissioned by Royal patrons. Neither Medicis nor Romanoffs and I guess I ain't Sir Peter Paul Ruebens neeever.'[81]

There is such eloquence in Ali's visual narrative, almost enough to compensate for his silence about the Revolt everywhere else. It is not surprising that he chose to paint his politics with brush, the way Lawrence painted his with pen. In their gift of the gab, these two artists would always find mutual grounds to meet. For those like John who were often the lucky recipients of Ali's letters – beguiling novellas that wove masterly words with masterful images – this affinity between the Englishman and the Syrian is compelling. 'They wrote with such self indulgence and flamboyance about streams of consciousness.'[82] If moved, they could, with only a handful of words or a painting, lift you up thousands of miles away and land you inches from them. At times they were in perfect sync, at others worlds apart. Listen to this rapturous exchange on Wadi Rumm!

LAWRENCE: Landscapes, in childhood's dream, were so vast and silent . . .[83] The avenue of Rumm . . . gorgeous in sunset colour, the cliffs as red as the clouds in the west, like them in scale and in the level bar they raised against the sky . . . Such whelming greatness dwarfed us, stripped off the cloak of laughter we had ridden over the jocund flats . . .[84]

ALI: A titanic apocalypse-geology of a collapsed volcanic system, granite and sandstone, the one chipped and slivered in smooth cliff-faces like polished metal edged in shimmery blues; the other a hallucination of brilliant orange/red/gold sculpted

filigree, like Hindu temples rising out of the pink desert floor.
People call it the desert but it's really full of life, vast horizons
studded with positive/negative polka dots of vegetable growth,
alternately darker or lighter as the sun makes his short solstice
trajectory . . . [85]

Now place the Arab in his desert and marvel at this recurring
Lawrencian-Jabrian dream: 'The essence of the desert . . . the
lonely moving individual, the son of the road, apart from the world
as in a grave.'[86] The wayward body of Omar al Sharif blurred by
heat and mist as he approached a thirsty Peter O'Toole. Do you
remember that scene? Feast then on Lawrence's first glimpse of
Feisal's men:

> Beneath every great rock or bush they sprawled like lazy scor-
> pions, resting from the heat, and refreshing their brown limbs
> with the early coolness of the shaded stone . . . Most of them were
> young . . . They were a tough-looking crowd, dark coloured, some
> negroid. They were physically thin, but exquisitely made, moving
> with an oiled activity altogether delightful to watch. It did not
> seem possible that men could be hardier or harder.[87]

It is a rhapsody that revels in Arabian limbs the way Ali sings
about Egypt's maleness: 'Sultry skin of every chocolate to café
shade, ideal bodies of a smooth mercurial voluptuousness built for
high speed action as for the steamy languor of the hammams.'[88] The
words dance for their writer, much like the Jordanian band of
Badiah (desert) soldiers in red and white *hatta wi' iggaal* (head-
dress) and Khaki robes do for their smitten painter.[89]

*   *   *

So where to from here? Where else? Towards the dominion of love
and sexual wants in Lawrence and Ali. This is a difficult one, for
in matters of the heart – and everything else, come to think of it –
Lawrence was at his most shifty magnificence. The trouble with
him is that in his bottomless well of love and hate, of motive and
counter-motive, of every kind of explanation for every kind of act,

his pendulum swung hardest. He used words like stunts and escape hatches, painting doors to truths and dead-ends – as many of them as the reader could count. To every question, multiple answers; for every endeavour, the medal and the whip; with praise, denigration. To posterity, he was a very generous man because in almost every eye-catching revelation or heart-stopping rendition, he offered more than enough hints to let loose the inquisitor's imagination.

His *Seven Pillars of Wisdom* opens with two passages that have the whiff of tortured whispers made in the darkness of priestly confessionals: a dedication to SA, aka Dahoum, Lawrence's 'donkey boy' during his archaeological digs at Carshemish, Syria, in 1911,[90] followed by a near-cinematic reenactment of bodily fever among the sand dunes. To Dahoum, he began:

I loved you, so I drew these tides of men into my hands
and wrote my will across the sky and the stars
To earn you Freedom, the seven pillared worthy house, that
     your eyes
might be shining for me when we came . . .
Love, the way weary, groped to your body, our brief wage
Ours for the moment
Before earth's soft hands explored your shape, and the blind
     worms
Grew fat on your substance
Men prayed me that I set our work, the inviolate house, as a
     memory of you.
But for fit monument I shattered it, unfinished: and now
The little things creep out to patch themselves hovels in the
     marred shadow of your gift.[91]

And then, and then, this: Chapter one, the very first page:

Some of the evils of my tale may have been inherent in our circumstances . . . Gusts of cruelty, perversions, lusts ran lightly over the surface without troubling us; for the moral laws which had seemed to hedge about these silly accidents must yet be fainter words. We had learned that there were pangs too sharp, griefs too deep, ecstasies too high for our finite selves to register . . . The men were young and sturdy; and hot flesh and blood unconsciously claimed a right in them and tormented their bellies with strange longings. Our privations and dangers fanned this virile heat, in a climate as racking as can be conceived. We had no shut places to be alone in, no thick clothes to hide our nature. Man in all things lived candidly with man . . . In horror of such sordid commerce, our youth began indifferently to slake one another's few needs in their own clean bodies – a cold convenience that, by comparison, seemed sexless and even pure. Later, some began to justify this sterile process, and swore that friends quivering together in the yielding sand with intimate hot limbs in supreme embrace, found there hidden in the darkness a sensual co-efficient of the mental passion which was welding our souls and spirits in one flaming effort. Several, thirsting to punish appetites they could not wholly prevent, took a savage pride in degrading the body, and offered themselves fiercely in any habit which promised physical pain or filth.[92]

A rather guilty climax to two very hard years of Arab arousal, no? True, 'some' and 'their' and 'several' manage a distance far enough to sink the actual accomplices in a murky pond of titillating ambiguities, but why does the reader have the strong feeling that this passage's author was more contrite participant than culpable voyeur? Could all this not be about a tormented soft spot for Arab heartthrobs? A noxious mixture of shame and ecstasy in a man who 'liked things beneath' him and 'took . . . pleasures and adventures downward'?[93] A man in whom puritanism and carnal longings took turns in teasing, even spitting at, each other?[94]

True there lurked always that will uneasily waiting to burst out. My brain was sudden and silent as a wild cat, my senses like mud clogging its feet and my self . . . telling the beast it was bad form to spring and vulgar to feed upon the kill . . . It was a real beast and this book its mangy skin, dried, stuffed and set up squarely for men to stare at.[95]

Some say absolutely, some insist absolutely not. To this very day, observers of Lawrence are still debating his sexual likes and dislikes. And one cannot help feeling that he would not have wanted it any other way: overtones and undercurrents, speculation, a near-definite *no* with enough room for a conceivable *yes* – and just as well if it were the other way around. The truth is there is no clear-cut evidence, no ironclad proof, no sightings, no credible witnesses – just a rape during the war years,[96] an undeniable taste for whippings in later years and rich words, as telling to one mind as they are guiltless to another.

The very thorough Jeremy Wilson, in his definitive *Lawrence of Arabia*, seems satisfied that the *Pillars'* dedication was as much to Syria as it was to Dahoum.[97] A bit of a stretch, considering that Lawrence seemed far more thrilled with Dahoum than he ever was with the Syrians, who he surmised were an 'ape-like people having much of the Japanese quickness but shallow . . . '[98] 'admirers (but not seekers) of the truth, self-satisfied, not incapable (as are the Egyptians) of abstract ideas, but unpractical and so lazy mentally as to be superficial . . . '[99] Besides, at first or fifth reading, do you not have the inescapable suspicion that somebody is in love? After all, according to Lawrence, his love for Dahoum – consummated or not – was deep enough to drive the 'liberation' of a whole people: 'I liked a particular Arab very much, and I thought that freedom for the race would be an acceptable present.'[100] That such devotion happened to be, in Lawrence's ingeniously elastic mind, a short ride away from love of mother country and self, must have made it all the more worthy of fulfilling. Cut through the thick of his adventure and you would dig up ambitions about building 'a new people in the East';[101] about catapulting to the helm a 'Sunni prince, like Feisal, pretending to revive the glories of Ommayad or Ayubid';[102] about ensuring – with British help, of course – that these same people 'remain in a state of political mosaic, a tissue of small jealous principalities incapable of cohesion and yet always ready to combine against an outside force'.[103] But shift your eyes ever so slightly to the edge of his designs and suddenly you are face to face with the literary pangs of a man in love. All these ups and downs, this brouhaha, this dreadful screw-up or great feat (your pick) was for the love of one gentle Dahoum – so that Lawrence could give freedom to Dahoum, who sadly had died some time before 1918, when Lawrence could hand it to him. *Wa min al hubi ma katal* (from a certain kind of love, death) goes a famous Arabic proverb. What made Lawrence think that freedom was his gift to give in the first place is one of those tasty Lawrencian morsels a Levantine can nibble on forever on a lethargic Friday afternoon.

There you have it. The very messy affairs of Lawrence's heart made even messier by a mind half-giddy about, and half-furious at, its dubious motivations.

*   *   *

To be sure, to all of this Ali could never rise nor sink – again, your pick. His sexuality was certain about whom it loved and wanted. It was free, confident, voracious, unquenchable. It declared itself unabashedly to its would-be lovers and sat very comfortably with its friends. His Dahoums lived silent and hidden behind the many closed doors of his lives in Cairo and Amman to appease society's sexual pretensions, not his own. And his was a far simpler quest than Lawrence's, a return to roots burdensome and mystifying mostly to himself. Comb through him any way you want, Ali came back to his part of the world a hotchpotch Arab. There were genuine, fully grown men in him, born and bred in every previous stop in his life. It would be easy to judge, as some have, his push and pull with Arabness as that of a viscerally Western man feeling his way uneasily in the East. In his sappy moods, his pen could jump metres over the top. 'Why are they so beautiful?' he asked himself on a day trip to the Jordan Valley in 2000, a good twenty-four years after settling in the Middle East. 'Is it because it gives us a glimpse of Islamic society, benevolent, accepting, fraternal, pluralistic, respectful, all encompassing . . . our hand-some people as God created them?'[104] If a little impatient, you would swear these were the irritating impressions of a casual traveller, a first besotted encounter with indigenous rhythms. Graphic depictions of 'solitary marathons in the midnight streets',[105] constant references to his Arab home as 'exile', descriptions of self ('the fond sentiments of the alien white man'[106]), from afar draw the rough contours of a wanderer who stood nervously on the outer fringes of the Arab world he inhabited. Ecstatic longings for and aloofness towards his origins took turns in Ali way before he returned to them and ever since. And so, call him a stranger in the Orient, a man by turns enthralled and unnerved by this land, and you would be half-forgiven, and yet you would not be half-close to understanding the outsider in him. Ali became a bit of a stranger in any place – any place – that kept him too long, eating away at his obstinate romantic visions and unleashing again the restless nomad. His thirst for the untouched native was not a yearning for that exotic *Other*, it was a search for the basis of identity before it had had the chance to cloak itself in imported layers. Ali was looking for that opposite Arab. 'What a contrast; their back country stalwart rootedness with my feather-like inorganic tenuous role,'[107] he remarked once about the difference between him and his Petra friends.

True, for him, squeezing his way into the sweaty armpits of the indigent Arab fold always carried with it large chunks of pure pleasure, along with a few moments of discomfort and some of sheer terror. But Ali always camped on the rough edges of existence and dwelled in its limbos. That is where he quickly ensconced himself wherever he went. For him, this was never a game, it was a way of life. His dilemma with Arabness was that of any Arab who saw too much of its complicated essence, not too little. Like his paintings, Ali's sensibilities were an interplay of so many shades of changing light and colour woven into the subtleties that permeated every interesting detail of life. Yes, he was much more at ease in the West – because the West let him be at ease. The East did not.

For Lawrence, the Arab world was not an existential problem, it was pure theatre, 'a kind of foreign stage on which one plays day and night, in fancy dress in a strange language . . . '[108] That is where he sought the role of a lifetime and, intoxicated with the

sheer audacity of his mission, he carried it to excess and became
lost in its wake.

> . . . The effort for these years to live in the dress of the Arabs,
> and to imitate their mental foundation, quitted me of my
> English self . . . They destroyed it all for me . . . Sometime these
> selves would converse in the void; and then madness was very
> near, as I believe it would be near the man who could see things
> through the veils at once of two customs, two educations, two
> environments.[109]

After all those joy rides in the desert, he mocked himself in Arab
gear mimicking Arab habits and tongues, just as he ridiculed
earlier 'the perfectly hopeless vulgarity of the half-Europeanised
Arab . . .'[110] It turns out, Lawrence was a man very faithful to the
immutability of *Otherness*. Cross fertilise, dabble a little, or plunge
outright, drink up some of that culture and digest some of these
mores, and all you end up becoming is a tortured parody. Perhaps
it could not be any other way for him, a man for whom any kind
of identity was as short-lived as yesterday, as claustrophobic as
today, as frightening as tomorrow. As if in constant flight from
the sameness of life, Lawrence sought momentary refuge in each
of his characters and ended up being a little bit of everything and
much of nothing. Edward Said gives Lawrence's fragmented self
a good summing up:

> In each of his activities he practiced Lawrence could devise a
> pied-a-terre for himself. In his letters . . . we see him . . . as the
> professional Arabist, the revolutionary, the intelligence expert,
> the imperialist politician, the classical archeologist, the classical
> scholar, the military tactician and administrator, the social
> critic, the literary critic, the historian, and above all the writer
> haunted by his own writing – in each of these he found a pied-a-
> terre, and yet in no one did he completely rest and in no one did
> he completely take possession. R. P. Blackmur goes so far as
> to say that Lawrence never produced a character, not even his
> own.[111]

Lawrence forayed into the East probably thinking that he could find his way back. He did not. And those memorable nights among the sand dunes did not help much either. Nowhere in Ali's own remembrances of embraces in the desert or anywhere else is there even a trace of neophyte remorse. In Lawrence, these feverish times seem to have stoked the fires of his 'standing civil war'.[112] But his ill-concealed self-flagellation for licentious behaviour, which was never too far away from his self-recriminations for political wrongs, provoked no visible reactions from Ali beyond the Revolt series. Perhaps Lawrence's acrobatics between tortured meae culpae and indecent swagger were eloquent enough commentary on the Anglo Saxon's troubled and troubling mission in the Middle East. And why respond when Ali could just sit back and enjoy a show he came to know so well. Flip-flops between asinine braggadocio and self-absorbed cross-on-my-shoulder guilt trips are tedious for most people, even if wrapped in mouth-watering phrases, but Ali must have liked all this hair tearing. He did it so often himself.

*   *   *

If Lawrence's politics ruffled Ali's feathers, Aleppo was always there to smooth them. For someone who cared so much about history and Jabri lineage and Aleppine roots, he must have been tickled by Lawrence's relatively merciful take on Aleppo, nasty though he was about so many of its neighbours. Lawrence liked Aleppo well enough to forgive it its knotty, cosmopolitan pedigree (unlike those of Beirut or Jerusalem), to join it with its querulous sisters Damascus, Homs and Hama, and to bestow on it, against all his evidence to the contrary, the precious title of Arab.[113]

A great city in Syria, but not of it, nor of Anatolia, nor of Mesopotamia. There the races, creeds, and tongues of the Ottoman Empire met and knew one another in a spirit of compromise. The clash of characteristics, which made its streets a kaleidoscope, imbued the Aleppine with a lewd thoughtfulness which corrected in him what was blatant in the Damascene. Aleppo had shared in all the civilisations which turned about it. The result served to be a lack of zest in its people's beliefs. Even so they surpassed the rest of Syria. They fought and traded more; were more fanatical and vicious; and made most beautiful things: but all with a dearth of conviction which rendered barren their multitudinous strength.

It was typical of Aleppo that in it, while yet Mohammedan feeling ran high, more fellowship should rule between Christian and Mohammedan, Armenian, Arab, Turk, Kurd and Jew, than in perhaps any other great city of the Ottoman Empire, and that more friendliness, though little licence, should have accorded to Europeans . . . The intensity of their self-sown patriotism tinged the bulk of the citizens outside them with a colour of local consciousness which was so much less vivid than the Beyrout-acquired unanimity of Damascus.[114]

Not bad, considering the spew that darted out of Lawrence's mouth about the Cairenes and his favourite people the Bedu. Whereas he found the former ' . . . horribly ugly, very dirty, dull, low spirited, without any of the vigour or the self-confident independence of our men . . . frenetic, querulous, foul-mouthed, and fawning . . . the fanaticism of the country is deplorable, and the treatment of women most unEuropean . . . and one could not stand or work close to them for a few minutes without catching fleas or lice',[115] the latter he took for

absolute slaves of their appetite, with no stamina of mind, drunkards for coffee, milk or water, gluttons for stewed meat, shameless beggars of tobacco. Their strength was the strength of men beyond geographical temptation: the poverty of Arabia made them simple, continent, enduring. If forced into civilised life they would have succumbed like any savage race to its diseases, meanness, luxury, cruelty, crooked dealing, artifice; and, like savages, they would have suffered them exaggeratedly for lack of inoculation.[116]

But, Khalappa, well, Khalappa, as the Hittites called Aleppo around two thousand years before Christ, was something different.[117] Like all its neighbours, it thrived and writhed under dynastic labels and periods with sumptuous rings and wonderful tempos, and reached the last century a robust if dishevelled ancient trading town awaiting Lawrence's verdict on who it was, is, and shall become. But Aleppo had survived so much and lived so long and hard, the future could not unleash anything with which it had not already met and sparred. Close your eyes and dip your fingers into the pages of any Aleppine phase, and you begin to spin, eyes watering, from myriads of shifting alliances, and marriages, and conflicts, and friendships; a deck shuffled so often and so completely, it keeps dealing out mega dramas and mini plots, a queue of villains and saviours turned invaders. For happy moments, Aleppo can remember Hellenist, Roman, Shiite Hamdanid, and Sunni Ayyubid times. Among its minders, it can name the only '*ad*' and every other competing '*id*' *house* in Islam: Umayyads, Abbasids, Hamdanids, Zangids, Ayyubids, Mirdasids . . . The Seljuks and Mamluks had their share of this city, too. For truly bad times, it would surely recall Hulagu, Timur and their Mongolian hordes, the bubonic plague, a few earthquakes, intermittent sectarian strife. For inspiration, it can always summon the Ottomans, the last of the lot, before it finally sits back and sighs.

Even in the very short span of seventy-four years (between 1186 and 1260), under Saladin's son al Malik al-Zahir Ghazi and his family, symbols of Aleppine contentment under Ayyubid wings, life was dizzy from so many nomadic journeys between good politics and bad. Forget for a minute the complicated web of events and ambitions, and take pleasure in the sound-effects of these Ayyubid and non-Ayyubid names: al-Zahir Ghazi, al-Aziz (son of al-Zahir Ghazi, ruler of Aleppo), Mu'azzam Isa (cousin, ruler of Damascus), al-Ashraf (cousin, ruler of Jazirah/Northern Mesopotamia), al Malik al-Adil (brother of Saladin and uncle of al-Zahir Ghazi in Egypt), Dayfah Khatoun (wife of al-Zahir Ghazi, daughter of al-Adil), al-Malik al Nasir Yousuf II (grandson of al-Zahir Ghazi), al Malik al Nasir Daud (son of Mu'azzam in Damascus ousted by al-Ashraf and al-Kamil), al-Malik al-Salih

Ayyub (son of al-Adil, exiled to Jazirah and then ruler of Egypt), Al Malik al-Salih Ismail (brother of Ashraf ousted from Damascus by Ayyub); Bohemond IV (Prince of Antioch and Count of Tripoli), Ghiyath al-Din Kay-Khusrau I (Seljuk sultan of Rum), Badr al-Din Lulu (Ruler of Mosul), Muzaffar al-Din Kokburi (Begtenginid ruler of Irbil), Leon II (ruler of Lesser Armenia), Louis IX (king of France) . . . [118] Now, how many Lawrences and Picots and Clemenceaus and Millerands and Berthelots and Curzons and Lloyd Georges did Aleppines need to make their days richer than that?[119]

It just so happened that Lawrence was describing this city when the Jabris themselves were neck-deep in pomp and circumstance. In 1983, Ali scribbled this cryptic résumé in his diary:

Ali Jabri born in mid-1940s in Jerusalem from an old Syrian family from the ancient town of Aleppo, rich in tradition and political significance. Family were statesmen and landowners. Father, a contractor, influenced an early interest in urbanism and civic design. Jabri grew up drawing from childhood. School in Alexandria in the last years of Farouk . . . [120]

This repeats the earlier biography, but a few more details to this or that sentence, a smidgen of colour, and the portrait begins to complete itself on his walls:

Ali Jabri born on August 18th, 1942, in Jerusalem, to Hala and Majddedine Jabri, scions of old Syrian family from the ancient town of Aleppo. At time of birth father worked in Jordan as head of East Jordan Municipalities.[121]

Jabris rich in tradition and political significance. Family were statesmen and landowners. Saadallah Jabri, Syrian nationalist leader during the French Mandate and prime minister in the 40s, is a great uncle. Ihsan, Ali's maternal grandfather and brother of Saadallah, was man of the Ottoman Empire . . . first Secretary to Mehmed V, the 35th Ottoman Sultan,[122] before switching to the Arab cause and becoming chamberlain to the leader of the Arab Revolt, the Hashemite Feisal ibn al Hussein, during his brief stint as King of Syria. In 1958, the desperately pragmatic Ihsan held the position of the President of the Council of Ministers of the United Arab Republic (the Syrian-Egyptian union) and Yemen, a ceremonial role accorded him by Egypt's Gamal Abdel Nasser in appreciation of his loyalty. Nafe', Ali's paternal great grandfather and older half-brother of Ihsan and Saadallah, one of Aleppo's richest landowners and one of its representatives in the Majlis Mabou'than, the Ottoman Chamber of Deputies.[123] In 1886, Nafe' and other Aleppine notables were accused of trying to murder the provincial governor Cemal Pasa, most probably as part of the latter's effort to undermine local notable influence against his reform program.[124] The men were never formally charged. Kamal, Ali's paternal grandfather, chosen early on to manage the family's waqf* and protect its wealth.[125] Father, Majddedine, a graduate of Robert College, Istanbul, held various positions of importance in Syria – head of Municipality of Aleppo (1946-1948), minister of works in several ministries between 1948 and 1958 – before he accepted the invitation of his friend Sheikh Fahd Al Sabah of Kuwait to move to Kuwait to help build that country.[126]

Mother, Hala, Bachelor's degree from Vassar College, New York. Went there against the family's wishes, after completing her studies in Switzerland. Older sister, Saadieyh, married in 1924 Musa Alami, one of Palestine's wealthiest and most respected notables, and divorced him in 1950 to marry his assistant Wasfi al Tall, who was to become in the course of the 60s one of Jordan's most prominent prime ministers.

Could these Jabris have been the vulgar, half-Europeanised Arabs to whom Lawrence referred? Because they certainly were – half-Europeanised, that is. They were also among the Muslim intelligentsia whom Lawrence dismissed as Western facsimiles:

They spoke foreign languages as often as they could, wore

---

* Waqf is a form of endowment traditionally used by rich families for inheritance purposes.

European clothes, were often wealthy, used to entertain and be
entertained by foreigners, and impressed themselves more deeply
upon foreign visitors than their numbers or home influence
warranted. Their political ideals were culled from books. They
had no programme for revolt, but many ideas for the settlement
after one. Such and such were the rights of Syria, such her
boundaries, such her future law and constitution. They formed
committees in Cairo, Paris, London, New York, Beyrout, Berlin
and Berne to influence European powers to go on spinning real
dreams.[127]

Imagine that! Why this Knight of Araby, this imitator of Arab
dialects, bearer of Arab garb, guest of Bedouin tribes, voracious
reader of political books and manuscripts, nonstop British plotter,
whisperer to Feisal, should have been offended by some Arabs'
wish to taste some of the same can be chalked up to imperial pre-
rogative. Lawrence was sold on Feisal as king of Syria, quite a few
of these Muslims were not. The Englishman was put out.[128]

But perhaps Lawrence's thoughts, if any, on the Jabris were as
mild as his about their city, because both supported the
Hashemites. For Lawrence, the pact with Feisal was cast in sand
and built on promises with broken bones. For the Jabris, it was
stronger with some Hashemite brothers than with others, lasting
well into that December day when Ali, finally, was lowered deep
into Petra. This is the reason the Arab Revolt series, for Ali, drew
several windows into a not so distant Jabri life. He hiked back-
wards through the towns, the desert, books, pictures, to understand the beginnings of this relatively recent Arab chronicle and,
perchance, catch a glimpse of his own family's past. What he
found was the sweep of history, where good intentions often fall
casualty of bad, and high ideals give way to low. This is why
Feisal, once a prince and a king, cannot see himself in these
paintings; why his Syrian kingdom, conceived without British
backing and with only half-hearted Arab consent, finds not a trace
in these paintings; why his Iraqi kingdom, born in 1921 with the
help of British guilt and energy and decapitated in 1958 with

*Saadallah and
Ihsan al Jabri.
Early 1930s*

*Young Majddedine
al Jabri in Syria.
Late 1920s*

unfathomable Iraqi cruelty, is not given even nominal space in these paintings – they are all shattered Hashemite dreams replaced by others with different names and different political persuasions. When Ali had to paint this Hashemite saga, he could only paint symbols of Mecca, where the Sharifain family started, and Jordan, which they never really coveted and where they never intended to stay.

From that very day, when the so-called pulse of Arab nationalism began to thump, and identity in every Arab quarter began to expand with lofty banners and shrink with parochial loyalties; when colonialism, with a straight face, pretended to care, and indigenous leaders pretended to cope and understand; when women, men, and children in their multitudes went very hungry, and remedies were very few and minuscule; when a new generation of men rallied behind so many national cries and splintered after a dozen failed escapes; when all of this was going on, the Jabris were there helping wield the levers of power, spinning a thousand and one marvellous possibilities and realising none.

Dramatic openings – again.

*   *   *

This is what Gertrude Bell had to say in 1926 about Ihsan, Ali's grandfather.

> The point is (did I write this before?) that the French are going to put the League of N. into a very tight place . . . a paragraph in Reuters yesterday saying that the French government was wholly satisfied with the rapid steps which had been made in the pacification of Syria . . . The Syrian nationalists making a determined effort to be heard by the League. One of them, now at Geneva, I know, Ihsan Jabri Beg . . . an able man who could put up a case good enough to make de Jouvenel[129] very uncomfortable. The League has refused to hear him.[130]

Gertrude liked Ihsan probably because, like her, he not only disliked the French, but he very much liked Feisal – the man she and Lawrence worked tirelessly to make king of Iraq after Syria was denied him. It is easy to understand how Ihsan, a pure bred Ottoman man, became bound to the Hashemites. He must have slept easy over this one. After all, Feisal's father, Sharif Hussein of Hijaz, a direct descendant of the Prophet and official Guardian of Mecca, had only recently broken off with the Ottomans in the hope of presiding over his own coast-to-coast Arab Kingdom. The Ottoman Empire was passé and Ihsan's younger brother Saadallah had already become wedded to the new Arab rage.[131] Bring in a nurturing Istanbul, that bonhomie that tied Sunni gentry to one another, and you have before you a devoted aristocratic chamberlain and his royal master.

Yes, the Jabris were more or less fine with a Hashemite king in Syria.[132] But like every other good feeling in those days, this one flowed from an awful blend of wishful thinking and depressingly far-fetched ideas. Somehow Feisal, his Jabris and their feudal friends, along with many of those rich mercantile townsmen and elevated sons of age-old Ottoman bureaucratic edifices, deter-mined to outbid the British and outwit the French.[133] Feisal thought he could reign over a newly independent Greater Syria that hugged restless Mount Lebanon, Tripoli and Beirut in the south-west, encompassed forbidden Palestine in the south and kept Trans-Jordan in the south-east.[134] A new Syrian Congress was 'elected' in 1919, and its representatives began to play like statesmen and deliberate on issues small and big. Even female suffrage, though shy, conditional and constricted, found its way to the hearts of a few enlightened men, among them dear, earnest Saadallah.[135]

Rashid Rida, the eminent Salafi scholar, argued that the right to vote was predicated on the condition of individual freedom, and so threatened husbands' control over their wives: 'Does a woman, under the protection of her husband, have the right to vote if he prohibits her from voting?' Jabri responded: 'Does he have the right to prohibit her from bearing witness in court?' Rida responded in the affirmative.[136]

(Brilliant debate, no doubt! It took women another twenty-nine years to win partial suffrage in Syria.)

But all this was so brief and so bittersweet. Feisal and Syria and the Jabris were not to be. Like a ping-pong ball Feisal let himself be thrown back and forth by the British, the French, and the Arabs. To many among his own people he was not enough Syrian and too much of everything else; to the French he was too Arab, too British; to the English he was only one pledge of a miserable three. In the end he was dispensable enough to sell out for the Zionists who were promised Palestine and unimportant enough to dump for the French who were promised Syria. But then how could Feisal compete with men and gatherings such as these:

> December 1, 1918, two years after the Sykes-Picot agreement had sliced-up the map with bizarre-looking borders and left the area with too many loose ends. The French Embassy, London. The French and British prime ministers sit down for a chat. Clemenceau starts the discussion with something to the effect of:
> 'What do you want to talk about?'
> Lloyd George declares: 'Mesopotamia and Palestine.'
> Clemenceau: 'Tell me what you want?'
> Lloyd George: 'I want Mosul [in Iraq].'
> Clemenceau: 'You shall have it. Anything else?'
> Lloyd George: 'Yes, I want Jerusalem too.'
> Clemenceau: 'You shall have it.'[137]

Apparently, after the deal between these two gentlemen was struck, the British prime minister was heard muttering to himself, 'Mosul has oil, Palestine is Holy Land; Syria, what is Syria?'[138]

But what did poor, put-upon Feisal expect? Only three years before, in 1915, a most revealing thought had overtaken Sir Ronald Storrs, the British Oriental Secretary in Cairo, upon hearing the full details of Sharif Hussein's conditions for joining the Brits against the Turks: 'We could not conceal from ourselves (and with difficulty from him) that his pretensions bordered upon the

King Feisal and Ihsan al Jabri

tragi-comic.'[139] Tragi-comic, indeed! Even Lawrence, who hated
the French enough to actively consider the possibility of Feisal in
Syria, could not help articulating, in typical character insights
that drowned niggardly admiration with profligate contempt, what
he and his superiors felt about the Hashemite bid and its agent:
'Feisal was born a brave, weak, ignorant spirit, trying to do work
for which only a genius, a prophet or a great criminal was fitted.
I served him out of pity, a motive which degraded us both.'[140]
This was hardly the last, or the worst, of the insults. The British,
who always found Sharif Hussein too stubborn for their taste,
began to find his nemesis ibn Saud of Nejd and his Wahhabis
perfectly charming substitutes. In the final battles between ibn
Saud and the infinitely milder Hussein, England forsook the

Hashemite and helped usher in ibn Saud as future king of the yet
to be Saudi Arabia.

> Incidentally, of course, we sealed the doom of . . . Hussein. We
> offered him a treaty in . . . 1921 which would have saved him
> Hijaz had he renounced [his pretensions] hegemony over all
> Arabic areas: but he clung . . . Ibn Saud is not a system but a
> despot, ruling by virtue of a dogma. Therefore I approve of
> him as I [would] approve of anything in Arabia which [was]
> individualistic, unorganised, unsystematic.[141]

Water under the bridge, all this. In any case, the British did not
need anyone to pat them on the back, they were doing so much of
that themselves. What is more, the very flexible Hashemites ended
up with Iraq and Trans-Jordan – by way of consolation prizes not
entirely disagreeable, even if Sharif Hussein himself ended up
Hijaz-less and throne-less living for a time in Cyprus.[142] With that
the gratified Lawrence announced that 'I take to myself credit of
Mr Churchill's pacification of the Middle East . . . The work I did
constructively . . . in 1921 and 1922 seems to me in retrospect the
best I ever did. It somewhat redresses to my mind the immoral
and unwarrantable risks I took with others' lives and happiness in
1917–18 . . . '[143] And thus his loving private parting words about
Feisal come as no surprise:

> Feisal owed me Damascus first of all, and Baghdad second: and
> between those two stages most of his education in kingcraft and
> affairs. When with him I am an omnipotent adviser: and while
> that is very well in the field, it is derogatory to a monarch:
> especially to a monarch who is not entirely constitutional . . . [144]

*   *   *

Such crowded political bazaars these British and French ones,
and the Arabs, always brilliant at haggling over the small and
petty, did not quite know how to negotiate over the large and
vital: there were too many unknowns and strange deals being
hatched over there over situations over here; there was that

very suave Haim Weizmann and the sneaking suspicion of a new Jewish home about to be built and an old Palestinian one about to be torn apart; there were small-minded jealousies masquerading as noble callings and low ambitions parading as high principles.

Truth be told, there is so little about the private lives of Ali's Jabris in these years. It is always a very misty day when the pen beckons them and their dead dominions. Cryptic mentions here, names in memoirs there, a reference in this book, a footnote in that. And the interviewees, so few, are either too vague or near mum. What a false notion of decorum or loyalty does not hide, exhausted memory smothers. Places and names and faces travel in intimate, disappearing circles. Still, the listener does walk away with some intimations and more than a couple of clues.

Away from Feisal and Syria, Ihsan retreated to Geneva in the 1920s. With him were Saadieyh (possibly), Hala, and his *freirah*,* the girls' German ex-governess and the second Mrs Ihsan al Jabri.[145] The first one, Subheiyeh, was said to be convalescing somewhere in Turkey, a much-needed respite that apparently lasted until her death.[146] For Ihsan, now a middle-aged, banished, anti-French activist, Geneva was altogether pleasant. He suffered the tumultuous change as the rich always bear it: with physical comfort and a certain amount of psychological strain. He hooked up with *Amir* (prince) Shakib Irslan, a Druze 'Arab-Ottoman gentleman'[147] and a more formidable thinking man, and began, to no avail, salvaging from the rubble of the old Ottoman Empire the beginnings of a so-called Arab-Islamic age.[148]

For the more pugnacious, younger Saadallah, an Aleppine lull welcomed him between every French pardon and exile.

Meanwhile, Saadieyh and Hala were well on their way towards lives as deceivingly serene on the outside as they were devastatingly turbulent on the inside.

*   *   *

---

* Freirah is the Arab Aleppine casual conversion of the German *Fräulein*.

Rumour has it that Saadieyh met Musa Alami under that huge tree in the Middle of Jericho.[149] She was seventeen or eighteen, he was twenty-seven. Soon after, in 1924, Saadieyh, the new bride, began her life between three grand homes behind the shrinking walls of Palestine.[150] In the summer of 1926, Hala went to stay with her at the house in Sharafat near Jerusalem. It was that same summer that Serene Hussein Shahid, Musa's six-year-old niece, heard the word suicide for the first time, from Hala's lips.

> One day as I sat close by her side painting her roofs, she said: 'I may commit suicide, you know!' Suicide was a word I had not heard before . . . I looked at her troubled face and pretended not to understand. Then she talked about death, and said: 'Do you know how I see your grandmother's guests in her elegant salon? I see their faces looking at me from their wooden coffins. We're all going to die, you know! You and me, too.'[151]

Hala was only ten or eleven years of age.

Telling, perhaps, but it is no more than a lonely incident on a lonely page in a lonely chapter about a distant Hala remembered in a friend's forlorn memoir of Arab Jerusalem. There are others about her, much like this one, that lie as debris in people's minds. On their own, each recollection reveals little, however much it tries, but when they all come together they do make you wonder. Among these are Hala's own creepy recitals to Diala about Ihsan throwing her stuffed doll in the forest in the dark night and telling her to fetch it to teach her courage; about Fraulein locking her up in the room with a dead body; about a slap across the face because she wanted the 'little doll with the feathers in her cap' and Ihsan wanted to buy her the big one. Diala recalls that 'she would tell these giggling . . . like Ali did stories that scared him that he was later calm enough to retell as a joke for others . . . If I was in the room, he would give me an anguished but humorous look to show it was awful, but with a smile on his face for all the laughing audience. They could both be the life of the party . . . the loudest laughter from their table.'[152] The storyteller can pair these shreds of Hala with those of others, such as the one of Ali when he was

*Saadieyh and Ihsan
al Jabri. Mid-1920s*

*Hala at the pool in
Saadallah al
Jabri's house in
Aleppo. Late 1930s*

only four or five years old in Aleppo, locked in his room, Hala
out, banging against the window and crying out to his upstairs
neighbour and kindergarten teacher, as she stepped out of the
building, 'Please, please, help me.'[153] Beyond this feeble attempt
at patchwork nothing much can be done with these fragments: the
mix is fascinating but it reads the way beautiful broken crystals
shimmer. And, of course, much like broken crystals it can draw
blood. To Diala, it has the taste of venom, pure hearsay pretending
to be fact about a woman who was as unhappy with Aleppo as the
city was with her.

'. . . She married her cousin,' Serene wrote about Hala long
after that Sharafat summer. 'She had a delightful family and a
beautiful home. Yet I never saw happiness in her eyes. What
more does she want? I often wondered, what more could there be
besides her intelligence, talent, beauty, education and background . . . Was her unhappiness a hereditary trait? Or merely
the whim of creation.'[154] Or both. Or because of hush-hush fears
and tight-lipped needs in a world that was cruel towards those
who were more than ordinary, far too special. People always
puzzled over Hala. To conventional eyes, there was always something biting into her, something not quite right. When all was
well, she was a tad too eccentric, when things went badly they
called her mad. But you never really hear too many specifics
about her, however much you ask. From the hum of low,
tentative voices comes chatter about how the piano, the dance
floor, six languages, Vassar and volatile Jabri blood made her
into someone very different, possibly even astounding: a woman
who in good times towered over everything and everyone, but in
bad slowly crumbled and fell apart.[155]

That was Hala, a freak accident in a tradition-soaked family
wound up tight from age-old feudal habits and Turkic moods. She
was blunt, fierce, stubborn, with a style so extravagant and yet so
tasteful, a spirit so generous, so carefree. 'Ihsan complained to me
about Hala,' Saadallah wrote in his Paris diary, on July 19, 1936.

Hala has come to Geneva and might travel to America . . . If she goes she will become a stranger to us . . . We have our traditions, our religion, our way of life . . . Hala called me to ask me about her travelling to America. I rejected the idea. She came back at me that she is twenty one years old . . . Europe and her schools and ours . . . are not enough for her. If she had been good at school, there would have been no objection. Hers is just obsession and silliness. And how nice for her to become a movie actress. God protect us![156]

Of all places on earth, this Jabri woman set her eyes on Hollywood. Why she only made it to Poughkeepsie, New York, halfway there, lies somewhere in the many lines missing from her shrivelled-up portrait.[157]

*   *   *

None of it ended well. Every piece of this Arab region became a headache and an eyesore. People's dreams carelessly flirted with reality until the two fell out and finally grew apart. Droves of people went to bed Syrian and woke up the next morning Lebanese.[158] That part of the Arabian peninsula – from the Red Sea in the West to the Persian Gulf in the East, from Jordan and Iraq in the north-east to Yemen and Oman in the south – sprawling with tribes and clans of different traditions and customs became one, and Saudi, under Abd al Aziz. Farther up, Basra and Nasiriyah in the south were nudged closer to Mosul and Kirkuk in the north; all were ordered to join the party, love Feisal and bow to Baghdad. Then, in 1948, Palestine went and Saadieyh right after it. Hand in hand with Wasfi, she said goodbye to Musa, only weeks, it seemed, after Palestine turned its back on him and them. Saadieyh's Palestinian friends were dumbstruck, appalled, that she would cross from such wealth to such modesty, from Holy Jerusalem to provincial Amman, from the West of the river to its East.[159] Actually, if it spoke of anything, this forty-three-year-old woman's love for Wasfi, only thirty-two then, spoke of passion and pluck.

Hala and Majddedine went from Aleppo to Amman to Beirut

and back again. They say she was bored, very bored, and restless. 'I am going to bear ten more sons to fight for Palestine,'[160] she half-consciously cried in Dr Oppenheimer's ear as Ali slid out from her womb on August 18, 1942. She never did.

Ihsan languished for more than a decade in Geneva while his brother Saadallah walked in and out of French prisons and remote Syrian villages, the dreaded sites of his evictions. A political leader in the making, he was bearing all the right humiliations and collecting all the right scars and wounds. A few more years and he would become one of old Syria's first men and certainly, unbeknownst to him and his kin, one of its last.

CHAPTER THREE

One Day You Shall Be Queen

He came from his country saturated with propaganda about
our savagery and of France's right to rule over us, saturated
with wild stories he heard and read about our country, the land
of magic and secrets. The more he swims in its unknowns and
looks upon its sons' pictures, the more he thinks he can explain
its caftans, its headdresses, its tarboush, in their strangeness
and primitiveness, as pretexts for humiliation and enslavement
of a frozen people, neither moved by duty nor accustomed to
responsibility.

> Saadallah al Jabri on the French intelligence officer
> who interrogated him on February 22, 1936,
> in Ain Diwar, his place of exile

'I am a member of the old ruling class, inevitably compromised
with the Bourbon regime. I belong to an unlucky generation,
swung between the old world and the new, and I find myself ill
at ease in both. And what is more, as you must have realised by
now, I am without illusions.'[161]

> Don Fabrizio in Guiseppe Tomasi di Lampedusa,
> *Il Gattopardo* (The Leopard)

Who would remember Saadallah al Jabri now?

*   *   *

1985. Spring. The Jordan Valley. The Ghandours' new mud house.

For hours Ali kept running up to the roof to check on the exact
spot to plant the tree, and then down again to see it up close. 'A
little to the right,' then he would come down. 'No.' Then up,
'Move it closer to me a bit,' then down. Up and down, for hours.

I was way over budget, no experience, this was my first engineering job, the crane was rented by the hour, it was hot, and we
stood there for hours, with Ali going up and down. I finally came
at him.[162]

Hazem, big and burly, bore down on Ali while the two stood in a
landscaped garden that he simply would – or could – not finish.
A shouting match, curses, and Ali storms out of the house.
'Fuming', he catches a ride back to Amman on a 'tomato truck'.
Greetings, introductions; no doubt the back straight, the legs
respectfully resting together at a slight angle, the hands clasped
together over lap – the way Ali always sat in company.

'Ali addjabri min Halab' – Ali al Jabri of Aleppo – and, what do
you know? The nonagenarian driver 'knew Saadallah'.[163]

*   *   *

From the very first moment of meeting Saadallah Abdel al Qader
al Jabri, right there at the beginning of the quest, one has the urge
to sprinkle on his story droplets from Lampedusa's mystical *Il
Gattopardo*, and gently tease out of it the Syrian version of the
surrender of an old, very tired order to its end. There are words,
times in Saadallah's diaries, rare though they are, that bring to
mind the breathtaking face of Burt Lancaster's *Il Principe* in
the mirror as it registered the truth and succumbed to its natural
cruelty. Small wonder *Il Gattopardo* was one of Hala and Ali's
favourite novels.[164]

'I have no chance, youth has left me, white hair has invaded,
old age has begun, the wrinkles have become visible.'[165] In that
summer of 1936 in Paris, when the Syrian delegation was
negotiating its way out of the French Mandate, Saadallah
mourned his ripening age as he waded into the fog of doubts
surrounding his country's future. He saw around him small men
with petty dreams – ' . . . among us are the weak, the cowardly,
and the greedy '[166] – men with 'no convictions, no solid idea or
unwavering thought. They accept everything.'[167] They were
hapless men with harebrained wives who threatened to go on a

Above: Sana'a
Below: City of the Dead, Cairo (Courtesy of Mr. Fadi & Mrs. Rula Ghandour)

This page: Fez
Opposite: Badia Soldiers (Courtesy of Mr. Mazen Armouti)

Above: Arab Revolt Series, No. 1
(Courtesy of the Royal Palace, Jordan)

Below: Arab Revolt Series, No. 2
(Courtesy of the Royal Palace, Jordan)

Above: Arab Revolt Series, No. 3
(Courtesy of the Royal Palace, Jordan)

Below: Arab Revolt Series, No. 4
(Courtesy of the Royal Palace, Jordan)

Self-portrait

Mid-shave
Overleaf: Sketch of Parthenon Frieze, British Museum
(Courtesy of Mr. Ronald Cohen)

hunger strike if their husbands did not send them back to
Damascus and who kept imploring the head of the delegation,
President Hashim Atassi, 'to hurry up with the solutions so that
we could go back to our country'.[168] He knew each of these men,
giants in Syria and midgets everywhere else, who were suffocating
Syria's prospects while furthering their own. During long months
of political nitpicking and bargaining over a people and their land,
Saadallah implored God to 'lighten my burdens, for I have had
enough'.[169] Saadallah could not have suspected then that *his* Syria
would last a mere instant after liberation, but he did know that
those responsible for defending it would ultimately fail it.
How appearances deceive! Here was a liberator unintentionally
declaring the future lost before it had even started.

But then, by that year Saadallah was a drained, middle-aged
warrior. Illusions had long ago abandoned him and optimism was
something he put on only for public appearances. Barely months
before that Parisian summer, Saadallah had been on the road to
yet another French-forced exile as punishment for his agitation
against their Mandate. He was sent to impoverished, isolated, cold
Ain Diwar on the edge of northern Syria. Crestfallen after his last
encounter with a French officer, he fills his page with a genteel
almost lyrical admission of fear:

> . . . A dump, broken windows, garbage, wood and stone, leaks
> everywhere, the wind howls. He said, 'Sit down.' Nowhere to
> sit, but on the stone. He raised his stick and cursed me. I have
> known no such fear in my life . . . All my pleadings . . . I began
> to anticipate the worst. I threw myself on the floor, praying to
> my God and keeping myself warm. I was between desperation,
> wanting death, and hope as a shield against harm.[170]

He died on June 20, 1947, eleven years after these diary entries.
He went haggard, worn and in intolerable pain from liver cancer.[171]
His fifty-four years carried him from the certainty of privilege to
the disquietude of want. Long before Ali was counting pennies, his
great uncle, this son of Aleppo's one-time Mufti (chief judge) and
descendant of Aleppine landed gentry, was in search of the next

gold lira to pay his mounting debts.[172] These difficulties in times of plenty may have been because of the hopelessly entangled Jabri inheritance issues and labyrinthine money problems that leave the shy inquisitor dazed, fingers numb from too much head scratching. It also may have been because of the high cost of Saadallah's political ambition and the modesty of his cash. Or it could have been because of his famously leaky pockets and extravagance. Still, those who believed Saadallah was a man of vast property and abundant wealth should be excused; it was only reasonable to assume that he was the happy recipient of endless waqf income and land rents. But it was not so.

Indignities had long settled over Saadallah's life in inelegant repose much like those particles of dust gathered on Il Principe and his family during their long carriage journey to Donnafugata. These began to accumulate years before the grand finale that broke his family's centuries-long sway. For Saadallah, away from the public eye, life bore many inadequacies. He was an unmarried, lonely man, who meekly responded to beauty and privately capitulated to his waning virility. Haemorrhoids and constipation ridiculed his youth and took turns in assaulting his vigour. He was one of eight brothers, some by his own mother, others by another, some very rich, some inexplicably poorer, and all obsessed with their share of the inheritance – Fuad against Fakher, Fakher against Murad, Murad against Fuad, Nafe's son Kamal (Ali's grandfather) against all.[173] He was a professional politician without a profession, who knew Turkish better than his own native tongue. Even in his younger days, Saadallah was a burdened man, sick of it all and anxious to find an occupation or maybe 'a village to which I can retire and find something to take away this boredom'.[174]

Only six months before his death, gossip started circulating that Saadallah had married Fawzieh, the sister of King Farouk of Egypt and the reigning Empress of Iran.[175] Prince Adel Irslan, a colleague, recorded in his journal: 'A fabrication . . . from beginning to end. The Empress is married. And even if there was trouble between her and the Shah, this certainly does not mean that she has become desperate enough to settle for Saadallah as a husband.'[176]

Towards Saadallah, this was one final insult to top a mountain of small ones.

Irslan may have been right, but would that he were more kind, for there were other more redeeming aspects to Saadallah's life. A handsome man of blond hair and blue eyes, 'a walking and talking fragrance'[177] with a weakness for beautiful tailoring, a good heart, and an impulsive spirit, Saadallah took a bouquet of achievements to his grave. He was a patriot, beaten, imprisoned and exiled several times by the French Mandate's forces.[178] Unlike many of his brethren in arms, including his own brother Ihsan, he became an Arab against his Ottoman patrons before he was one against the French.[179] He went the proud bearer of precious official titles, the highest among them those of foreign minister, speaker of parliament, and prime minister.[180]

He did not die a saint – only a bullet could have granted him that – but he did die untarnished by the dirt that usually collects on the names of politicians when they have lived too long. Patrick Seale did not err when he described him in *The Struggle for Syria* as 'the bravest and straightest of the [National] Bloc leaders and perhaps the one man whose reputation and authority had survived the trials of the preceding years'.[181] It was to Saadallah's memory that his nieces, Saadieyh and Hala, turned when they wanted to indulge in Jabri pride.[182]

In this withering man gathered many good things and a few bad ones. Iron resolve, integrity and a call higher than money,[183] mingled with small outlays of vanity, weak governing skills, a terrible temper and a susceptibility to dispensing favours to family.[184] As prime minister, Saadallah seemed too faithful to his class or too weak before its demands. He did well at liberation but far worse at governance. His fellow politicians fared no better. Between formal independence in 1946 and the military coup of 1949 were three years of internal tumult and external intrusions that exposed the impotence and conflicting ambitions of the ruling clan. Much of what was good in appearance turned out to be much less impressive in fact. There it was, sizzling Syria, pleading for guidance in such trying times; there they were, its old guard, with the meekest of answers on offer. Towards the end of a drawn-out battle for independence, Syria was at a crossroads – its townswomen were demonstrating for their rights while its village women were selling or leasing out their daughters for scraps of a living;[185] its Islamic fundamentalism was still young and only one among many paths; its younger generation was still infatuated with modernity and its promise; its prudent men and women were agitating for a semblance of economic justice for the many without it – and the boys at the helm followed all the wrong road signs.[186]

Upon his death, *al Ayam* newspaper declared Saadallah a humble man, mentioning a monthly income of a mere 30 gold liras from his family's waqf.[187] This could have been the truth, or it could have been the reporter's way of eulogising a spent man. In any case, the farewell itself could not have been more apt, for only a few years after Saadallah's death eulogies were being written for his entire class.

*   *   *

Two years after his uncle Saadallah's death, on the morning of his seventh birthday, August 18, 1949, Ali was walking to his summer camp on the main road towards the church in Aleppo. Suddenly, Majddedine and Hala arrived in their car, picked him up and left. Ali's cousin Alia remembers seeing him enter the car and vanish.[188] It had been a little over a year since the 1948 Arab-Israeli war and five months since Syria hosted its first military coup. These events were the first to trifle with him, in what turned out to be fate's lifetime hobby of picking on Ali. After three years at Victoria College in Alexandria, he was chased out again in 1952 by Egypt's own coup. Majddedine and Hala sent him first to Switzerland then, two years later, to England, where he stayed until he was eighteen. After being swept up on his way to camp, Syria was never home again for Ali. Europe became everything essential to him, three-quarters of an identity, more than an orientation, a way of life.

*Ali, six years old.
1948*

*Ali skiing in
Switzerland. Early
1950s*

Ali never quite understood why his parents decided to send him away at the delicate age of seven, when they had determined at the time to stay in Syria. For years, he harboured silent suspicions that he simply was not wanted. Majddedine could not have been too pessimistic about Syria – he would soon become a minister of public works again. The din of change was easy to hear but the undercurrents of upheaval had been quiet. The coup of 1949 was momentous for Syria and the Jabris, but neither could have understood then how far reaching for both of them it would be.

*   *   *

Still, it was in that year, 1949, that Syria began to shed its Noachian habits and indulge in new unnerving addictions. Coup begat coup, and with every new tremor a little more of the old went and a little more of the new grew. Down there in the ash heap of history reside the many explanations for this sweep of the broom. Rummage through it and pick out any number of the reasons you usually hear for the collapse of time-worn dominions: those about the decaying teeth of a feeble class and its weakening bite; about blue-blooded liberators, once nationalist heroes, now incompetent administrators; about hungry upstarts, brash and unwise, who tinkered too much with fate and brought its wrath upon them and their enemies; about military chaps too happy to join the revelry and too eager to stay there long after everyone had gone home. Any halfway decent history book on Syria will tell you about the runaway rhetoric of a mendacious leadership, the disgrace of Arab disunity, and the 1948 Arab defeat in the first Arab-Israeli war. It will tell you about characters like wily Akram Hourani, the peasants' man, who colluded with uniformed men to expedite his and his constituency's ascendance to influence. It will tell you about a depressingly immature democracy that could not absorb external pressures and accommodate internal political rivalries. It probably will also share with you American nervousness about Tapline's oil pipelines running through an unstable and increasingly unfriendly Syrian terrain. Syria's, in a way, was an

Ali and Majddedine, mid-1950s

Class photo Rugby School, 1959–60. Ali is in the middle row, 2nd from right

acute case of excess: too many Sunnis at the top, too many others at the bottom; too many destitute peasants down below and too few landowners above them; too many political hacks manipulating too many agendas; too much interference by neighbours and too much tampering by distant powers.

That such tumult found its first release on March 18, 1949, in the person of Husni Zaim, a remarkable combination of lunacy and silliness who perched, corrupt and self-satisfied, at the head of the Syrian Army, is proof that even the most portentous of developments can contain within them all the elements of low comedy. Zaim ushered in the brilliant age of Syrian militarism for many noble reasons, not the least gallant of which were cases of rotten ghee in the digestive system of his ramshackle army, with his full name written on them. It turns out Syrian soldiers were not only firing with defunct weapons but, thanks to Husni, they were literally letting loose the full fart-load of his corruption into Syria's lovely country air.[189]

Who can resist the sweet taste of a story that wraps Syria's entire mess in one Marquezian episode? Who would not gape at the sight of a million good reasons for rebellion squashed under a truckload of a clownish general's stinking motives? Who would not be struck by the poignant symbolism packed into a bizarre Husni Zaim ousting a clueless Shukri al Quwwatli?[190] In truth, Zaim's person and purpose foretold the insolvency of Syria's military rule, much like President al Quwwatli's revelation to Musa Alami on the eve of the 1948 war exposed the bankruptcy and shame of his. 'Our army and its equipment are of the highest order and well able to deal with a few Jews,' al Quwwatli confided to Alami. Undeterred, he continued: ' . . . We even have the atomic bomb . . . Yes, it was made locally; we fortunately found a very clever fellow, a tinsmith.'[191]

Digest that, and you can swallow almost anything.

It was rumoured that, very soon after his seizure of office, Zaim was ostentatiously displaying himself in front of his house's mirrors and crowing to his wife, 'One day you shall be queen.'[192] Yes, it would have been a wondrous thing to hear him utter in his

Syrian vernacular: 'Eh, mou toukbrini, eh wallah byoum areeb lah tseeri malakeh.'

Husni Zaim lasted a measly four months in office, but the military era which his coup blessed into existence still kicks and screams around us to this day.

*   *   *

The dawn of Syria's new age was neither swift nor tidy. Like Saadallah's death, the old regime's was wrenching. Five coups d'état took place between March 1949 and February 1954. From 1949 to 1958, when a returned President Quwwatli and his mates handed over the republic to Egypt's Gamal Abdel Nasser – all lace and perfume on the outside and poison on the inside – eighteen different cabinets had been formed, most of which died almost immediately after slithering out of Parliament's penetralia.[193]

During these nine years, the country's old keepers scrambled for the smaller roles, while newcomers grabbed the bigger ones for themselves. Overgrown, unruly children that they were, Syrian politicians played politics as if it were a game of musical chairs, pushing and shoving their way to their little thrones.

Saadallah's demise had spared him the sad spectacle, but his brother Ihsan, never as dignified a figure as his brother, seemed more than happy to play his part in it. Those few political memoirs that remember him mention little, and much of it is top heavy with sarcasm. In 1954, Ihsan took the vague mumblings of a bumbling President Hashim Atassi as an official request for him to form a government. When he proceeded to consult with his parliamentary colleagues, the response was a repressed giggle.[194] In 1958, his endorsement in the Egyptian Parliament of the Syrian-Egyptian union, as head of the official Syrian delegation, apparently was a performance laden with such exaggerated reverence that it reminded Khaled Azm, one of old Syria's sharpest statesmen, of Ihsan's days with King Feisal.

How I would have liked to see Jabri in his Ottoman tarboush and his black suit, holding the folded flag, as if carrying the medals of a dead man in an official procession, then bowing to kiss the flag and raising it in a cinematic melodramatic gesture to the chair of the Speaker. Memory takes me back to 1920, when Jabri was chief chamberlain to King Feisal. I imagine him somberly walking down the stairs before the king and then standing and shouting at the top of his voice, 'His Majesty the King,' then throwing himself on the floor while the king slowly came down the stairs to greet his guest.[195]

These theatrics were preceded by Ihsan frantically running around the hotel in search of Marouf Dawalibi, another Aleppine representative, who had the folded Syrian flag which had been specially brought for the occasion. Failing to find Dawalibi, Ihsan ordered all his suitcases broken open. Many years later in Cairo, when Ihsan was a wilting nonagenarian, Ali saw 'a tyrannous old grandfather raised in the Byzantine courts of Constantinople . . . made of cold-steel – not in terms of strength of principle or moral purity but in sheer sadism of will'.[196] Would that the old man's masochistic knack for farce had not concealed itself so well from his grandson. It would have made Ihsan more human and their relationship less tormenting to Ali.

Ihsan's sycophantic exhibitionism was not for naught. Gamal Abdel Nasser was impressed enough to bestow on him the ceremonial position of President of the Council of Ministers of the United Arab Republic (the Syrian-Egyptian union) and Yemen. Sadly for Ihsan, the unhappy union lasted a very short three years. Soon after Syria pulled out of the marriage in 1961, the Yemeni Imam Ahmad bin Yehya sued for divorce. And that was that for this Jabri, a political anachronism who had tenaciously clung to relevance way after his expiry date. He settled in Cairo until his death on March 7, 1980, at the age of ninety-eight.

On the military plane dispatched by Syrian President Hafez Assad to bring Ihsan's body back to Aleppo, Ali, sitting beside his grandfather's coffin, wrote: 'The late Ihsan Bey El Jabri, President of the Council of Ministers of the United Arab Republic and Yemen, oddly small, his head to the tail of the old plane, flying

Ihsan al Jabri with leopard

feet first back from the town of his twenty-five-year exile to the
stone parapeted house rented for half a century surveying the main
square of Aleppo named after his greater brother Saddallah.'[197]

Ihsan probably would have been flattered by Assad's gesture
and furious at Ali's eulogy, but, in truth, both spoke of that same
essential quality in him: he and his time were unimportant enough
to the new Syria for him to qualify for a decorous return to his
country.

*   *   *

If the Syria of the 1950s – unsure how much of its familiar past it
wanted to keep and how much of an uncertain future it should
surrender to – had been too dismissive towards Ihsan, it was too
wary of a much younger Jabri. Hard as he tried, Majddedine,
with all the necessary credentials and all the right skills, could not
secure a solid role for himself in this ever-changing place. In the
span of eight years, between 1948 and 1956, he became minister
of public works five times in five different cabinets, most of which
could not manage more than a few months' worth of life.[198]
Much less enthusiastic than his father-in-law about unification
with Egypt, he finally packed his bags and went off with Hala to
Kuwait in 1958, never to return.

By September 1961, when the military's increasingly restless
top brass staged a coup and severed the union with Egypt, Syria
had finally made up its mind and was ushering in a new batch
of leaders.[199] They came mostly from the countryside, over-
whelmingly from the middling class, increasingly from the Alawite
minority, definitely from the military and, sure enough, all were
marching under the Baath party's flag.[200]

Land redistribution had begun in earnest in 1958 and the first
wave of landowners – 3247 of them, a negligible 1.1 percent
presiding over one-third of Syria's cultivated land – were the first
to feel the earth literally shrinking under them.[201] Thirteen years
and a succession of land reforms later, Ali would have this to say
after a few memorable visits to government offices to sort out
which plots still belonged to him and his family:

Sheikh Fahd Salem al Sabah of Kuwait and Majddedine in Kuwait.
Late 1950s or early 1960s

A million dusty bureaus. The pigeonholes and mektebs (offices)
of a depleted, exhaustedly febrile agricultural bureaucracy – endless complications . . . [One] land reform cabinet after cabinet.
Debts, repealed laws, reversals, and litigations. The blade of the
grain, the ear of the corn, the seed of the wheat all transformed
. . . to institutions, law, and social tablet. Feudal collapse still
unreplaced by anything anywhere of a comparable harmony. In
the centers of town transactions, the marble dirty facades of the

palace of justice and ministries of this and that, people flock like flies feebly fretting their way through vast deserts of articled papers and legal hassles.[202]

The wonder years of Hafez Assad the Lion Heart had only just begun.

*   *   *

On that same visit in January 1971, on his way from Lebanon to Syria by car, Ali, who by then had long been holding a Jordanian passport, was stopped at the Syrian border. The taxi driver had gone into the Syrian passport control to stamp his passengers' passports and came back calling for Ali.

> 'They want the Jordanian,' [the taxi driver] said too innocent to be deliberately sardonic . . . In I went. Torrents of abuse:
>   'Are you any relation to Saadallah al-Jabri?'
>   'Yes, he is my great uncle.'
>   'Eh tidrab bi halsahneh.' (I curse your face)
>   'Your father?'
>   'Your mother?'
>   'Your nationality?'
>   'No, you're not, you're Syrian!'
>   'Be quiet you lying dog!'
>   'You're for the army!'
>   'You're a draft dodger!'
> Protests from me. Appeals to some sentimentally held belief in the values of civilised exchange. Useless. Grabbed and man-handled by several rubber-stamp-geniuses . . . right on the front steps in front of the lines of waiting cars. Pushed and pulled amid slogans and curses, turned into instant ancien regime Dog on the Run. The people's state will make you pay for your birth and responsibilities. Called in through one echelon after the next. Same questions, same dogmatic insistence on everything I was denying. Soon realised the hopelessness and calmed down with minimum effort.

Ali was kept for a night in a Syrian cell. Mustafa Tlas, Syria's Interior Minister and the husband of Nawal al Jabri, a cousin, bailed him out the next day. One cannot but wonder if the face of his uncle Saadallah lulled Ali to sleep, as he rested his head on Dickens' *Bleak House*. Only forty-nine years earlier, in 1922, Saadallah had this conversation with the French judge presiding over the trial of Ibrahim Hananu, Aleppo's nationalist leader:

> Judge to Hananu: 'You claim that you fought against France in the name of the Syrian People. Can you bring me one Syrian who has given you this mission?'
>
> Silence . . . and then the voice of a young man who stood up and said to the Judge: 'Your honour, I, Saadallah al-Jabri, a son of this country and one of its educated ones, I, and thousands along with me, gave Ibrahim Hananu the mission of fighting France, which entered our land without right. It is our right to launch an armed struggle against this foreign occupation. And the criminal, your honour, is he who violates people's safety and their freedom and not he who fights for his country's independence and faces the Senegalese's bayonet in his quest to liberate the land of his ancestors.'[203]

The irony would not have been lost on Ali.

*   *   *

Walk around Aleppo now and you beg for more than the washed-out remnants of what was. The city limps through the days grey and harsh, even on a bright autumn morning, reeling from decades of indifference. You hear the *ahs* and *oohs* of beguiled visitors, but fatigue sets in when you first arrive and stays with you every time you step out. Those austere monuments that jeer at the opulence and grandeur of their Islamic cousins in Cairo and Istanbul still stand. The Citadel, the oldest living daughter of Aleppo, resuscitated and beautified by Al Malik al-Zahir Ghazi in 1209, 'soars above the city like a great cone of chamfered top',[204] guarded by snoring, plastic-slippered men, the ubiquitous sentries at the gates of Arab heritage. Visit it one minute after three o'clock in the afternoon and you are politely informed, 'Sorry, even history needs a nap.' The town's winding, narrow, busy souks still breathe and feed their people. Like a spiteful stepmother, this regime milks these children of bygone wombs for all their worth and then leaves them to fend for themselves against the corrosiveness of filth, against age and yellow caterpillars and the ice-cold winters. Yet, this city has seen so much devastation over the centuries that probably it is secretly laughing itself silly at its sheer good luck today, for what is benign neglect when measured against the harsh blows that stamp so much of its history.

Majddedine and Saadallah, both true lovers of this ancient birth-place, can be seen in the town's centre by those who want to find them. Saadallah is the name of the square to which the adjacent park, one of Majddedine's surviving creations from his municipality days, sends wafts of cool air to soothe its haggard face.

Scores of paintings survived Ali. None has been found of Aleppo.

CHAPTER FOUR

Faded Levis, Biba . . . Mouloukhieh,* UAR

'Mummy . . . I have many problems to iron out and many failings
to put right . . . '   Ali in a letter to Hala, March 25, 1963

'Poor daddy found very little happiness in me, his only son.
You yourself have impressed upon me the feeling that I was a
bitterness to him.'   Ali in a letter to Hala, January 1971

'Mummy passed away. Diala's tears. What will quench them?'
                    Diary entry on the day of Hala's death, 1984

It is said that when Majddedine went to Stanford in 1964 to
retrieve Ali, he found the age-old Jabri masks scattered in the
clutter of his son's life and there, in a sun-filled corner, sat
the liberated sexuality of a painted face too intoxicated with the
promise of the Sixties to recognise its maker. In a haze of
dreaminess, Ali was finally glimpsing a destiny other than his
own, but as he reached out to embrace it, he found himself staring
into a pair of despairing eyes. It took Majddedine three weeks to
find Ali. It took Ali one naked, drowsy, half-conscious moment
with his father to declare himself lost – forever.

   This is a fragment from an encounter no one knows well enough
to tell. It is nothing more than an isolated shred of a half-truth
that went with its keepers. They are all dead now – all. The con-
frontation between father and son may not have happened this
way, but it was like Ali to be stuck somewhere between tragic irony
and comic bad luck as they got together for that perfect movie
moment. Nineteen sixty-four. California. Cool is still a toddler; it

* A very popular dish in the Arab world.

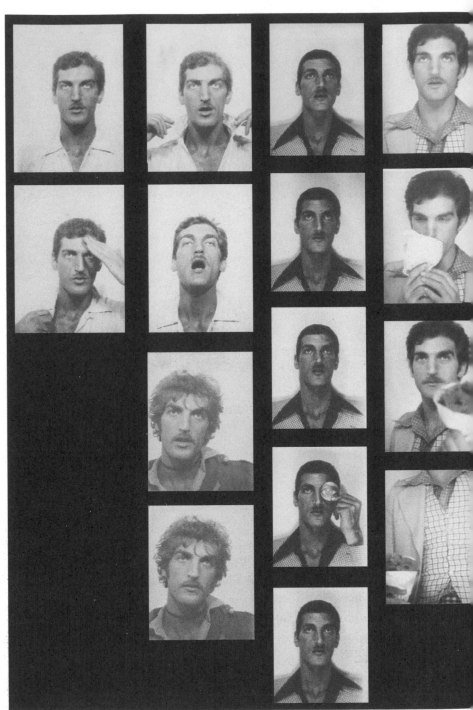

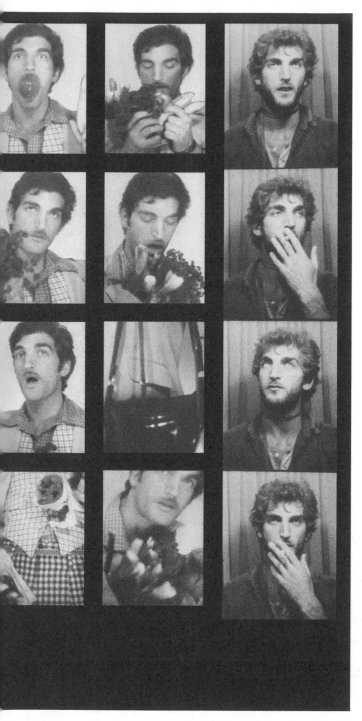

*Passport
instamatics
1970–71.
London diaries*

does not recognise the repressed flutter of the heart for its kind. It is September. Some friends have graduated and moved on, others are still away for the summer. The 'most gifted group of artists'[205] is breaking up. Ali is behind shuttered windows and locked doors. He has been dipping in and out of his secrets all afternoon. Alone. He is stoned, seconds away from yet another epiphany, when who should pop through the door but daddy.

Every time the truth about Majddedine's 'rescue' effort in California makes an appearance its many siblings come humming along. There is the one about Ali wanting to join the army or the navy,[206] or the other one about Sir Maurice Laing, Ali's English guardian since he was twelve, dropping in on Ali on his way back from West Canada and finding him ' "down at heel," his shoes being worn out, his clothes tatty . . . '[207] Possibly, the impression mild psychedelic happiness leaves on the clueless. There is yet another about Ali failing Stanford and joining a beach commune. Ali could never stay long enough with a story to give it form, and this one, as with so many others in his bag of memories, nestled comfortably somewhere at the bottom of a dream. 'You know I never tell a story the same way twice. Does that mean I am lying?'[208] Justine asked Arnauti in Ali's favourite *Quartet*. His stories, like hers, never wanted to revisit the same place more than once.

Except that . . . except that, not too far beneath the hearsay about Ali's supposed turmoil at Stanford, there is a loud murmur of a truth that is worth telling: Ali was happy there. He fell into the lap of California an eager child with an infectious sense of play. Those red lines that reminded him whence he came and where he was certain to go were beginning to blur in the hectic cadence of delirious youth, artistic fervour, and slippery avocado parties. The Sixties were upon him but they were still innocent and fresh and mild, and he was light and insatiable. He had that nose. He could sniff a new wind long before it had even gathered its unruly elements and begun to travel. And the approaching winds were so lovely and so exhilarating in America.

*   *   *

You can reassemble parts of Ali in California more than forty years ago. There are enough yellowing letters, enough dogged reminiscences to take you back, if only to help heal an affair hideously mangled by Jabrian heavy hearts.

There are these faded impressions from Michael:

> To me he seemed a bit mysterious, exotic even; thin and elegant in expensive shoes, tight white jeans, fine shirts, his hair fair and combed straight back, showing up with fantastic drawings, some fashion fantasies or costume designs, some Aubrey Beardsley-esque grotesques, once a whole series, rather morbid, drawn from medical textbooks of exotic diseases, many venereal in nature, exquisitely rendered in watercolour or coloured pencil . . . erratic in attending classes (though marvelous in any studio work involving drawing) . . . regarded as somewhat of a prodigy within the art department . . . his talent was obvious. Quite . . . [209]

Beth's descriptions deepen the character lines somewhat: 'the frequent flicking of his Dunhill lighter . . . Marlboros . . . a suave elegant continental style: tailored slacks, Italian shoes . . . blue or pink Oxford cloth shirts . . . a white sweater with a stripe and another with an Inca pattern . . . '

Grass – oh, yes – but none of its wilder cousins. 'White wine and linguine and clam sauce at Renato's . . . beer pitchers at St Michael's Alley while we listened to Miles Davis, Dave Brubeck . . . ' Plenty of parties of 'drawing or painting for hours with . . . Ray Charles, Booker T & the MG's, Motown, surf music . . . La Dolce Vita soundtrack . . . '

Ali was 'one of the innocent ones in our immediate crowd . . . I think . . . actually a virgin, but he may have had a secret life or incidents earlier in his teens . . . '[210] There is that toe sucking party for a perversion: 'A bunch of us . . . all curled up fully clothed on a friend's bed one afternoon, giggling like crazy and sucking each other's toes. We got hysterical . . . and that is as far as it went.'[211]

Things were good, it would seem. School was bad, very bad. Up and down it went, with sure sightings of the rare A on the way up

and a whole mess of Withdrawals and Incompletes on the way
down. Towards the end, Ali fell all the way to the bottom, chased
down by too many Fs and the occasional C.[212] He simply could
not make it to those classes, write those papers, or complete those
assignments. A future in architecture was pure fantasy now. The
money was either plenty or scant, depending on Majddedine's
project cycles. But things were good. He was running fast, Jabri
dictums always scurrying behind him, never quite able to catch
up. One after the other they fell away, old and ignored. The art
was near astounding, his talents obvious, the impressions they
left permanent. In the 1962 Oil Painting and Life Drawing class,
Ann remembers

> Ali painted for hours at a time, creating and recreating figures
> on canvas . . . jewel tones, blues and greens among them . . .
> figures . . . often women in dramatic dresses elongated, sinuous
> forms, beautiful stylised and full of movement . . . I remember
> a large green and blue portrait . . . a Goya or Velasquez . . .
> loose brushy background and a couple of female figures . . .
> exaggerated hair ('beehives' and Bardot were available for
> influence) . . . His work was influenced by the stage, drama,
> and a sense of the royal court . . . often with the sense of parody.
> He used large canvases at 3x4. I never saw him paint small.[213]

What else? Stanford's Ram's Head Theatrical Society. Ex-
perimentations, new clothes, a campy elusiveness awaiting Susan
Sontag's 'tentative and nimble' guide [214] and searching for others
to share its 'fantastic sense of the absurd'.[215] No *Acid Kool Aid
Tests* yet – that comes later – no Perry Lane, no trips with Ken
Kesey. Andy Garcia's Mother McCree's Uptown Jug Champions
were already here, but the Grateful Dead were still more than a
few months away.

It could never have been blissful for Ali – he was not made for
bliss – but at times it probably came very close to that. He pleaded
with his mother to forgive his waywardness and gave pretence its
due. He swam to her shore every once in a while on postcards of
solicitude. This was all Ali could offer, it was clear, but, for Hala

and Majddedine, it was nowhere near enough. His accomplishments were too few and the pleas too many.

'My parents suspecting me of running round with stars and gays and other dreadful perverts,' he wrote to Beth on October 10, 1964, soon after Majddedine and Hala hauled him back to England.

> I don't know if true, but they said FBI called up and told them . . . They'd shriek at me I [could do] nothing but laugh in semi [hysteria] between fits of crying . . . My mother says I've killed her joie de vivre and her health – that I would be a menace if I were near my sister. That I'd disgrace the family name at any moment if I went home with them . . . I kept having terrible sort of semi-psychotic impulses that I'd go crazy or commit suicide . . . I am too strong for the former (I know I am too cowardly for the latter).

The thoughts that must have crossed their minds as they hunkered down in room 59 of San Francisco's Fairmont Hotel and looked for Ali for three weeks! He had simply vanished. William Branch's article, 'Parents keep lonely phone vigil for missing foreign student', must have horrified them:

> After a 9,000-mile journey to the Bay Area, the anxious parents of a 22-year old Stanford University student from the small Middle Eastern nation of Kuwait are trying to locate their son who left the campus after flunking out . . . The student looks and acts startlingly like a typical young American artist intellectual . . . a long way from his true role as the son of a wealthy and prominent contractor . . . [216]

For this and everything else, Ali would pay dearly for three hellish months.

*   *   *

The price he had to pay was called Coates. At twenty-two, Ali was deposited in the care of a grammar-school teacher and his wife, a Dickensian couple living in a tiny house in the middle of England near Rugby, Ali's old public school.

(I am writing in an overcoat) . . . A very grim industrial town –
rows and rows of smoggy, blackened redbrick Victorian houses
in winding estate developments. Thousands of sooty chimneys,
people walking around in depressing thick clothes – the image
of a gloomy totalitarian state . . . I being taught mathematics by
the husband . . . the nearest movie theater is 35 miles away! I'm
not allowed any reading but I have a bible in my room (I'm not
being melodramatic) and a book about the Bayeux tapestry.
Don't write to this address! [217]

Jabrian wrath could not have found more distressingly burlesque
lives and characters to inflict on Ali than the Coates': 'Prototypes
of good, clean, God fearing, Christian *virtue.*'

The man, Mr Coates, is a retired teacher and a lay-preacher,
no less (a layman ordained to preach in church, as opposed to a
formal priest). The wife is a typically respectable Englishwoman,
absolutely smothered in clipped vowel sounds and middle-class
niceties (little fingers always raised over daily rituals of tea at five
o'clock, continuous knitting, hot water bottles, Christian prayers
and such). They are very good people and it is suffocating to live
with them. We say prayers at every meal and they read the bible
out loud before dinner every evening. I have to take part because
my parents imposed it on me as one condition for letting me out
of their sight. Since my parents instructed the couple not to let
me out of their sight for a moment, they take me to church with
them twice a week . . . They live in proverbial simplicity and
frugality, some 25 miles outside of Rugby on a country road.
Every day I am tutored for four hrs. in math and two hrs. in
biology . . . They are totally innocent of fads, fashions, intellec-
tualisms . . . Theirs is absolutely the height of the self-contained
burgher mentality – no awareness whatsoever of art, of painting,
of emotion, of racy, even dissolute, youth, no concept of even the
vaguest expression of hedonism. The house is shabby-genteel and
a monument to their hideous taste – 1940 wallpaper on every
wall, mahogany furniture with tenderly darned anti-macassars,
prints of ducks in Woolworth sunsets, sentimental imagery of

English landscapes and boats and things in fading sepia tints. It sounds classic and therefore fun in a pop way, but it's not even that – just plain ugly, ugly. I'm not judging them in terms of these outside appearances – they are only manifestations of their pugnacious solidity and down-to-earthness – qualities that I admit I lack but which drive me nuts in such overwhelming evidence . . . My room looks out on sort of backyard where a solitary neighbour puts her baby in a pram. There aren't any children to play with, no dogs to take for walks, no cats to stroke and turn on, no movies, no books, no magazines, no empty chatter or flippant amusement. Everything is as gray and serious as the mashed potatoes we eat at every meal.

There he was, a full-grown man, twenty-two years of age, suffering his comeuppance as if a troublesome teenager. The letters must have made for painful writing then, but forty years on, Ali's reenactments are so utterly hilarious, the reader would be forgiven for misreading the wretchedness of his actual situation. No wonder Beth hung on to the letters.

My parents made me stop smoking . . . The Coates don't drink or smoke and they told me firmly when I first came that they think such habits are signs of moral collapse . . . I miss my clothes. My mother took away all my suits and ties and wonderful American shorts and levis (which she said made me look perverted) and gave them to charity organisation. When we got to Rugby they took me to a seedy little shop and deliberately picked out of the dumpiest, baggiest, drabbest clothes they could find. They did this, they said, in order to [help me] overcome my sense of vanity. A horrible fight broke out when I tried to protest. So here I am looking like a 45-year-old British clerk – you should see me wrapped up in my overcoat, gray-brown, huge padded shoulders, several inches thick, the hem well below the calves. Also, floppy gray flannel trousers with 3" turn-ups; a thick prickly woolen coat, and solidly toe-capped 18-lace shoes. I'm glad I've still got a sense of humour . . . The town is crawling with Mods and Rockers, all unbelievably raffish and cool-looking in Cuban heels and paisley shirts, long straight hair . . . It was mortifying to see all this elegance and fuck-you-all-stick-in-the-muds-atmosphere and yet be helpless myself. I wanted to run to them, turn cart wheels in the street and give Mrs Coats the third.[218]

He did not.

In December, in an about turn typical of Majddedine and Hala, Ali was instructed to go to Austria in January for a skiing break.

Oxford did not accept him, but Bristol University did. He joined it in the fall of 1965. Dr Albert Hourani and his wife Odile became his new guardians; he would grow very close to them over the years.

*   *   *

There is the odd gem here and there from Ali's California days. Many of the paintings he sent to Kuwait he inexplicably destroyed when Diala returned them to him in the 1980s. Many of his early progeny disappeared this way. 'What is life but sheer vanishing sands, no trace in the end without creative output,' he ruminated to Diala in 1975.[219] If only he had followed his own wise counsel.

In the corridor of Diala's apartment in Amman stands a woman. At first glance, she is grace in total disarray as she ponders last night's *faux pas* and declares herself satisfied. It is a partial study by Ali of Velasquez's *Las Meninas*, 'The Maids of Honour', one of the few survivors from Stanford. The face is Hala's, says Diala.

*   *   *

Whispers tell of how Majddedine's furious hands fell on Ali behind the walls of London's Dorchester upon their return from California. There is no echo of those slaps in Ali's voice, no trace of them in his papers, only sibilations from the few who know almost nothing. But in the shadow of that sorry day the deep wrinkles between father and son had begun to breed again, smothering estranged faces and squeezing the life out of two broken hearts.

Pictures of Hala during that time in London show an ashen face, struck dull white by her son's display of forbidden colours. Those anguished trips of his between remorse and rebellion; her

cri de coeur that this son was not quite how she wished him; his
eyes that caressed the handsome face of a waiter; those disappearances in the bathrooms of London restaurants – did she see it
then, the eclipse of a certain kind of Jabri life? Could she hear
them then, the disquieting sounds of death as she prayed for the
days to stay still? As she stared into that camera, was she peering
into the end?

It would always matter to Ali that he was not enough 'man',
not enough Jabri, not enough Arab, not enough of anything, in
Majddedine and Hala's eyes; and such a waste it was for him and
them, for every time he tried to inch closer to their vision, he
became helplessly disfigured in his own. There was so little Ali
could do and so much to mend. In the end all he offered were
halfhearted gestures and overeager prose in the occasional letter.

'Mercy for Ali and forgiveness from Diala,' was Majddedine's
last written entreaty to Hala in London before he was wheeled
into the operating room and death, in 1967.[220] He finally understood and forgave.

*   *   *

Nineteen sixty-five. Bristol University. The Sixties drawing close
to midlife. America is far away now. Soon after being let loose
in what Hala and Majddedine thought was quiet, conservative
Bristol, Ali explored and tested and teased and tortured and
celebrated and reinvented every part of him.

Ali and Bristol, between 1965 and 1970, need a whole new kind
of stitch work. The notes read like vivid film rushes. There are
transformations here, a character coming into focus with all its
oddities, a mind crawling out of old holes and digging itself into
new ones, happenings that have a beginning and a finale, friendships that stayed with Ali till the end. There are explicit memories,
like Sara Waterson's, that sketch raw, precious vignettes of Ali in
each of these five years. There are recollections by Antonia, Kate,
Diney, John, Frank, that bring context to an elusive man whom
lapsed time can only deliver to us in fractions.

*   *   *

An orgy of clothes, junk sales and thrift shops. The wardrobe becomes a fertile womb to a succession of Alis. He flirts with all his longings, 'brutal and dangerous . . . male and butch . . . camp and feminine'.[221] Gold swathes the hair and edges the blue of his eyes. A touch of Americana tickles his accent, a gentle Oriental breeze lingers. All this, and Ali Jabri for a name.

There is never any money.

It is the Saturday night dance. A woman is in love with him. Theatre on the piste. Antonia is watching Ali from the balcony as he hypnotically plays the floor. 'Who can dance like that?' she asks.[222] They meet later that year. Antonia! Here is one name that travelled with him wherever he went thereafter.

The last song is playing. The dance is about to end. He is cheek-to-cheek with Sara. He knows this can never be. She wonders.

Who is he, really? There is mention of pedigree; land as far as the eye could see and countless villages – again. The hair has grown so long but now 'he is hacking at himself, very brutally . . . have to almost shave it all off'.[223] He is in anguish and isolates himself in Badock, his residence, for two weeks. He is back in his straight-jacket and sensible shoes. Bell-bottom trousers, silk scarves, flowing shirts, mark time in the closet. He refuses to say what this is about.

Diney graduates. She moves to London and Ali starts visiting her and Kate there. They are already very good friends. 'Adventuring into the forbidden,' she calls it – their Sixties trip. 'We set each other off, Ali, Antonia and I. We understood each other very well.'[224] She does not meet Sara. Antonia does not either until much later in 1968, when Ali was in Kuwait. Ali's bit of compartmentalisation. He liked it this way. Neat. 'Not sure why. He could not control anything in his life and this is the only thing he could manage, I suppose . . . '[225] This is a reasonable thought by Diney, but what was there to manage? Maybe Ali just preferred an existence carved into bits and pieces, parts of a whole, each nursed into a life with a beating heart and things to tell.

It must be 1966. There is not a cobblestone in this town that does not know him, wide-eyed helplessly curious child. Like the wakeful nights, Leigh Woods and that truckers' café under the

Ali at Bristol, mid-1960s. Courtesy of Frank Drake.

flyover on the other side of the docks love him.[226] In 'flowing robes,
veils, and beads,'[227] he walks the town at midnight with Frank.
Last week he went to pick up Sara to go to the cinema. He
'dropped some hashish on the carpet . . . a crimson patterned one
. . . He refused to go out until we'd found it (how could we enjoy
the movie without a smoke!!?) and got into a terrible state over
it, crawling around on the floor and getting more and more
hysterical, whilst I got crosser and crosser.'[228]

There is a surviving letter to his parents. It is strained, formal,
hobbled by the pain of previous years.

> We're supposed to spend at least one month in Italy . . . at one of
> several language courses, Florence being the recommended one.
> I would like to prove capable of doing this, if I can show you that
> I am taking my studies seriously and I am being careful with
> money.[229]

Horace Walpole is Ali's dissertation subject. Walpole! Eight-
eenth-century man about town. Serendipity – the word – is his to
claim. Accidental sagacity, he called it.[230] It is not surprising
that Ali should have chosen Walpole. The son of Prime Minister
Robert Walpole, he was a wit, a lover of art, architecture, gossip,
the author of the Gothic *The Castle of Otranto* and the incestuous
Mysterious Mother. He was possibly a connoisseur in male love
and one of Sontag's more famous campy picks. 'Ali's dissertation
grew and grew to uncontrollable proportions, causing him much
anguish, and was as florid and overwritten as the works of his
subject ("too much purple prose!" I remember his tutor writing on
the first draft which made us all chortle – Ali included).'[231]

A news item in Bristol's evening newspaper mentions Ali and a
shoplifting incident – doubtless this was nothing more than wealth
redistribution at its most sincere. The article describes him as a
'native of Jerusalem'. Ali is miffed by the description, complaining
that 'it made him sound like a Semitic shop-keeper'.[232] Pity he
should have been caught. They are all doing it but he is very good
at it. Frank laughs: 'He was the most outrageous thief, not in any
contemptuous way but in a daring way.'[233]

Ali has fallen in love with the impossible – a man, a dear friend. This one could never love him back. It would not be the last time Ali yearns for the unattainable. Nobody knows.

Nineteen sixty-seven. Ali becomes friends with a group of Moroccan acrobats and almost runs away with them.

Disaster. The Israelis walk into another piece of him and declare it home, and Majddedine dies, waving goodbye to Kuwait, to Aleppo, to that old Jordan Valley road, to every Jabri, to every companion and stone.

What now for Hala? What now for ten-year-old Diala? For Ali? The man in armour, this Jabri pillar, is gone. There is an abundance of files about dwindling land in Aleppo and receding wealth in Kuwait. Fortunes are vanishing quickly. Ali is stuck in Kuwait. He stays with Hala and Diala for nine months, and teaches English at the American Community School of Kuwait. Summer is hellish. While Diala and Hala spend time in Beirut where Majddedine is buried, Ali moves to a room at the Hilton, takes up a job at the American Embassy, and waits.

The scramble for a living starts for all of them. There is talk of sending him to the American University of Beirut. His letters to Sara are miserable. His letters to his mother are not. He keeps alluding to Arab stirrings in him.

> So many new insights and realisations have dawned on me about the Middle East. Love it or hate it, here one can more fully develop one's human resources, one's whole stretch of consciousness, than anywhere else. Perhaps because one suffers more here, one struggles more against ignorance and limitation. It is quite simply a greater challenge than living under anesthesia in the West. Here one can put so much energy into larger roles . . . [234]

Was he telling Hala what he thought she wanted to hear? Probably. Did she believe him? Almost certainly not. Hala could not cut a path for Ali to anywhere. After Majddedine's death there was even less of her to give. Saadieyh starts paying the bills. Wasfi and Saadieyh! Could they be mummy and daddy? 'Toi et Wasfi, vous me

donnez un niveau éthique morale que je trouve inspirant,'[235] he
writes to Saadieyh. A woman of consequence, a man of power.
They are up there on that social ladder, at the top of that political
pyramid. Ali glimpses it, a Jabri life that can be again.

Nineteen sixty-eight. Summer. Saadieyh forks out the money,
and Ali starts his trip back to Bristol. He stops in Jordan and takes
up a summer job at the Jordan radio.[236] At Bristol, he moves into
one of the flats at 19 Caledonia Place, Clifton, where John Dollar
was already settled in another one. John had met Ali sometime
in 1967. He first saw him in the canteen of Badock, 'shuffling
along . . . Threadbare jeans, strange aloofness, almost exaggerated
expression of boredom and a desire to be elsewhere.'[237] Always a
desire to be elsewhere. They soon became friends.

Ali and Clifton got along very well. It was an 'intense social
world of experiment; so free for just a short period of time'.[238] He
is tripping all over the place, going on wild mental excursions and
self-discoveries in a tempest of hard living. For Sara, there is
something perturbing about all of this: 'Face paint and make-up,
mirrored caps, and rags tied all up and down his arms and
legs . . . '[239] He was going way, way out there. There may have
been a woman one night, one last hurrah for Hala and Saadieyh's
sake, but his other cravings were no longer in hiding, openly
seeking others with a hunger like his own.

There is hardly any money, but things are good.

Nineteen seventy. August. Bristol is over, the diploma is in hand,
but the results are lousy. 'J'ai passé . . . J'ai passé avec une grade
humiliante,' he laments to Saadieyh, 'très mal fait, j'étais tout a
fait pris d'une sorte de crise.'[240]

Before plunging into the stubborn aimlessness of his London
years, a handsome six of the nineteen seventies, he goes on a
Bristol-to-Beirut trip via Europe. A prophetic declaration kicks
off the very first of his diaries: 'It was extraordinary to understand, assimilate, stand there at the sally railing slowly digesting
the fact that no I'm no longer in my comfy room back in Clifton.
That is no more. I a pilgrim.' Before long, with typical great
timing, politics pisses on his plans yet again. Soon after he reaches

Corfu in Greece, Jordan's civil war drags him back to London. Every friend he has – Diney, Antonia, Frank, George and Mary, John, more than one Roger, a Pete – acquire permanent space beyond the Bristol daze.

Ali would often return to Bristol for short visits and leave head-deep in his usual heart-rending nostalgia.

> The beautiful winter landscape of England glides by like velvet after that low soft full sun, a clarion clarity in the pale washed sky over Bristol and then slow gradual winter's solstice shading into dusk . . . and something like anguish in a constricted throat. Clifton to be left so once again.[241]

*   *   *

For six years, Ali erased himself out of every corner Saadieyh painted him into, all while depending on her benevolence for everything in his life: the job at the Jordanian embassy as a student adviser, the rent, the pocket money, the trips . . . You have read the letters. Ali was desperate to stay in London. She wanted him near her. Why he thought he could rebel against his aunt while remaining utterly dependent on her may have had something to do with his outlandish hope that his pleas, if obsequious enough, would save him from the harder way out: a genuine effort at independence. But Ali, well into his thirties, latched on to his hopes much like a prostitute holds on to the prospect of a good lay. If maturity is measured only through the sobrieties that chip away at careless youth, then from his Stanford years Ali had not grown a day. His chronic money problems, the yawning gap between his talents and his ability to make a living, his perplexing allergy to deadlines, his pubescent behaviour when coping with filial duties, remained with him.

His diaries and letters in the 1970s are one long, enthralling ride through the yesses and noes of his desires, his dreams and fantasies, his useless procrastinations and escapes. It never really worked out the way Ali wanted it, but then again he could never decide what he wanted – some of this, a lot of that, less of that, more of this; multiple visions and a neurotic fear of committing even to lunch; a troupe of mind-sets, often at peace with one another, more often at odds; an on-off love affair with the improbable and a constant dread of the inexorable.

Oh, sweet mama here I come; oh, darling sister here I'll stay. England? Oh, yes, please, please, England.

L'Angleterre . . . beloved country, you green leafy pasture . . . juicy citadel of chlorophyll . . . [242]

A throat-tightening meaning for me . . . the sight of an English village church nestled among green fields and thatched cottages, where the cows browse to the very door of the belfry, that familiar Norman silhouette rising so protectively in the gentle English light . . . [243]

And what about the quietude of Oxford on a late September afternoon?

Golden evening sun slanted through the foliage . . . slush trees, pastures, fencings . . . strolling spinsters, inscrutable activity of vesper . . . domesticity. Englishmen strolling with girlfriends, late summer roses turn to light . . . [244]

Not to mention the confetti of dear faces and treasured bric-a-brac.

Faded Levis, biba . . . Antonia's brown sambrown z-pronger, my old abandoned railway hobnob boots, checkered socks . . . Julia's latex white knickers on mirror.[245]

In London, 'one gets rid of the burdens of the past that perch on one's shoulders like vultures.'[246]

But the treadmill of it all in this city.

It is hopeless . . . ! No future, no money, little time for creative work. It's a blighted future here in the long run . . . Here I am about to turn into this hideous 9–5 gray-faced shorthaired hunched back wage slave. Worry, worry, worry. Where is I-Ching?[247]

What is depressing is the dirt everywhere and the artificiality and sadness of the life of the urban masses moving like cattle through the streets . . . I begin to understand how ugly life is over here, if one does not fight for survival. Bristol was a beautiful cozy place . . . existence over here is like living in poison.[248]

A sprinkle of Arabhood, a touch of Islam? Yes, thank you!

My ancient world tenaciously hangs on to me, ancient mud-wattles, palm fiber reeds and rushes, a mess of dates and curdled goats milk cheese, Bedouin flutes piping from a desert of insane loneliness, glimmering ruins buried in the sands of time, the shepherd flocks go clonking by, camels graze in Oriental twilight . . . Too much Romanticism, I hear you say?[249]

I was lucky, really, to have those years in Aleppo with Nana whose saintly risings at dawn to read her Koran, and whose radiant imparting of simple things like the Fatiha to me distilled an unfading, innermost feeling for our religion that no amount of illiteracy in our glorious native tongue, no decades of impoverished exile among the barbarous western masses (oh yeah?) can erase.[250]

But, oh, God! The suffocating embrace of a religion which wants to be everything, be everywhere in that 'strictly strident xenophobic tight-minded place, if possible with a sheikh intoning the Koran in my ear . . . '[251]

What about the artist's needs?

Do I pursue these before losing them forever, swallowed by age . . . never to taste their youth in mid flight. Duty now unflinchingly or later when more detached and voluntary? I-Ching must be consulted again . . . [252]

Mummy . . . I have come to feel the possibility that the terrible sense of loss and isolation, adrift in the West, might find one answer in at least a partial contact with my origins . . . I would like to test its viability for myself . . . It is important to have at least a glimpse of what one sprang from, in order to make peace with one's own elemental composition.[253]

Make peace with one's own elemental composition! He must have struggled with that one.

> Naturally, I think of you and Diala . . . let me add that from my silent distance these last few years, I have felt far from blameless regarding your solitary situation . . . at least I should be writing to you and offering my support, even if you wanted nothing to do with me.[254]

The I-Ching. No sympathy there.

> In human life, the individual achieves significance through the discrimination and setting of limits – these are the backbone of morality, unlimited possibilities are not suited for man.[255]

And dear Diala,

> what can we do, you and I, but accept our rather dissimilar fates with equal resignation. You have been cheated of that so-called higher education and me with my lazy habits and laconic frame of mind, hardly knowing where to apply the misspent fruits of all that expensive nurturing our poor parents blueprinted on me. Irony! Irony! Sometimes I curse the way they cut me off from my origins (though that is partly accounted for by political factors hardly to be blamed on them. After all, they did not exactly engineer the great socialist revolution of the UAR single handed now, did they?) . . . [256]

But then how much could he give? ' . . . I'm simply too irrevocably a dropout mentality.[257]
And then there is that

> Jabri curse, that what for other people might be an enviable position of prestige, security and a definite role to play ends up being the screaming mini heebie-jeebies C-R-U-N-C-H.[258]
> The family is such an accursed institution in so many ways. I'll admit I'm dreadfully prejudiced, but I do think that some kind of Spartan system for turning out sturdy-limbed, mass-produced, well-adjusted, hang-up free zombies would be so much

Ali coming out of Ridgmount Gardens, his residence in London.
1973–4. Courtesy of John Dollar.

better than all these twitching psychic-cripple aberrations like
the Jabris, late Aleppo, mouloukhieh, U.A.R.[259]

Why in my despair do I juxtapose with such extremeness the
goodness of staying [in the Arab world] with the treachery of
return. Could duty not be performed equally validly later on
when the 1920s decade has gone and I am ripe for new roles.
Surely one last period of vagabondage . . . [260]

Where will it be? Kuwait, or Cairo, or Amman? 'I would settle in
the Middle East, I really would like to!'[261]

But 'homelands what homelands, I mean even Jerusalem
where I was born, I can't put a foot in – no more than you could
announce your imminent residence in Zurich'.[262]

I think to accept that Arab way of belonging, that lack of
individualism, the stifling salon values, Mme Zameet* (busybody) and Mme Drat [farts], Ala'l wil il [the gossip], so and
so . . . well that would need a certain amount of dying in one
sense . . . [263]

To make it worse,

one can't rely on friends in high places and hardly marriages of
5th cousins twice removed, never before set eyes on, to scrape
one out of whatever dungeon one finds oneself in, for having
photographed a picturesque policeman, or whatever. 'You there!
You didn't salute! 28 years + confiscation.'[264]

Besides,

for the moment I am as deeply planted here as could be, what with
the job, my habits, a certain daily rhythm, an acclimatisation to
the culture . . . [265]

Six years lost in a forest of options and not a shrub of a solution.
That was Ali: the nightmare in the dream, the laugh in the gut of

---

* Zameet has no actual Arabic meaning, but the connotation is that of a
busybody.

calamity. He could dowse his life in syrupy sentimentality, lift it up to soak up a tad of romanticism, and then peel away all the sagging skin and choke on the bitter facts. Reflect again on these narrations about the burden and privilege of being born a Jabri, about the suffocation that intrudes upon the temptations of the East, the hardness that lurks beneath the copious liberties and freedoms of the West. It was not so much that Ali was befuddled by his peripatetic yearnings – although the obvious risk in choosing these quotes is of giving precisely this impression – but that he always saw the ironies in each possibility. His weakness lay in his refusal to settle the debate and choose a side. But as the clock ticked towards the mid-seventies and the dreaded one-way ticket back, some of Ali's wants became discernible under the thick layers of his shifting dislikes and *amours*. About certain things, he was immovable: how he wanted to live, whom he wanted to love, where he would prefer to be. This is why the East was an ogre and London was ideal.

True, in the East there was shelter, a past much older than yesterday, a future longer than tomorrow. But the East was where the many islands of his self would have to drift discreetly, silently, in the glare of day; where a family and its place would torment this hapless man, carrying him between fleeting moments of joy and many longer ones of disgrace; where that clichéd veil of mystery lifted only before the harsh face of oppression. The East was an anchor which sank the heart and drowned all reverie with it. Whereas London throbbed with ready sanctuaries. It was respite, escape, distance, man's love of man untamed, cuddled. It was about 'grabbing what cannot be'.[266] Every conceivable burden he could isolate on the margins, in his journals and letters, nursing them there, while the rest of his life he would release unfettered to indulge its every want. Of course some of it was about the flesh: 'parties, saunas, mescaline, blotter samples, deep throats, poppers and juicers, whisky to the ear lobes, Ace of Hearts, the Black Queen, divine music, tanned Californians, tongues and bodies and flaming creatures . . . Heat!'[267] Some of it was about the minutiae of the anonymous day: a sandwich lunch on English grass under a rare sunray, the opera, hours of sketching in the British Museum, the occasional weekend in Gloucestershire with Rick and his girlfriend. Some of it was about the beautiful studies of Parthenon carvings that hang on Ronnie's walls today;[268] about exhibitions of Assyrian artifacts and quick sketches of King Ashurbanipal,[269] the 'Arts of Islam' at the Hayward Gallery,[270] about dinner at 12A Ridgmount Gardens, his home with Antonia.

> After these several years at Ridgmount, the place has taken on a certain glow, full of beautiful and interesting things, books, plants, little old finds from the old markets like Portobello, both Antonia and me being very into third-world awareness, we both love natural materials, rattan and grass mats, woven basketry, cane furniture, African prints, exotic memorabilia . . . the flat is small but it contains a whole universe of colour patterns and geographic reminiscences . . . not least being my nostalgic collection of Arabia-looking pictures and objects scattered throughout.[271]

Some of it was about him and the mirror before a casual outing:

> Heavy black boots, dark levis, well-worn black suede levis jacket and white check shirt romantically collared and cuffed, a conscious habillement à l'Ingres, though rough and tumble counter culture style . . . It is only packaging, as we all know, and full of falsehoods, svelte exteriors . . . [272]

Wilde's 'One has to be a work of art or wear a work of art' would have been used here – because Ali was both – had it not been quoted mercilessly and into the dustbin of worn-out campy truisms. Look at the pictures! Look at those instamatic passport pictures on which Ali was hooked. They nuzzle inside his diaries next to the dry leaves and flowers that marked the passage of his seasons, staring back at you every few turns of the page.

Some of it, as Allan puts it, was about 'an interloper . . . a painter's eye, a spaced out kid', groping innocently in the dark 'for the new, for the other side'[273]: 'black friends from uptown . . . the Twenties at 2[am] . . . reggae, ska, the Jamaican shuffle, the bloos, the Pattie, RockSteady, the West Indies . . . Head throbbing with rhythms and cross currents.'[274] Some of it was about all fingers on the pulse of a city and change, on seemingly mundane images before they became the icons of the day or the harbingers of the era yet to come: Angela Davis before her trial in February 1972, right beside a strip of Muslim men kneeling in prayer, both towering over Zola, Cézanne, Gandhi and Lenin struggling to share space with the happy faces of Nancy Reagan and Frank Sinatra. Flip the page back if you like. Here she is, Hannah Arendt, lecturing on the *Origins of Totalitarianism.*

But the East was a quandary inside a conundrum inside a tangle all tucked into a muddle. Had he been ignorant about or indifferent to things Arab, there would have been very little to explain. But Ali, unbeknownst even to Antonia ('I don't recall he was at all involved with that part of the world, outside of his embassy job'),[275] was up to the minute about the region, intellectually engaged in and palpably in command of the specifics of its history and situation. His daily diary entries and lengthy periodic postings to Diala teem with commentaries of unusual prescience and sensitivity delivered with a sombre pen or presented in packages of beautiful satire.

In nuanced positions unusual then for witnesses on either flaming side of the Arab-Israeli fence, Ali saw victims and culprits exchanging places on any given day. While absorbing the lessons of Terence de Pres' reflections on the Holocaust, Ali glued collaged images of Israeli military boots over Palestinian heads. Very quickly, lest the author and Ali be accused of the crime of likening unfathomable genocide with run-of-the mill atrocities, his were not deliberate juxtapositions, but dispersed annotations on the schizophrenia of human tragedy. Very sympathetic per-spectives on the Occupied Palestinian Territories ('The Jordan River dividing along its sinewy meanderings East Bank from West, Islam from Judaism, ancient Arab agriculture from . . . exploitation-Israeli computer planned occupation forces – heart breaking to gaze at the hills on the other side . . . ')[276] did not preclude outrage at the massacre of Israeli athletes in the 1972 Munich Olympics: 'A culture once noble and elevating has become

synonymous with the silence of cowards and the brutality of men
too envenomed to partake in the human community. Each detail of
cause and effect on the Arab side adds to the shame.'[277]

After close to a century of this Palestinian-Israeli debacle –
stripped naked now by the mulish resistance of facts to scavenging
myths – views such as these are still cursed by many on both sides
as the political myopia of traitors and fools. That Ali held them
over thirty years ago, when pleas for empathy and sanity were few
and far between in the deafening din of hatred and bloody tit-for-
tat, is evidence of the wisdom and blind compassion of this Jabri.
Wisdom and compassion, it has to be said, that did not express
themselves only in the comfort and privacy of his journals.

Cairo. September 1974. A gathering at Ihsan's Nile apartment:
Ihsan: 'You should come and live in Cairo and forget everything
about England.' Ali: 'Ludicrous fanaticism . . . Why should I
consider myself only Arab . . . ' Guests indulged in self-centred
victimhood at the hands of the West, while finally I burst out:
'What about the 6,000,000 Jews that Arab school children learn
to forget.'[278]

Ali knew much, and he knew it well. His protestations against
home as 'exile' were not too unlike those of countless other Arabs
furious with a culture embarrassingly reactive and anaemic,
governments with an endemic shortage of successes, and societies
at once timid and tyrannical. They made it easy for their sons and
daughters to flip-flop between love and disdain. What place bathed
so freely in overwrought odes to dead glory while stewing in the
ignominy of today? How many fellow Arab travellers have lamented,
like Ali, the casual slaps of officialdom on their humiliated face?
Amman airport, June 9, 1973:

I am so anxious to get off the ground, for God's sake. Typical
customs-inspection security grilling, officials all pervasive suspicions and unable to accept very easily non-mother-tongue-
fluent foreign looking bona fide national entity. 'Where do
you work,' and 'who the hell are you,' gruffly badgered in best

intimidation style. Whereas real foreigner remains untouched. The postcolonial nationalism hang up.[279]

Check out his tagged drawing, sent to Diala in a 1976 letter, of a 'fragile bored youngish'[280] bourgeois Arab beauty. Blending sharp insight with a blade-like wit that shattered the glazed existence of his victim, Ali exhibited an astonishing feel for the post-oil boom ascendance of the vacuous and inane in Arab culture. With that subtle sarcasm of the learned, the once rich, and the terminally condescending, Ali could bring out the red in the palest of cheeks at the slightest of slights – and there were many. This one, he confessed, was provoked 'by my hypersensitive awareness of her [a close friend of his] and her mother's not particularly extensive interest in me: big game, they're after, not sincere small-time juniors from the Ambaschiata di Kharabishti (embassy of gibberish) . . . '[281]

This is the Arab world that stalked Ali's insomniac nights. It was real, familiar and oozing a mixture of wickedness, allure, and inescapable duty. Ali's head, as François suspects, was pegged to the West, but his heart kept nagging its owner to go East.[282]

*   *   *

'This year is so crucial. I have to either get back to the Middle East or – get back to the Middle East,'[283] he disclosed to Diala and his mother at the end of 1975. By April 1976, a stale, sour air was seeping through the cracks of his dead-ends. It was time. On a mild afternoon in April, upon returning to his office from the fashion show for the London Designers' Collection at Chelsea Town Hall for which he did the drawings, Ali broke down.

I burst into my little office [at the embassy] with its neat piles of hopeless pedestrian transactions and sad papers from unknown sons and daughters of Arab families in such different circumstances to what I had just come from, my little Middle Eastern pin-up pictures and calendar manuscripts . . . and the old barely surviving geraniums I've almost given up nurturing on my backward-facing window-sill, and promptly burst into tears. I could see my whole situation, the helpless limitation of it, the day-after-day treadmill of it, the contrast with the week of hectic glamour I'd just tasted, and the all-pervasive feudal pattern in the hierarchy of protection under the king, the elaborate system of submission to social machinery by which we accept our fates as cogs in a larger whole . . . [284]

Antonia begged him to marry her, so he could get his British citizenship and stay. He did not take her up on it. 'I think he just did not know how to make it here.'[285]

One evening, years later – it must have been in the early nineties – while munching on nuts at a dinner party at Rula and Fadi's, Ali told me: 'I came close once to marrying a woman – Antonia.'[286] That was the first time I had heard him mention the name of someone from those other lives, those other places.

*   *   *

The choice of Arab country was easy. To Diala and Hala, he fretted that 'it can't be Jordan, where I'll be like some cocktail canapé on a toothpick under aunty's fingers, and it could scarcely be Kuwait, where you have enough worries without a down-and-out among you – so it has to be Cairo or Aleppo. The latter looks just too remote and threatening.'[287] In December 1976, Ali went to Cairo to visit Ihsan. On a seeming whim, the Cairo period began.

CHAPTER FIVE

Ah, Ya Hamada O, King of My Heart!

The solace of such work as I do with brain and heart lies in
this – that only there, in the silences of the painter and the
writer can reality be recorded, reworked and made to show its
significant side.[288]

Darley, in *Justine*,
Lawrence Durrell's Alexandria Quartet

She leans back in elegant black and white against the piano,
barely in her twenties. It looks like a large sitting room, tasteful,
pleased with its few accessories. The Tamara de Lempicka Calla
Lilies and the embroidered cloth that hangs over the piano are
backdrops to spread-out arms and contented eyes that declare, 'I,
too, am Egypt.'

This is probably one of Ali's finest. Umm Kalthoum, the
crooning legend who pulled at the heartstrings of Egypt's
bashawat and *fellaheen* (gentry and peasants) alike, way before the
advent of Gamal Abdel Nasser and long after, is in her youthful,
life-size splendour. In the languorous, confident pose of this adored
woman, once a poor daughter of the Delta, the spectator stares at
one of the continuities that mocked Egypt's noisy walkout on its
past, for though Nasser belittled every expression of the old mother
country as tainted, passé, borrowed, this voice, this hypnotising
voice, he welcomed to the bosom of his new Egypt.

Take your time with this painting. It deserves it. Had Ali been
fascinated only with the faded emblems of urbane, cosmopolitan,
Francophone, Anglophile, unveiled, bejewelled, *Je-ne-sais-quoi*
Cairo, then Asmahan, the Syrian Druze singing princess, who
eclipsed Umm Kalthoum before her fatal car crash in 1944, would

have stood instead in that portrait and still brought roaming eyes
to a halt. Leila Murad, even, the singing Jewish paramour of
debonair Anwar Wajdi (our own Clark Gable), who soothed the
aching hearts of men and women made silly by an abundance of
love, would have done just as well.[289] But Umm Kalthoum was
different. Umm Kalthoum was *bint al balad* (a daughter of the
country and countryside) – the girl who trekked to the glittering
centre from its muddy periphery and sang herself from the bottom
to the top; the peasant who came to town and serenaded it into
happy submission; the native who crossed from the rich brown
earth to the white alien crowd and dared pronounce herself equal.
Umm Kalthoum was Gamal's just as much as she was theirs. She
sang to him the way she sang to those before him. This fresh,
modish Umm Kalthoum – just like her older, beehived, bespec-
tacled, white-handkerchief-in-hand self – she, too, was Egypt.

There is nothing accidental about this painting. Umm Kalthoum at that age, in those clothes, in front of that piano, in that
pose, was not a casual choice for a portrait. This celebration of
an image of her which, by the seventies, could be found only in
the rare nostalgic store or magazine profile, has Ali's embrace of
irony painted all over it. Every grainy particle of this young Umm
Kalthoum spoke to Ali about the nagging questions of identity: if
she could, with such apparent confidence, make her sense of self
so limber and fluid, could not he, Ali al Jabri, a savant in the
ambiguities of belonging, remould his selfhood as she did hers?
Could he not dart out of the alien white crowd straight into the
arms of the brown earth? Could he not cosy up to it, know its
suffering, smoke chicha with it, become part of it?

*   *   *

Evening. February 11, 1977. Less than two months into his
sojourn in Cairo, on a bus to somewhere, Ali issued this homage to
his Arab identity.

Feeling attenuated, radiant, somehow transfigured . . . great
internal gulps of longing and identity as the breezes of Egypt in

Overleaf: Body of Human Waste, Cairo
Above & below: Into the Night, Cairo

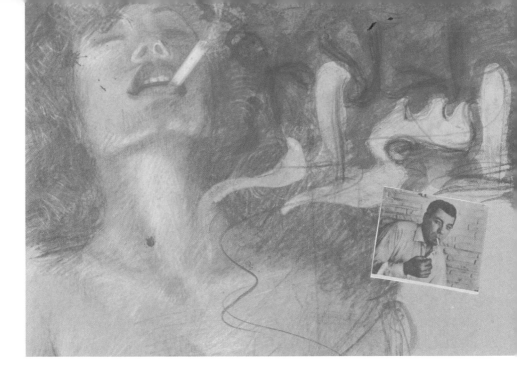

Above: Woman in Red
Below: Woman in Black

Nasser Series No. 2:
Private Crimes

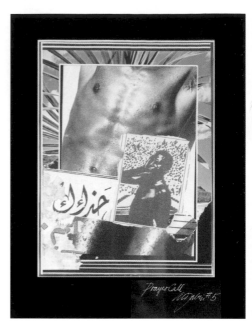

Nasser Series No. 5:
Prayer Call

Nasser Series No. 7:
Midnight Call

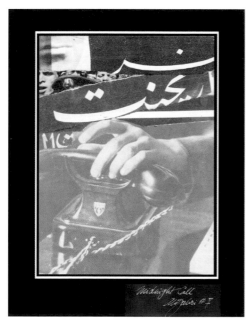

Nasser Series No.8:
Golden Age

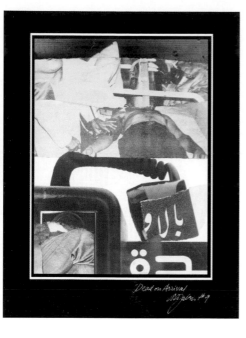

Nasser Series No. 9:
Dead on Arrival

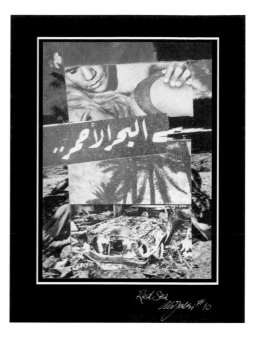

Nasser Series No. 10:
Dead Sea

Nasser Series No. 11:
By Agreement

Nasser Series No. 12:
And Now

Opposite: Shajarat al Durr Mausoleum (Courtesy of Mr. Fuad &
Mrs. Nidal (Ashkar) Na'eem)

Above & below: From Ali's Cairo Sketchbook
Overleaf: Um Kalthoum

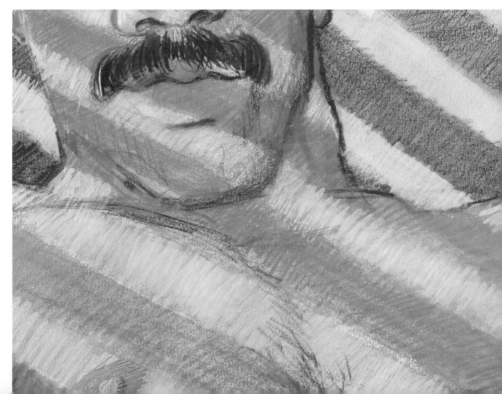

the evening caressed my face through the open window and it seemed that figures and architecture and details of town life and customs of the Islamic world composed one harmony of homage to itself.[290]

Beseeching words – sincere, no doubt – but they carry within them the syrupy romanticisms that always seized Ali on his very good days. In those early weeks in Egypt, the possibilities were wooing his future, and his initiation into Arab life was pregnant with delectable probabilities. He was feeling his way into the myriad personalities of Egypt and it seemed the walks between them, however daring and reckless, would bring him closer to home.

A vast demonstration surging through Ramses street Tahrir, the main square . . . Slogans! Chanting! Thousands of youth, Egypt in full cry . . . I rushed to the railings, asked 2 youths just outside stripes, What is it, what is it? The transport problem? Any glance at Cairo's traffic and mass transport situation is enough to comprehend a demo! . . . It's also everything else, they added . . . *Ya Sadat, Ya Sadat*, you are a millionaire while we starve . . . Bread, Bread! We are your children Egypt, hear our cry . . . Hukuma Hurra [free government] Ta, Ta, Ta, Ta, Ta . . . where are you now Oh, Nasser, Ya Gamal, Ya Gamal . . . and on high shoulders the young lion leaders, café au lait champions in glasses, afros, Marxists perhaps (need to be) . . . Felt totally involved, totally one with them, though I presume looking foreign in my white floppy jeans & sneakers . . . and yet so safe and secure – is it possible? – under the mildest most humorous most loving people protesting its tragic humiliation! The army aloft, the accusing condemnations of the socialist doubly shtickk. And the foreigners say Egypt is cattle, they cannot speak? Let us now be heard!! . . . The Arab world in its tragic misdirection at the hands of money and mediocrity. Where is austerity? Where is scholarship at the top? Where is the grace of history? The tradition of the spirit? Islam itself an empty vessel like the Christian clergy keeping them in sufferance. Hours later the troops arrive . . . motion and counter motion like waves of the sea – ½ laughter, half genuine hysteria . . . That evening dinner at Jean Pierre with the posh double barrel name [Peroncel Hugo] Le Monde Cairo correspondent[291] in his extraordinary luxe Garden City apartment only inches away from it all, now scenes of debris, torn out pavements . . . and here as the guests came up the glittering S.S Empress pure Art Deco, Ascenseur Schindler . . . The Louis XVI bombe buffet . . . The selected intelligentsia of the stricken city gathered for its midnight supper . . . served by the same docile and gentle Egyptian faces and hands that massed the late afternoon streets. But let's be fair, this was not 'Let Them Eat Cake . . .' merely inescapable karmic divisions of life as she can't help dividing the sons of the earth.[292]

The rummaging in the depths of this country began. For sissies, the slow, tentative dip into nativity. For the timid, the careful sampling of local tastes and prearranged journeys into the mouth of the gutter; for them, in-and-out Europeans and insipid bourgeois Arabs, the gloves, the nose-holding, the fish-bowl gazing at indigenous moods and colours. Ali stripped naked this dusty, ageless, burning, hard *Misr* (Egypt) and kissed his way down to its 'princely cracked brown feet'.[293]

A sense of total isolation and frantic immersion in my art work . . . trekking daily to the scene of the crime, on funky taxis, brown drivers, Om Kalthoum, the photorealism of pullulating streets, the snatch of robes and draperies and headgears extraordinaires, all oblique-shot . . . surcharged immense multiplicity and the plunged envelopment in it all is *total*. A kind of descent into black states of soul, a despair in my exile (always exile) in the land where no possible relationship of clean reciprocity seems to happen – it's all 'how much?' or 'what can you provide?' or 'what is your status?' . . . We are kind of outer Mongolia pierced by a blurred noon-climax heat . . . [294]

Hopelessly in love, my passion the people, my ecstasy the faces, my despair beside the Nile, the desolation, the lack of contact, the finality. 'I am drugged on Brown flesh.'[295]

Egypt was forced open. There were no slow, leisurely slurps of distress or pleasure, no split hairs between the higher callings of the intellect and the lower motivations of carnal want. That difference between the persistent matter of identity and incessant urges of sexuality, that distance between untainted Arabhood and potent manhood, never made their case with Ali. It was either the two together or nothing at all. For some reason, he could not venture into one without foraging in the other. In the end, there was rarely an elated feeling that did not end up a disappointment, rarely a stunning discovery that did not bring with it a terrible truth, nowhere a sight of luscious Egypt that did not float on a sea of hands roughed up by too many years of muck and hard living.

Beneath the silver crescent in the very early hours after midnight. Perhaps it was that misadventure with 4 youths and a knife that triggered my decline & a loss of appetite. The sickening of impulse, a gorged assuagement in the throbbing streets no longer exotic but imbued with the savagery of motive.[296]

*　　*　　*

Upon arrival, Ali parked himself in a back room in apartment 12 of Abu El Futuh Building at 78, Rue El Nil, Gizeh, Cairo. It is rinky-dink now, a rather rundown building with corroded detailing, but it must have shone in those early gloating years of Nasserism. This Nile-view lodging was offered to Ihsan Pasha al Jabri for services rendered between 1958 and 1963, back when Nasser thought Syria (and the whole Arab world with it) was his for the taking.

What a strange friendship this was! What strange friendships Arab Nationalism paraded before the enthusiastic Arab crowds! Here was the quintessential Aleppine feudal lord – haughty, Turkic, and Francophone – losing villages and estates to Syria's new military order, all the while sucking up to Egypt's own petit bourgeois, land-grabbing army man.[297] All that space between the haves and the have nots, all that arm wrestling between panicky idle beys and righteous hotheads and berets, gone, forgotten, bread crumbs under the carpet, in the name of Arab brotherhood and unity – so long as it played on the other side of the border. But then, if Ihsan could, with such ease, drop an Ottoman sultan for a Hashemite king, why could he not, after the passage of so many years, ditch royalty and declare himself a Nasserite? After all, they started it. Feisal and his brothers, once the Hashemite kingdom in Syria came to an embarrassing end in 1920, did not seem too keen on Ihsan. Why should he not then return the insult? Nasser, like Sultan Mehmed V and Feisal, was king of his own hill. What difference did it make that they were born into it and he had barged his way in? So why not Nasser, the man of the hour, the saviour of the day, the power that be, Ramses of the people? And Nasser, liberator and uniter that he was, so loved converts, new believers, even if they were sorry, old geezers. There was always a place for them, something to do, like the ceremonial presidency of the council of ministers of the union between the UAR and Yemen. The union died a sickly toddler, but the post lasted a lifetime on Ihsan's résumé.

If there was a better choice than Abu El Futuh on the Nile in Egypt, Ali could not think of it. Cairo, granddaddy, this apartment, they seemed such a perfect alternative to that other dreaded Jabri in that God-forsaken destination – Saadieyh in Amman. But if Ali thought life with Saadieyh would be nightmarish, life with Ihsan turned out to be positively freakish. Jabrian reprimands angrily awaited his return in the wee hours of the morning, while Jabrian rituals hounded him from sunrise to sundown. Suspicions sneaked up behind his unquenchable urge to submit to every passing whim and scared the wits out of his need to satisfy every desire. The scramble between filial responsibilities and razor-edge nightly trysts among the tombs and living shacks of Cairo was bound to start out funny and end up in the very vicinity of the pathetic. Scarcely two months after Ali's arrival at Abu al Futuh, the diaries began to make references to Ihsan's outrage at 'my disgrace to the home', to tirades by the neighbour ('the swarthy stud') in the middle of the night – probably at the frequent sight of a dazed and naked Ali wandering onto the balcony – to Saadieyh's

Gamal Abdel Nasser and Ihsan al Jabri

'ghastly anxious calls from Geneva'.[298] All these harrumphs, of
course, while Ali, with draft board, brush, and pencil in hand, was
'dithering between Islamic regions & the good old *Mathaf Masr*
(the national museum) and not wanting to seem shy to Mohammad (the guard). Ah ya Hamada O king of my heart.'[299] It was war
between that most addictive ubiquitous Egyptian arse and a blind,
narcissistic, hypochondriac, chair-bound, Ihsan. The arse won.

> Beauties teeming down every vista . . . Driven to distraction by
> the asses. The Egyptian ass is a taut-sprung marvel greater
> than the pyramids as a feat of Bio Engineering and to the touch
> ever more rock hard in its silkiness.[300]

There Ihsan sat among 'the endless official photographs sus-
pended in their outdated Edwardian leaning out angles with the
captains and the kings . . . '[301] lobbing his complaints at this odd-
ball Ali about his dilettantism, his late hours, the missed dinners,
the dubious habits, the unannounced disappearances. The rules,
the commands, the conditions, became a daily transaction between
a sadistic, controlling patriarch and a thirty-five-year-old grandson
in mortal fear of the 'dreadful incubus of Juddo's (grandfather's)
possible displeasure'.[302]

> He told me that he was upset that I left and that he wants me to
> stay as long as I like . . . He sat me down and gently, with serenity
> and thoughtfulness, told me . . . that I ought to stay here, but
> under the following conditions:
>
> The six commandments:
> 1. I should take up my Arabic lessons again.
> 2. I should have dinner with him every evening.
> 3. I should commit no sins? (What does that include?)
> 4. That I should return home before they close the gates at
>   10:30 or not go out at all.
> 5. I should tell him where I am going before I leave the house.
> 6. I think I have mixed the numbers a bit. There were no more
>   than five?

This is how the two made up after the first row that threw Ali out of Abu El Futuh in October 1977. A month or so after this send off by Ihsan, Ali was settling into an Egyptian *Awwamah*, a bare, rickety houseboat that belonged to friends of Saadieyh's. Now he could

> gaze with serene detachment straight into Juddo's pokey-furniture-infested balcony only a few thousand social levels further up the bank . . . The poor old dear (alias Angus Scrooge McDuck HE) is, I hope, peacefully aslumber after the nightly ritual of the 200 medicines, prescriptions, tablets, ointments, and doctor's phone numbers that keep his sense of physical wellbeing, not to mention 'faites vos jeux messieurs' Jabri Baccarat-alive and well.[303]

*   *   *

More than two years after Ali's death, paintings were found in the many hidden cartons he filled with his life. None of his Jordanian friends had ever seen these before. He always showed some of the Cairo diaries' sketches and drawings, never the paintings; of all his works, these speak most openly of forbidden love. Nudes, you could call some of them, luminous masculinity in the hours right before or the seconds just after. They betray a total surrender to his men, their chaotic city, and their gruelling lives. This is what he always wanted: a raw, rough, skin-to-skin existence in a land swarming with virility, kindred Cavafian spirits on Alexandrian shorelines, 'a coffee and a hard to find florida[304] at the Saidi-Sudan café.'[305]

> 2 guys walked past, cowboy silhouette dark moustached and with tight jeans. Their talk was yet mine in the level of inflammation, plein dans les rues, they made me feel like it (they always do!). I got the tall one up the elevator, no lights on the landing and his cigarette lighter flaming just in time in the pitch black with our deep dancing shadows behind the brief glow to reveal what eye behind the peephole in the door must have found macabre – the door didn't open thank God . . . [306]

Pity for him that the rewards and penalties were always so un-
comfortably intimate with each other. Love often came in with
switchblades and strolled out with booty, paintings were sold for
pocket money, and shower-less days and unwashed knickers kicked
the life out of the romance of simple living.

What is going on? Egypt land of perfidy and lies? Did 25 years
of Gamal Abdel Nasser totally corrupt your soul through the
insidious gnaw of ruination and poverty – they want money, I
want love! – or is it me who hunts for the dark gutter's silver
lining finding only the fascination of the unobtainable? Tastes,
the bitter keenness, solitary marathons in the midnight streets
. . . hideout haunts, the City of the Dead, among tombs, domes,
sand piles, crumbling mortar . . . the sweet music of Muslim
mortality made miraculously into living flesh by the music of the
living among the early shadows of morn . . . I am suffering from
the intensity of the system, of the body of ideas, of the religion,
of the upbringing, of the biology of the human psyche-scape.
Here in Islam's centrifugal navel – beneath the aqueducts of
medieval Arabia, the shadow of the citadel, the rearing of the
proud edifices of glory to the past, all bitter sweet, all dust in the
mouth.[307]

There were no breathers in this Egypt, no time-outs. These
purifying deep dives into reality and dejection followed by those
uppers – quick, illusory and exhilarating – took him through the
cycle of sadness and euphoria, up and down, day in, day out, over
and over again.

*   *   *

What Arab can think of Egypt and not ponder the man that was
Nasser? Gamal. The Gamal. Here is a demigod who can still ruffle
Arab feathers. At the mere mention of the name, breath quickens,
mouths go dry, and hipbones shift uneasily in their sockets. In
Egypt, minds are calm when debating the good and the bad about
him – he spent eighteen years with them; they know him – well.
But try in the rest of the Arab world to draw up a balance sheet

Ali painting among the Mamluk tombs in the City of the Dead.
1988. Courtesy of John Dollar

and you will hear hisses and boos from even the most temperate voices.

Of all the indictments that occupy every other page of Ali's Cairo journals, 'Egypt of perfidy and lies' is the most heart-breaking. True, it was his frenetic ways that helped him find this Egypt. He admitted as much when he threw the noose around Nasser and then loosened it by confessing to the culpability of his own hunts

for the 'dark gutter's silver lining'. But Ali was not swimming only
in Cairo's human cesspools in his dual pursuit of noble ideals and
physical cravings, and the maladies that gorged on the flesh and
spirit of this people did not stop at the gutter. What he saw were
not only the typical corrosions that make the inhabitants of misery
everywhere siblings. Egypt in its entirety was reeling from years
of intoxicating visions of greatness and the depression that con-
sumed it in the nauseating morning after. Love him or hate him,
in the seventies, you could not look at this country's unfulfilled
promise without picking on Nasser. Even now, thirty-eight years
after his death, you cannot begin to fathom Egypt without
probing the legacy of Gamal. Two long decades of muscle flexing
and magic wands and poetry – which harangued the bigotry and
gluttony of the old Egypt and celebrated the equality and dignity
of the new one, which threatened to win back Palestine, which
feigned revolution and traded on it – have their place in every tear-
stained portrait of this *Umm al Dunya*, this mother of the world,
as its children call it.

Every kind of scar marks this charred Arab landscape. The
memory of Nasser is one of them. Every Arab nurses a gash or two
from every manner of perceived or actual betrayal. Conspiracies
here are a daily occurrence. Some are for real and deadly, most are
the stuff of desperate imaginations eager to explain away every
failure and self-induced humiliation. In this place of constant
upheaval and chronic injustice, politics intrudes on every household and the pain it inflicts is very personal. This is why those who
loved Nasser still cherish his name and those who hated him still
curse it.

The Jabris themselves were of more than one mind about him.
Hala, apparently, was a fan, and Ihsan, we know, started as one
and became a full-blown crony. But Majddedine and Saadieyh
were more beholden to the rival house of the Hashemites. While
the former seemed intrigued by Syrian unification with Iraq,[308]
the latter belonged heart and soul to King Hussein and his Wasfi.
A house divided upon itself, as usual. Even Ali's scattered selves
owe something – however tentatively – to Nasser, because if it had

not been for his entry onto the Egyptian stage in 1952, Ali might well have stayed on at Alexandria's Victoria College. Instead, he was dispatched to the West and, at the tender age of ten, he could not take with him more than the weakest of Arab sensibilities; more poignantly, he could not take with him more than the most fragile of family ties.

About Nasser, over the years Ali put together conversations between rowdy metaphors and talking images, here reducing him to his essentials, there stretching him into his full pharonic self.

A bunch of officers from the army yachted off the waddling porno-addict monarch [Farouk], imposed rule for the people and sweeping reforms. The rich fled, the foreigners migrated, Swiss bank accounts got the draft and giant estates were carved up into liverwurst and that is what the fight was all about: Black Brown civilisation versus honky whitey with his socio-industrial programme to lay waste to your resources and suck it, dear, like dry, thereby imposing transworld imperialist control to fight Commie menace – sulfur dioxide, never mind . . .

Gamal Abdel Nasser got up in his own machine, surrounded by yes men & stooges in zoot suits & loud ties. Propaganda blitz-krieg on the air-waves, socialist rule and rigidity behind the bars . . . Bleak monster edifices to house Soviet-style bureau-cracy, but the peasantry were hearing their names called and little Ahmed presumably no longer had to serve Lady Phyllis her evening tooth powder . . . and the poor were made to feel more dignified as they continued their unchanged diet . . . [309]

The whys, the hows, and the wheretos in a whirlwind trip. You can, if you must, quibble with one or two facts but you would be missing the point. The beauty of these comments on history is not in this or that detail, but in the filmic quality which takes you smiling through them and finds you inadvertently nodding at the end.

Never underestimate the hypnotic charisma of pride to a people long brought low without it. Every time Ali's little Ahmed reached deep into his history he found majesty, and every time he bounded to last week he felt slights and letdowns. Little Ahmed would remember the grandiose bluster of Khedive Ismail who ached to 'turn Egypt into France, Cairo into Paris, and his court into Versailles',[310] while he tried to trick luck out of a meagre living. He would remember 1882, when Colonel Urabi rebelled and failed and Lord Cromer first entered his house and stayed.[311] He would remember those lucrative years of imperial Britain, of good works and good business: the chirpy sound of a climbing stock market that added little to his livelihood, those asphalted roads and streets on which Lady Phyllis travelled, the telephone on which she lapsed into incomprehensible prattle, while his own starved schools churned out ignorance and blather.[312] He may have even come across a backpacking T. E. Lawrence on a Cairo street sometime in 1912 looking sullen and ill from the sight of too many ' . . . querulous, foul-mouthed little Ahmeds'.[313] Yes, there never seems to be an end to the boo-hoo-look-what-they-did-to-me whining of Arabs. But playing the song over and over again does not make it any less true, it just makes it old and tired. And for little Ahmed, there was no song he preferred to dance to than this one. Nasser may not have been inexorable, but there was a reason for him, fertile soil for his star.

Take Saad Pasha Zaghloul, Egypt's premier nationalist, and all that hoohah about Egyptian independence in 1922. Such hard work went into it, peasants and workers felt they did their bit. But, after all the blood and sweat, *Brownie* still languished on this side and *Honky* cocktailed through life on that; the British played nasty, King Farouk played roulette, and parliaments came and went, their members scampering fifty steps back for every two inched forward. In this Egypt, there were some smart men, some competent men, but their liberalism was too young and too erratic. Worse still, rumours had it the palace was too corrupt, too drunk and oversexed, and the English were too manipulative, too cynical and too arrogant. The Egyptians rightly became confused and angry. Then, to top it all, the 1948 Arab-Israeli war blew up, Arab politicians chanted Palestine, Arab rifles fired every which way but straight, Israel was born and around 700,000 Palestinian refugees found themselves miles away from their homes.

And thus rose Nasser of the poor man, of Arab dignity, of Egyptian pride; Nasser the liberator of Palestine, the champion of justice and democracy; Nasser of heroic defiance and sure answers. So rapturous was all this that the Arabs were soon twirling trance-like around their magnificent dreams the way Turkish Sufi dervishes rotate around their magnificent selves. Heads moved, lovesick, to Nasser, much like they swayed to Umm Kalthoum's *Amal Hayati* (The Hope of My Life). The faithful in Beirut swore that his face could be traced on the surface of the moon. That voice, that flawless mastery of the ordinary man's Arabic, the way he gracefully seduced it upward and gently cooled it down, the way he swung it lyrically to the left and raced it back sober to the right. Nasser! He said so much and with such power, whole nations, millions of people, walked so tall at the end of every speech that they could not see the mush they were treading in way down below.

What is in a word? Everything if you are from this Arab neck of the woods. 'A form of verbal magic,'[314] Navid Kermani calls it in his little marvel *Silent Sirens*. Listen to the Koranic recitations of the sublime Sheikh Abd al Basset Abd al Samad and touch the awe in your silent tears; listen to the riveting poetry of Al Mutanabi and feel the slow swelling of the chest and the quick lifting of the head; listen to the fiery orations of Gamal Abdel Nasser and rise up to own your destiny. A towering man, Nasser, among mighty men, but he could never have become the giant that he was had he not first been a poet. A lifeless phrase in his possession, such as 'ya ayyuha l-ikhwa' ('Oh, brethren'), could become fodder for a rhetorical fire, 'electrify audiences and link [him] to a 1,400-year line of ancestors'.[315] As Kermani reminds us, just as ordinary people during the Prophet Mohammad's time 'found it hard to distinguish between poetry and revelation',[316] Nasser's masses could not differentiate between truth and poetry. Heresy? Nowhere near it. This is not about the veracity of blessed messengers, it is about what is in the Arabic word that elevates mere mortals into the company of unforgettable men. Sit today in the midst of any audience watching old reels of a speechifying

Nasser and, like Kermani, you will feel the air heat up from the fumes firing out of inflamed nostrils.

> . . . the crowded cinema [watching Nasser 57] . . . vibrated with excitement. When, in the final scene, Nasser addressed his audience in the classical vocative, emitting familiar classical phrases from a masklike face, the tension in the audience was palpable. And, at the end of the speech, when, from the pulpit of Azhar University, Nasser the Socialist, cries out 'Allahu akbar' four times punctuated by short, pregnant pauses, the wheel comes full circle and he is back where his own history began: he becomes a prophet.[317]

This was the glorious Nasser, the voice that could turn a dozen spoken words into an epic of chivalry.

Look now at the picture of Nasser at the foot of the plane, with Sadat a distant, tiny figure a few steps up. Look at Nasser in military garb issuing a sombre salute. Look at the civilian and uniformed men that hover around him. You have his whole epoch right there before you. Just in case you have not grasped the symbolism, Ali's comment at the foot of the photo – 'The Golden Age' – highlights it. To those who love Nasser, the picture, on its own, may communicate the aura of his calling and greatness. To those who do not, it starts out as a visual synopsis of the heyday of Arab militarism and quickly deteriorates into a parody of it. Ali could have chosen a thousand other pictures of Nasser, yet he chose this one, because for the innocent it managed to say very little but for the knowing it said it all – blandness and satire looking the same and acting as one.

This picture does not exist by itself. And its message is clearer when it is seen in its context. It is number eight in a series of twelve collages Ali did in the early 1980s about the malevolence of Arab politics and its intrusions into the simple life. If they seem dated now to some Arab eyes, it is because we have come so far and huge slabs of the truth have been picked up along the way. If they seem offensive to others, it is because those others have been sleeping undisturbed behind their travelling blinds. With the sinister dark glasses that peer out of *Private Crimes* in number two, the visiting card that announces the *Compliments of the Intelligence Services* in number three, and the telephone that rings at midnight under a shut mouth and torn scrap of a crowd in number seven, Ali strings together iconic images of Arab authoritarianism, the tools it uses, the menacing representations of state which usher in number eight and a saluting Nasser.

It is not known when this picture of Nasser was taken, but it could only have begun to acquire its meaning after 1967. By the late 1950s, Nasser's successes shaped many Arabs' shopping list for a made-to-order superman: the diplomatic triumph of the Suez war was tangible, unmistakable; the withdrawal symptoms of a furious and blundering British Empire palpable, gratifying; Nasser's land reforms were more than cosmetic, reasonable; the democratisation of education genuine, earnest; his bid for membership of the club of powerful nations audacious, admirable; his brinkmanship shrewd, exhilarating; his call for Arab oneness exciting, invigorating; the man's disinterest in money fresh, obvious. Even by the mid-1960s, when the gloss on Nasser's rule had worn off, when mistakes were piling up and achievements were running on empty, this picture of Nasser would have winked only at those who never bought into him in the first place.

But by 1967, history had delivered its blows and myths lay seriously wounded or dead on the surface of the battered body politic of the Arab world. For many Arabs, it was time for funerals, for bowed heads again. It was time for *Dead on Arrival,* Ali's number nine in the series: the last gasps of a sickly regime which should not have been born in the first place. It did not matter if Nasser intended war or whether Israel tricked him into it. That he would pick a fight or slide on his bluster and bravado into the trap of one, when his and every other Arab regime were so distressingly and knowingly unready, revealed the extent to which he and his entourage were feeding on their own crap. Six seismic days of a sunny June exposed the gross ineptitude of the military leaderships which had spent years pounding into their citizenry numbing, fearsome assertions of the potency of their ways.[318] ' . . . Seventeen years ago . . . It seemed, or it started to seem, like the people's era had begun to dawn, lit up by the army's sun,' bemoaned Arab journalism's man of letters Ghassan Tueni three months after the disaster of 1967. And then, ' . . . the army, the instrument of the people; the army, the leader of the revolution; the army, the factory of heroes . . . '[319] crumbled like a paper tiger atop the falsehoods that had created and sustained it.

At full volume the hype and lies seeped from a shrinking Nasser, like the piercing wail that escapes a fast-deflating balloon. 'Nasser . . . a moment of madness,' the Egyptian novelist Tawfiq Hakim lamented in his *Awdat al Wai'* (The Return of Consciousness), 'a leader mesmerises an entire nation, "expropriates its mind," creates fake victories and wastes the bread of a poor society in pursuit of a pan-Arab mirage.'[320] The façade cracked open, and out tumbled the humbled spirit of a traumatised nation. Behind every extravagant fabrication sat rows of stingy statistics, and under each miracle sighed a thousand shattered hearts. Where to, Nasser? Those land reforms that talked up revolution and divided up the land *comme un petit bourgeois*;[321] that bogus 'Arab socialism' that made you mama and papa; that intense love for political parties and trade unions and workers' and peasants' rights that lived only by your consent and hailed only your name;[322] those assassinations and imprisonments of activists, thinkers and journalists;[323] that rhetoric which sent millions of Arabs into a frenzy, eyes glazed and tongues lolling, while state coffers were emptying, schools were turning into three-shift factories and employment was becoming a byword for government charity;[324] that bombastic Arab nationalism that mistook its drivel for sacred writ and presided over the neighbourhood like the old colonial masters.

Not everyone partook of this hard look in the mirror. When it came to the failures of revolutionary Egypt, there was always plenty of blame to go around. For the scandal of 1948, Nasser and his boys indignantly blamed a decrepit monarchy, corrupt feudalism and a high bourgeoisie led by Western collaborators. But for the tragedy of 1967, he, man of courage, found safe refuge behind any one or two or all of the usual suspects: bad luck, America, Israel, an immature people, reactionary Arab regimes, fifth columns, Abd al Hakim Amer, Nasser's number two and chief of the Army . . . All these, yes, absolutely, but never Nasser. For the wins, he took all the credit, boasted all he wanted about the sheer power of his wits and will, but for the cock-ups, never. And for the utter shame that was and is 1967, his people concocted something infinitely better: an unquestionable triumph. The whole aim of Israel and the West in this war, his defenders argued, was the brilliant system of Nasser. Keep him and his regime, they insisted, and you will have won the war. For the 1948 *nakba* (catastrophe), regime change was the noble calling of patriots and brave men; for the 1967 *nakssah* (relapse), regime change became a conspiracy of cowards and traitors. Interestingly, in the initial moments after the *nakssah* – an ingenious euphemism if there ever was one – Gamal seemed to be in agreement with his foes. His first move was to announce his resignation – considering the extent of the rout, a forgivable case of the jitters. But then the masses made a presumably spontaneous countermove, thronged his home, demanded the resurrection of *al-rais* (the boss), and shook him out of his blues.[325] How could he refuse? A mea culpa was quickly folded into the back pocket and a half-resuscitated hero started to recast his defeat as a figment of the enemy's own imagination. Too bad! Just when an individual act of surprising decency was about to find a respectable spot for itself in Arab history, it graciously surrendered to the yearnings of a people in a chronic state of denial and crawled, a negligible footnote, to its home on the margins of the past.

Look at him in Ali's picture one last time. Downcast now and somehow dishevelled in his military uniform, a tragic figure, he stares into oblivion and salutes American wheat which made the bread that fed the majority of his townspeople,[326] salutes Egypt's youth squandered in fake jobs at empty desks, salutes his new slogan 'No Socialism Without Freedom', his secret eyes and ears that monitored loose tongues on every street corner, an obliterated Air Force, a shamed army, thousands of dead soldiers, a con-

quered Sinai, an occupied Jerusalem.[327] Cronies hang about, while
the puny heir apparent looks on and waits. They all look kind of
silly. Typical of every Arab wisecrack about this people's never
ending quandaries, this photograph has all the elements of a
tragedy inside a joke.

The cruel senselessness of it all! Each cutting in Ali's *Red Sea*,
By Agreement, and *And Now* – the last three collages in the series
– comments on the fakeries of regimes that spilt Arab blood and
stepped on a whole people's humanity in the name of Palestine
and the military fight that was sure to bring it back. The collective
wreckage in this photomontage visualises Edward Said's evocative
recital about the chains that shackle 1948 to1967:

> As one looks back at these things in the context of 1948, it is the
> immense panorama of waste and cruelty that stands out as the
> immediate result of the war itself . . . A vast militarisation over-
> took every society almost without exception in the Arab world,
> coups succeeded each other more or less unceasingly and,
> worse yet, every advance in the military idea brought an equal
> and opposite diminution in social, political, and economic
> democracy.[328]

In his Body of Human Waste sleeping in a seeming stupor next
to its baby somewhere on a derelict Cairene pavement, Ali
captured the punishing rewards of those two decades' apocryphal
attainments.

Nasser! 'Walahee, ya akhee (by God, oh brother) he made me
proud to be an Arab.' You can still hear this refrain, even in
the most highbrow discussions in Arab salons. What is in these
words? Something quite extraordinary, actually: a near-constant
suspension of disbelief when it comes to Nasser's daring works of
fiction, even by those who were never particular admirers of *al-
rais*. It takes a special talent to convert sceptics of your performance everywhere into ardent believers in your bombast;
to persuade them that actions may matter but that it is only
through the power of words that Arab pride and dignity can truly
measure themselves; to convince them that the distance between

what is being said and what is being done does not count. Many labels have been attached to this artistry, which makes Nasser and his mimics Houdinis and the Arab people such a susceptible audience; Edward Said's the orthodoxy of hypocrisy[329] is by far the best.

Nasser is not dead. He is life-sized now in Egypt, a symbol for some, a bitter lesson for others. The audit is being continually revised, and people regularly plump for a place on either side of the fence. Elsewhere in the Arab terrain, he still breathes in this poster or that square, in this Yasser or that Saddam. No, they are not all one and the same, and no one – no one – came even close to Nasser. Some, like Arafat, relished near-death experiences that became great escapes and taunted their people's cause with an arsenal of misdeeds and mendacity. Some, like Saddam, thrived on a brutality unvarnished by even a second's worth of regret. And some, like daddy Assad on whose face 'a fathomless cynicism and a terrible knowledge were written',[330] became professors of cunning, pioneers in the art of transforming soldierly realms into family enterprises.

To all of them, Ali bequeathed a set of collages completed after the 1990 Iraqi invasion of Kuwait. While he planned his departure from Jordan, with shelves emptied and boxes filled and sealed, Ali plastered together images of the devastation wrought by decades of 'People's Rule'. The interplay between macabre and caricaturish pictures and visual *double entendres* sums up *or-else* Arab democracies presided over by ghoulish hangmen, sanctified by subservient pseudo-ideologies, emboldened by super-power collusion, and perpetuated by terror. These political compositions were mercy killings that ridiculed monstrous legacies to death. They have no hidden messages or allusions to other better systems or leaders, just the fatal blows that start with the spectator's first snigger.

*   *   *

The Cairo of the 1970s was awash with the discarded fairytales of yesteryear. In living piles of debris, they ran rings around a

careworn city. Everywhere the visitor went, vistas of shrunken
dreams were on view. The new pharaoh was busy hacking at
the old tall tales and weaving his own golden yarns. No surprise
there; in the shadow of many a larger-than-life man prowls an heir
waiting to downsize him.

Where to start but with the ignominy of 1967. To this bleeding
wound, Sadat administered the psychological victory of October
1973. True, no occupied Arab territory was recovered, but no
additional land was lost and a remarkable feat was extracted from
an apparent draw. There was something so cathartic about an
Israeli drubbing at their hands. What with Israel's initial surprise,
the US airlift, and retired Israeli generals hastily brought back to
active duty, it turned out that the Arabs could deliver a long over-
due slap. Now that Egypt's chin no longer dangled close to its
clavicle, Sadat's path was paved all the way to Camp David and the
land of the *honkys*. In place of Nasser's forlorn Arab Egypt, Sadat
concocted one that pleaded for inspiration from the not-so-distant
past. In the words of Fuad Ajami: 'The new, triumphant Egypt
stood for a "free economy", a more responsible order, an Egyptian
Egypt. "June's Egypt" had lost its way; "October's Egypt" re-
gained its soul. The talk of revolution vanished: Misr . . . was to
become the new symbol. The Egyptian order began its march
forward – to the past.'[331] And like that pre-Nasserite order, this
one's enchantment with the West had no anchor, knew no bounds.

> The tragedy of [khedive] Ismael's world view and later, of
> liberal nationalism, was its incapacity to stay at home with its
> own world, to keep a safe and respectable distance from the
> West . . . What begins as a dialogue . . . ends in embrace and
> surrender. Then the legitimacy vanishes, and the adherents are
> exposed as collaborators.[332]

In 1977, for anyone who cared enough to notice, it was this Egypt
that was making the rounds, seesawing at full speed between the
pull of indigenous sensibilities and the lure of Western trappings,
clamouring for foreign accolades and neglecting local consent,

selling modernism to the outside and nurturing extremism on the inside. Ali's thoughts stalked this never-ending spat between the Egypt of the earth, which writhes with its people's destitution and torment, and the Egypt of flights of fancy and pseudo-hip sights and sounds.

Two drawings. One bright, one dark. Against a background of flaming red, the sultry woman smokes her cigarette. We do not know in which book or on what screen Ali met her, but she looks like she has just stepped out of a sixties novel by Ihsan Abd al Kouddouss, the closest Egypt came to a male Françoise Sagan. The lady is white, bourgeois, young, modern, city dwelling and seductive in that particular way Egyptian cinema likes its women. The tail end of *secrets* touches her neck, the small photograph of a hey-baby type of man giving us an indiscreet lead into one of them. She was *high li* – high class, as Egyptians in jest sometimes like to say it – this posh side of the Nile the way it so wanted to see itself. Under her is the sinewy woman in a black caftan. She could be centuries old or born only yesterday. She is looking at us sideways from a background of Arabic alphabets, a sliver of a Koranic verse and flakes of Arabic poetry.

> I wish I were the candle of her nights
> so that she could see me burn in my tear.

There is one thing that makes these two faces special, that makes them more than an artist's casual observations of a country's varied expressions. These faces did not talk to each other. They still don't, and they never did. This is a very old silence, and one still listens to it in the open air and glimpses it in fiction. Arabic literature is peppered with themes of embattled identity and dislocation, peopled by Arabs who traipse between neighbourhoods five minutes apart but inhabit worlds utterly at odds with one another. They even creep into foreign literary inventions born and bred in Middle Eastern locales, including that one that always left Ali feeling so giddy: *The Alexandria Quartet*.

*   *   *

At the end of Clea, the last act in Lawrence Durrell's *Quartet*, a delicious exhaustion overcomes the reader from being so long in the company of sensuous, opaque characters who float, noncommittal and self-obsessed, over the length and breadth of Durrell's Mediterranean Alexandria. A suspicion begins to grow towards the last few pages of Justine (the first), a nagging question, really, that soon enough matures into a lasting impression: in this splendidly hedonistic city there is space for every hotchpotch Alexandrian but practically none for the Arab. He is an extra in a coastal burg crowded with steamy foreigners.[333] The mesmeric prose about the 'anarchy of flesh and fever, of money-love and mysticism',[334] ignores him, the plot pushes him to the many hidden shadows of the town. He is an overlooked son squeezed out of the scene by an indifferent father too in love with his other children. This is Durrell's 'Alexandria . . . where somehow the camels and palm trees and cloaked natives existed only as a brilliantly coloured frieze, a back-cloth to a life divided in its origins.'[335] There are the Hosnanis, of course, but Christian Copts that they are, they predate, and by centuries, Amr ibn al Ass's seventh-century Arab (read Muslim) invasion of Egypt.[336] And even within this wealthy Coptic house Durrell's partiality for Alexandria's cosmopolitan grain is written all over the two brothers. Between the urbane, dashing, worldly Nessim and his ugly, churlish, violent brother, Narouz, the contest is very quickly settled.

Durrell's Alexandria was in Egypt but not of it. His was a predilection for foreign specimens, wanderers, Alexandrian voices born of a mélange of origins and living in a town from which he could hear 'the noise of the sea and the echoes of an extraordinary history'.[337] The rest of Egypt, 'famed by the bleakness of faith which renounced worldly pleasure: the Egypt of rags and sores, of beauty and desperation',[338] he was content to leave to its Arabs. Fingers have often been wagged at Durrell for conjuring an Alexandria that was a stranger to the real one and its Arab natives,[339] but that his 'dream-city' seemed so unmindful of them was all the same to him.

However, it was not all the same, say, to Nasser, himself a

native-born Alexandrian. And for him this was not only about Durrell, but about his Scobie and Nessim and Justine and Perswarden and Mountolive and Pombal and Ali's Lady Phyllis – the whole lot of them. It was not only about Alexandria, it was about Egypt, for in Durrell's saga about rootless lives laying claim to Alexandria were echoes of all the preclusions by, all the condescension of, foreign communities laying claim to an entire Arab expanse. The little Ahmeds that hung on as fringe accessories to the frame of the *Quartet* became the stuff of Nasser's own political narrative. And just as Durrell's text had so little room for Ahmed, Nasser's was not interested in Clea or Balthazar. That they and their friends were equally uninterested in belonging to his Egypt made the ending inevitable and Alexandria that much poorer to live in, because the cosmopolitan city's demise was 'felt not only by the Greeks, the Italians, the French, the Armenians and the Jews who departed, but also by the "Egyptians" who were left behind'.[340]

Sadly, there is nothing in this depiction that would dare call itself original. Not forty, fifty years into this unending debate. True, when first traversing the *Quartet*, picking up on the absence of the Arab and other Durrellian proclivities, there is no pressing need to wade into sources beyond its pages to glimpse silhouettes of empire and the issue of identity that unavoidably walks in their wake. But that is the public arena where the *Quartet* and its undercurrents, and Nasser and his riptide, have been living for many years now. And from the start, everything about these two clashing fictions was so utterly contemptuous of the *Other*. Each hunkered down in its bunker, crying foul and building chasms. 'We are Arabs,' crowed Nasser; 'they are Arabs,' lamented *al ajnabi* (the foreigner) on his way out, as if Arab identity was a one-size-fits-all mask for every Egyptian woman and man. Neither storyline cared to notice that in this Arab Egypt, sculpted by Nasser's chisel and hammer, many Egyptians were left by the wayside. And thus the merciless erasures of old Alexandria would become a genuine attempt at repossession in both narratives, celebrated by one as furiously as it was decried by the other. In 1977, Durrell mourns the 'deadening effect' of 'Nasser's flirtation

with Communism'[341] and *Arabization* on 'a place for dramatic
partings, irrevocable decisions, last thoughts . . . '[342] Years later,
Edmund Keeley declares the new Alexandria 'squalid . . . now
Arabic once again – Arabic and little else . . . '[343]

> If you walk along the esplanade leading to where the wondrous
> ancient Pharos used to stand (now Fort Kayet Bey, grotesquely
> restored as a museum celebrating the Egyptian navy), you will
> encounter odors and sights that will amaze you . . . Its modern
> palaces – homes for the established members of the foreign
> colony that brought much exploitation and snobbery, some
> progress, and a strong cosmopolitan flavor to Alexandria
> from the mid-nineteenth century until Gamal Abdel Nasser gave
> Egypt back to the Egyptians – are now shuttered tight with no
> outward sign of expectation . . . [344]

He is right. And yet away from such sorrowful verdicts, Ali's
paintings bore witness to the monuments, the citadels, the
mausoleums, the mosques, the people, the streets that betrayed
the vibrancy, the vividness, the diversity, the multiplicity of Egypt's
cultural fabric. In his superb recreations of Mamluk heritage, in his
renditions of the beauty that lights up the dimmest of Egypt's
hideouts, in his drawings of these black and white women, is
plentiful evidence that the real Egypt dons more than one face and
speaks with more than one tongue.

In truth, Nasser's choreographies of Arab resurgence were, as
elsewhere, the story of a society exorcising itself of its colonisers'
legacy. But with each insistence a little more of the country's
nuance was quashed and a lot more of its contradictions were used
as ammunition in the battle for identity. By the time of Sadat, the
ill will between those searching inward for satisfaction and those
looking outward for inspiration had sprouted in every crevice. In
the name of Islam, harassed traditions staged a comeback; in
the name of modernity, Western look-alikes pushed back. In the
name of purity, protagonists spread angry notions of indigenous
authenticity; in the name of openness, their antagonists en-
couraged beguilement with consumer frills and pastimes. In the

name of God, the sword was shorn by his self-proclaimed soldiers; in the name of unity and majority rights, minorities were taught daily rituals of allegiance and instructed about the merits of quiescent devotion. In the name of stability, every secular voice, every rational thought, every truly progressive notion was silenced and ordered to stand down – by both camps.

All this wrangling was disheartening to Ali. What he was living through in Cairo and encountering in Alexandria and painting in both, neither warring side would have recognised. Many who knew him thought him Durrellian, but his fascination with lush native textures has no parallels in the *Quartet*. There is no trace of it either in the state's (and its Islam's) monochrome idea of its own Egyptians. Ali's own feelings about Alexandria tried to puncture holes in the nihilism that swore this city was dead and done for.

The time of Cleopatra . . . polyglot jumbled genetics producing something uniquely Alexandrian and piquant, the mixture of Egypt, the end of the Nile, the Mediterranean Hellenistic culture, the din of clashing cults . . . diversity of orientation and the black tumbling locks and the brilliant gaze of a tough city feeding on the pleasures of the flesh and the commerce of hard come on![345]

In these insights of Ali's, Keeley may find the 'inner eye of an Egyptian poet, one who can see the vital imaginative resources that remain hidden from those confined to a European perspective'[346] – and a xenophobic one at that. In these Cavafian quarters, something of the mythical Alexandria had not quite departed. There are those who would dismiss Ali's sentiments as romanticism eavesdropping on imagined conversations between an emasculated past and an impoverished present. But every drawing and word from that time evokes the humanity that lives and sings and steals and prays and plays and makes love in the deep fissures of that ruptured society. For him to have recognised only the dissonance would have meant too many omissions and exclusions in his gargantuan exile. His obsession was to elude these and snuggle up to the bosom of estranged human beings. He did, and, in the end, he still took with him the screams and howls of vexed identities that tore the upper part of Egypt from its lower, that alienated the haves and cast out the have nots, that housed different Egyptians in separate colonies with walls, high gates, and watchtowers.

> Exhaustion sets in from the pressures of a society brutalised by its crowdedness and tough conditions. Way up above, the Saudi princelings and visiting luminaries holed up in fortified luxe hotels where the hungry street boys like 'Suddenly Last Summer' gaze through the plate glass at the blond (dinerette?) as the forkful of animal matter enters the glistening open cavern of lipsticked lips . . . [347]

Here were two of Egypt's faces, one conceived by some dreamers' wishful thinking and floating on tiny islands of make believe, one fixed hopelessly to the ground. Two Egyptians inextricably intertwined and forever living apart; they pass each other in the street, the first fleetingly glances with a mystified, curious sort of fear, the other stares back in dismay.

CHAPTER SIX

Don't You Dare Call My Works Paintings

The Syrian-Jordanian artist Ali Jabri is able to reconstruct on paper at once the poetic soul of the Arabs and their violent sensuality. But he is an exception in all the Near East.[348]

Jean Pierre Peroncel Hugo
Le Radeau De Mohamet/The Raft of Muhammad

'What in God's name are you doing here, Ali? Why don't you go back to Cairo or to London? Why don't you get out?' I cannot remember the number of times I asked him this. He never ever answered. I only heard the pain, you see. It would come out in inaudible mutters – moans, really – that gave away 'the helplessness of it all'.

Like most torrid love affairs whose broken hearts bleed on the surface of every reminiscence, Ali and Jordan, in rewind, are steeped in anguish. The good times and good graces survive only in fragments, barely easing the sadness that permeates his Jordan letters and diaries. I fear that even the skimpiest survey of these will reduce me to a mere archivist of lamentations and regrets. There are memories – friends remember, I remember – but they are peep holes into pieces of him, recollections that sometimes say much more about us than about him. At their most talkative, they respond to his claustrophobic perceptions of circumstance and self. At their most mystified, they are scratching away at their chins, looking for hints and clues about this man called Ali.

I know. The 'I' has been a stranger all this time, what is it doing here now?

I don't know. I somehow feel compelled to change voices, to lay

Ali al Jabri with the author, 1998

claim to me in this last bit of Ali, to concede perhaps that somewhere in this patch of him, in these Jordanian years of his, I had
a space all of my own. If I have something to say, I am thinking, do
not say it from way out there. Come closer!

*   *   *

From very early in his days in Jordan, Ali knew that something in
everything about this place was not quite right. The spirit was
jaded. What looked like novelties from afar, up close turned out to
be yesterday's chewed-over adventures. And age . . . age, that
most fearful of Ali's adversaries, was attacking his austere midriff
and hanging loose from his high cheek bones – or so he imagined.

  Certain things were assumed as unending prerogatives: health,
  youth, the unconscious elastic tissue skin dew and clear eyes . . .
  though a destructive tendency was always there underneath . . .
  Suddenly within two years in the Arab world . . . my life has
  taken on a bitterly ironic turn . . . losing physicality . . . emerging

limitations in the body . . . the enforced curbing of desire. Accumulative experience reducing the freshness of impact . . . [349]

Those tired anemic eyes, the look of the Jaundiced Face! The thinning hair . . . the whole temporary mask of youth & beauty stripping and peeling off like last year's cucumber facial.[350]

There was a harshness to this Jordanian desert, a severity that shunned the sensualities of the Nile and its inhabitants. Illicit desire here was a lustful breath away from public opprobrium. It would have to be pursued way beneath Amman's rectitude, far from its gasps. Under the reproachful gaze of Saadieyh and society, new compartments would have to be added, clandestine lives would have to multiply. Even the closest of Jordanian friends would not be told, the subject hovering like an open secret every time he disappeared, every time he refused a lift home after dinner, every time he said he was coming and never showed up.

In this Jordan, profound questions were going to meet a terrible fate and the chase after aunt and identity would, in the end, come to nothing. He knew. Yes, Ali knew long before Saadieyh's death in 1998, the *point finale* of all his futile searching, that he and Jordan were not going to make it. In 1982, on his flight back to Amman from Paris where he went for a museum course,[351] Ali 'cried and cried . . . Dear God how do I go about now to pick up the pieces. Where the direction? The courage, the guts, the hope and what is to happen to the line of poor Majddedine? . . . And here I am awake in the sunny lands of dust and flock . . . '[352] where, even in a farcical joust with one loutish, out-in-the-boonies Jordanian, the improbability of a good life became stark.

Burble, burble days later . . . Interrupted narratives . . . quick dash to the capital to rescue ailing aunt from the blues . . . Poor lady, she's my only source of family affection – everything else is a detached rush of potential imagery, or culture-clash, or downright boorishness. A gigantically fat grocer in native gear, ensconced in his flyblown shop, demanded to look at my day's work as I passed; scanned it squintingly down a bulbous egg-

plant nose and finally jerked back at me: 'Ya draw my big
Arse!! Ya Hear?? Ya know dat deep 'ole right up my arse?
My bum 'ole? Draw the 'ole right up my arse!!' Barked at me
(exquisitely unknown) a total stranger. My mouth fell open then
I hurried on.[353]

Looking back, all the signs were there. They coloured in faint
black every aspect of his situation. London and Cairo were
temporary stops, transit lounges, to slow his final trip to Saadieyh
and Amman. Jordan was the end of the journey. Long ago, back
in London, he had resigned himself to the inexorability of life in
the Arab world and his aunt's control over him. So this was where
incessant explorations would be brought to a halt, where duty
would finally shape meaning and usher in the menial chores and
the grand tasks. This was where smallness of country and cosiness
of people would make anonymity a thing of the past, private space
a rare delight, the dress code simple pants in khaki or beige, shirts
in blue or white. For a man enamoured with youth and titillated
by the unknown; a man at his freest living in wild shirts, funky
jackets, to-die-for boots, a man at his happiest when swinging
between a question mark and its infinite answers, Jordan, every
which way he turned it, looked like a dismal prospect.

You would have thought that there would be a natural affinity
between this beleaguered country and this besieged man. Both
were still so young and so vulnerable, coping with identities picked
up from many places and cooked up by many hands. 'Outsiders
conceived of its borders and identity,' Joseph Massad tells us of
Jordan.

They led its national army well after independence; people whose
roots within existing memory lie outside the new borders of the
country, rule and continue to rule it; its population consist in
its majority of people whose geographic 'origins' within living
memory are located outside the borders of the nation-state (. . .
Palestinian-Jordanians . . . Syrian-Jordanians, Hijazi-Jordan-
ians, Egyptian-Jordanians, Iraqi-Jordanians, Lebanese-Jordan-
ians, Turkish-Jordanians, Circassian-Jordanians, Kurdish-

Jordanians, Chechen-Jordanians, Armenian-Jordanians) . . . [354]

You would have thought that among these there would be a comfortable corner for this Syrian-American-Continental-English-Egyptian-Jordanian-Arab. You would have thought this mix of nationalities would have softened the reticence of the desert and added a cosmopolitan flavour to a nascent Amman. It did not.

*   *   *

There is no point in regurgitating the blows and counter blows between Saadieyh and Ali, which erupt like boils and linger as scratch marks on the face of *The Ottoman Widow and Her Nephew*. But I hardly know how to write about Ali in Jordan without writing about him and her.

I keep flipping through the turbulence of their relationship from the moment Wasfi died until Saadieyh succumbed, in the early 1990s, to the serenities of Alzheimer's. I go back to what I wrote in the early pages on how Ali foresaw, even before Wasfi's assassination, the great void that would separate her expectations from his demands, how he predicted the rancour that would tear into their love for one another. And yet, Ali moved to Jordan and latched on to her till the day she went. It would be easy to say this was Ali. It was in him to wail about the traps and demur at the sight of that open window. To many of us, he was a man far more fascinated by the pain of complaint than the relief that comes with solutions, a man for whom maze-like walks through the darker geographies of a half-imagined reality were infinitely more intriguing than a stroll on the flatter surface of the real thing. Never a straight stitch by this tailor, we thought, only embroideries. [355] All this was true, but there was more to him and Mrs al Tall and Jordan, something unspoken.

Every time I think about Ali and Saadieyh, three episodes from the early eighties diaries come to me.

March 13, 1980. Ihsan Jabri is in his coffin and Ali is sitting beside it on the Syrian military plane that was taking them both from Cairo to Aleppo. A small item appeared in the Baath News-

paper the following day on 'the funeral of the late warrior Ihsan al
Jabri . . . The deceased played a leading role in the fight against
French colonialism and held several official positions during that
time.'[356] The *ancien regime*, a harmless corpse now, could return
to its native soil for a proper burial.

I drew hastily the whole way, hardly taking notice of anything else
but the coffin itself with its stapled or thumb tacked depository
tickets and pass-papers and identifications and cargo-permit
contents: One 107-year-old statesman from a distinguished line.
Extinguished. All systems negative. The pulse simply finally
came to a gently curving halt . . . His daughter [Saadieyh] was
with him at the time. Aleppo, airport, lounging commando troops,
family cousins, younger males. The dash to his house in town.
The hubbub. The rhythm. Toothless Jalila in her ruined state
so long after the luxe she once knew in the pashadoms and
sumptuous villas of Egypt as a diamond-flashing blond heiress
from the North, now hag, red-bleached dried grass hair, the
mouth an empty socket of ritual grief, impoverished and kicked
by a junior monster son. Next to her the black veiled head of
Khaldieh, his nurse and attendant housekeeper for 25 years, the
coarse peasant family from his country estate, also ruined in a
way by the passing of her master . . . the 2 of them, 2 women's
heads a miniature vignette of croaking grief like the Greeks,
framed in a window at the top, while in the streets below at the
corner of the square named after my great uncle [Saadallah]
opposite the park bestowed by my father, an electric tension
before the eye of the storm as the city prepared for the whiplash
of violence and civil war with a death toll of 750 was it?[357]

These characters, each with a present that is a bitter enemy to
their past, each hurling at Ali and each other the shards of a
wrecked family, are more than extras in Ali's restaging of the
funeral scene. They are the leads through whom the Jabris' entire
drama is captured. In the coffin lay the expired century, Jabrian
descent from aristocratic glory to middle class ordinariness. On
the face of Jalila were all the scars borne by expectant youth

I. International-
style: overhead sun-
glasses (Travel)

2. Hair: Jean-Marc
Maniatis, Paris.
Auburn rinse (not
Henna)

3. Macquillage:
Heidi Moravetz for
Lancaster.

4. Bronzage:
Abu-Dhabi plus
Charles of the Ritz

5. T-Shirt:
Arnaud de
Rosnay for
C. Dior.
(Edition:
Petropolis)

6. Motto:
Internation
Badge-Cult
Affirmation
of Origins

7. Avoirdupois:(I)
International
Crash-Diet,
(Food-Boredom)

8. Avoirdupois: (II)
Local Variety
Hip-Measurements
(Starches & Pastry)

9. Psychology:
Boredom/Restlessness/
Ambition/Boredom/

IO. Social Structure:
Affluent Upper Bourgeoisi
Connections: considerable

I. Nuclear Background:
Extremely close-knit
family pattern, siblings
ocal upbringing. foreign
nish.

.NoseI: Ramallah
Nose2: Lausanne

3Scent: Chloe, Karl
agerfeldt.

I4. Intellectual Apparat
us: Harrold Robbins,

I5. Habitat: Mid-East,
urope, United States.

Behavioural Index:
ium, Benzedrine,
Librium, multi-tranqus
ithdrawal-sleep motive

7. Marital Status:
iting forthe Big One.
Currency: $$$$$$$$$$

Previous page: Aqaba Boat (Courtesy of a private collection, Beirut)
Above: Anatomy of a Rich Girl (Arab, late 20th cent.)
Opposite: Ihsan al Jabri

Above: Ma'an House (Courtesy of Mr. Fadi & Mrs. Rula Ghandour)
Below: Petra Stone (Courtesy of Mr. Fadi & Mrs. Rula Ghandour)

Below: Ali's installation for 'Disorientation' at the House of World Cultures, Berlin

garde bédouine

Opposite: Bedouin Guard
Above: Jordanian Taxi Driver
Below: Pella (Courtesy of Mrs. Widad Kawar)

Above: Nabi Yosha' Shrine (Courtesy of Dr. Ghaith & Mrs. Zein Shubailat)

Below: Cherry Blossom

ravaged by a merciless history and filial cruelty. In Khaldieh's tears was the bitter memory of lost estates and the loyal servitude of their peasantry. His father's park and Saadallah's square were two lonely reminders of the once good fortune of the family.

Saadieyh, Hala and Diala did not attend Ihsan's funeral. Hala had not talked to her father for decades and Diala hardly knew him. The reasons for Saadieyh's absence are unknown, but she did fork out enough for the funeral to vent about it months later to Diala. Her niece's response could not have been more revelatory of the estrangements that had long been nibbling their way into the heart of this family: 'I am sorry we are so helpless. But please do not blame us if you spent on Juddo's funeral. Please do not blame me in particular . . . If you chose to pay for the rightful grandeur of the dead, do not blame those barely living, especially not me.'[358]

The 'grandeur' of dead Ihsan would have to be paid for now to elevate it to 'rightful'. He himself had pretty much abandoned any real pretence to it in the last days of his life. His public demeanour may have kept that very stiff chin up, but his private conduct was palpably less interested in keeping up appearances. It may not have been purely by chance that Ali tucked his wistful passages about the funeral under a copy of the letter Ihsan sent to King Khalid and Crown Prince Fahd of Saudi Arabia sometime in the mid-1970s.

In the Name of God the Merciful

His Majesty King Khaled ibn Abd al Aziz, King of the Kingdom of Saudi Arabia, and His Highness Crown Prince Fahd ibn Abd al Aziz, possessors of the greatness of brilliance and ability and political wisdom, a long life may God give them and their protective shade over all of the Arab countries.

I am daring after a long reluctance to ask your greatness, with two extended hands, the one holding my eye which is threatened with blindness and darkness, the other holding my sick heart, in the hope that I might have a little of the Azizian care. Here, I remember how when I was general secretary to Sultan Mehmed V in Turkey, sitting in its cabinet meeting during a discussion on bestowing the Al Mashirieyeh and

Wilayat Hassan on your father, the late founder of the Saudi
Kingdom and the knight of the trees of its greatness, King Abd
al Aziz Al Saud, God rest his soul and make of his grave a light
to guide the entire Arab nation . . .

I humbly wrote to your father, His Majesty, to refuse Wilayat
Hassan and the Turkish Mashirieyyah through which they
meant to strengthen Salameh bin al Rashid in the areas which
he had taken over then.[359] My worst bout of luck was when I lost,
in a great fire that burnt my entire house, the letter your late
father, His Majesty, sent to me . . . When, after many years of
absence, I returned home in 1951, I wanted to kiss your late
father's forehead and hand and introduce him to myself. His
answer was royal and most true, as he sent me a private plane, a
Dakota, in the same year, and invited me to Hijaz to perform the
Hajj. I went and had the great fortune to kiss his forehead,
and he, God may have mercy on him, sent me . . . an enormous
amount of money, which, God is my witness, I declined, not out
of false pride and caprice, but out of love and loyalty and my
wish not to compromise the friendship that linked me to your
late father who had just started to spread light and justice in the
Saudi Kingdom . . .

I came knocking on your door to ask for your help for an old
and faithful friend to the royal family, asking the almighty God
to support you and give you long life so that the Arab Island can
be a source of light, and happiness, and prosperity . . .

Ihsan Allah al Jabri [360]

Extraordinary words from the former chamberlain to Hashemite Feisal whose own father ibn Saud had driven from Hijaz.
Extraordinary words from this devotee of Nasser, the Sauds'
nemesis. Why did Ali attach it as a keepsake to his 1980 diary?
Was it to remind him how much Jabri valour Ihsan had managed
to forsake, how far down the ladder history had pushed his family?
Or was it, for him, something more benign: yet another souvenir
of the complicated historical ties between the Jabris and Arab
royalty?

Two years after Ihsan's death, Ali was on the metro in Paris:

> In my old leatherette, very unshaven but hardly caring about the
> respectable appearance bit with the ubiquitous portfolio +F's
> [François possibly] big aluminum suitcase stuffed almost to
> breaking point & 4 drunks got on. Bums who've crashed all the
> social restriction barriers on a Samuel Beckett wavelength, and
> the biggest sort of dangled in my face only jestingly threatening
> with ripostes about 'il faut pas s'y prendre la vie' . . . but the
> contact though distant somehow triggered me off and I started
> to cry comforted solely by that mild looking married lady unmade-
> up for once in unpretentious bedroom slippers who perhaps
> wondered what a grown unshaven man was doing sitting on the
> metro with tears trickling down his face as I thought of my
> father & mother and sister and the helplessness of it all on this
> fateful planet.[361]

Two years after this incident, on October 23, 1984, Ali recorded
this small note in his journal: 'Hossa Hamad phoned us this
morning . . . about mummy. Mummy passed away.' Hala had been
dead two days in her house in Kuwait before the neighbours finally
broke down the door and found her. Earlier that same year, on
her last visit to Amman, Hala had finally agreed to see Ali. Her
physical deterioration shocked him. After she was buried in
Amman, Raghida recalls Ali murmuring, 'She is buried in this
insignificant grave, no proper stone, no epitaph, no nothing . . .
After all this grandeur. And my father is out there in some unknown pit somewhere in one of those Beirut cemeteries.'[362]

These episodes, for me at least, say all that needs to be said
about Ali's Jordanian predicament. In their shadow, mystifying
dependencies become fathomable. There was a solitude in him,
an aloneness, a crippling fragility, all bred by torrents of furious
events and familial retrenchments. It was not in Ali to leave all
this behind. He was all about a sorrowful past. An unburdened
future was for dreams, it was for others.

For him, it had to be Saadieyh, always Saadieyh.

*   *   *

Almost immediately after Ali's arrival in Amman in 1978, they
clashed. Against her wishes, he wanted to spend time in Aqaba. In
retaliation, Saadieyh cut him off, refusing to offer him her house
there. 'Down & out, absolutely broke . . . and nowhere to go after
severing all contacts with the treacherous poor old aunt. Miracle,
this job drops on me at the Holiday Inn: pool attendant! Beach
boy: oh perfection, oh fate!'[363]

A Jabri for a lifeguard! The spectre of scandal ran all the way
into Saadieyh's panicky mind and changed it. Ali got the keys, but
this harangue had a different feel to it than the long-distance
pushing and shoving that had bruised his 1970s. For him and her,
this one had all the features of a daily routine, all the makings of
an ugly habit. In her bellows and his screams he could hear the
frightening answer to that one nagging matter: family. All his
pleas for love, for money, were becoming the stuff of steely quid
pro quos and hard transactions. In no time, their relationship
started to swim through farce one day and trudge through smut
the next. Nowhere was this ghastly theatre more compelling than
at Saadieyh's very own Jordan Museum of Popular Traditions.[364]
She had always dangled it like a carrot to speed up Ali's arrival in
Amman, offering it as a meeting point between their shared ideals
and artistic interests. It seemed like a perfect proposition. Their
collaboration had worked once before. On the hill next to Saadieyh
and Wasfi's Sweileh house, they had built the prime minister's
mausoleum, now somnolent and ramshackle – the child of Ali and
Saadieyh's talents. They envisioned it and built it together in the
mid-seventies, both inspired by Nabi Yosha's (Prophet Joshua)
shrine in Salt, northwest of Amman. It did not win the Agha Khan
prize as they had hoped, but it paid eloquent tribute to beauty in
the homegrown, the understated, the simple. This mausoleum is
Jabrian grace and taste at their finest.

And so, very soon after landing in the city, he went to work in the
museum as some sort of creative adviser, and very soon after that,
their partnership deteriorated into a shrill duet.

Yesterday she executed a commando raid on the flat seizing the

Wasfi's Mausoleum. Early 1990s

portable black Sony from the white bedroom . . . undoing on the way the bedspread to plainly indicate her disapproval . . . In front of the Museum and her imperially ravaged staff, it becomes a painful humiliation for me to have to carry on knocking myself out for Museum . . . When the acknowledgement is so slightingly absent and the censure never out of sight . . . for what? . . . [365]

Terrible things are going on! Aunty thinks I am rasping her for money (personally) she seems to be mixed up between professional services rendered and family impecuniousness. She starts screaming she already sent ma 2 thousand!!! Blue moider! But forgets I am trying to get my professional self 'together . . . '[366]

Madame came back from Damas proceeded to scream at me on phone when I requested home trip for approval or rejection of drawings . . . 'Your mother. Your sister!' . . . Is this museum treadmill turning my life into a ghastly dismal failure? . . . [367]

Inconceivably vulnerable position at the museum with no contract only a verbal agreement from an extremely capricious directress . . . [368]

What do I do about Sitt's [her ladyship's] fear of scandals inducing her to cut my salary and this month not even issued a bean . . . [369]

Slaving all day in that fucking museum and for what? To come out dirty, tired, ugly, old broken in health friendless & broke?[370]

Illness, low morale, depletion, lack of inspiration, poor work, loss of direction, museum frustrations, Diala, Aunty, money running out . . . [371]

There is no trace of Saadieyh's voice in this invective. The telegrams between her and Hala, the odd letter to Diala, the trickle to Ali, betray little more than the frustrations of an overwhelmed benefactress. Her friends' shy conjectures summon the very tentative face of a lonely woman – temperamental, tight-fisted, yes, but lonely and desperate for Ali's constant company. Even Ali admitted, every once in a while, that his sweet Saadieyh was indispensable. Every house he walked into in posh Amman, he walked into as the nephew of the Sitt. And there were all those trips together, those gatherings with the Hashemites, lunches with the powers that be, dinner with Sadruddine Agha Khan.[372] There was the museum course in Paris and the training sessions at the Smithsonian, the Metropolitan, and the Getty Institute – all care of Saadieyh. There was Saadieyh paying the late rent:

The cheque for rent three months late for two thousand . . . & what would I have done if aunty hadn't helped, Allah yahfazek [God keep you] my dearest Saadieyh and how many times . . . [373]

There was Saadieyh saving the day when he was stuck at Cairo airport's passport control:

Scared while they leave you to rot in the slow-drip juices of paranoia surrounded by scuffed skirting & the dreadful late twentieth century criminality of US import glass plastic serried chairs & football match on universal radio while cat kept me solace on lap and aunty distraught finally came to rescue.[374]

Like that, they jounced from the moment he set foot in Amman.

It was always my dear, darling aunt, or that damned old wretch. Not surprisingly, years before she died, Ali had figured that, where it most counted, she was not going to deliver. As she began to travel into herself, he fretted to his friends that 'the house is gone'.[375] He was right. The Sweileh house was gone.

That house had meant so much to him. It took him all the way back to those care-free days – the leisurely breakfasts by the pool, the flora and fauna of the beautiful garden, Wasfi's library . . . Nothing evoked the majesty of Saadieyh and the eminence of Wasfi quite like that house. Nothing brought him closer to them quite like that house. It is where he and Diala stayed every time they visited, where they came to know and love Wasfi and felt Saadieyh's kinder heart. It is where, before Majddedine and Wasfi's deaths, most everything in life was one-step short of dandy for Diala.

Sometimes I dream I am back in Sweileh, or Um al Nu'aaj, as my aunt Saadieyh liked to call it. That was its original name, as the white stones studded across the hilltop looked like ewes

Diala in the Sweileh House. Late 1970s

(nu'aaj) seated across the barren land that overlooked the road to Damascus to the North and the road to Jerusalem to the West.

There was no shadow to those days and years of innocence . . . I was introduced to a magical world of country living in Jordan as it was meant to be . . . The house was still small and there were these amazing fluffy cats, Shirazi and Siamese everywhere, and the two wolf dogs, Seif and Deibah (sword and wolverine). I would disappear with them for hours . . . There were splendid peacocks, sometimes allowed to parade their jeweled selves across the estate, and gazelles, exquisite creatures that had their own enclosure, as did quails, and geese and country chicken with their resplendently coloured roosters.

There was a beautiful house by the sea in Kuwait; there was London at the Dorchester . . . childhood was replete with content-ment and Wasfi and Saadieyh's home was added to this as my rural Paradise. Summer mornings were cool and misty then and I would be the first to wake as the sun rose over the Bedouin tent on the hill I could see across the trees from my bedroom . . . ecstatic Seif and Deibah who would be grinning up at me to encourage me down for our early morning ramble to pick posies of fragrant white jasmine, and hearty geraniums along with the big tea roses Wasfi had planted to make rose water out of. Then I would creep into their bedroom with the big square balcony and the white mishrabiyah panels across the windows and leave brightly coloured posies by each bedside table while they still slept, using the small Khalili [Hebron] glass vases Saadieyh had brought with her from Palestine.

Our joyous mornings would begin when they woke up; as Jamil brought Wasfi's coffee and Saadieyh's hot water and honey, followed by a troop of cats . . . who would all occupy the bed as Wasfi turned the big Zenith radio on to hear world news from the BBC. I would occupy the big bentwood cane rocking chair that I found perilous but exciting as we planned our days before Wasfi went to work in that first beautiful Jaguar with the Jordanian flag fluttering at the front and the guards following. Or he would get up and sit on the couch overlooking the hills on the road to Jerusalem and the garden beneath him with that huge white bird cage among the rose bushes, full of brightly coloured birds, and silently drink his coffee enjoying the view as he ate the grapes Aminah, the young girl from Nablus who worked in the house, would cut from the young vines. I would sit quietly by his side as I would by my father's side on the verandah in Kuwait, enjoying the pure and companionable silences of shared early mornings.

In later years more was added to the house in Wasfi's lifetime. Proper built indoor stairs, and then Wasfi's madafah or guest-house was added right by the house, with its own fireplace and a terrace full of orange and lemon trees. After he died, Saadieyh had his photographs mounted on the walls of the madafah, as well as all over the house, in his memory . . .

Another year it was the big Arabic salon with the domed roof with small skylights that had been built by an elderly artisan from Jerusalem just before we lost it. The floor of the Arabic sitting room and the terrace beyond it were of Jordanian marble, as pink as the walls of Petra and as beautiful. Saadieyh had simple couches made alongside the walls, as an Arabic seating arrangement, at one time upholstered in pearl grey raw silk she brought from Aleppo. You could sit down under the gorgeous fairouzi coloured opaline chandelier and look across the expanse of pink marble terrace to the oblong pool edged with Jordanian stone slabs and flanked on all four corners by a Grecian/Roman head that had been found on the farm of one of Wasfi's friends, and now looked sternly out across the valley as swallows and nightingales dipped and soared across the water and the water of the pool met the sky in infinity. There was a huge carved stone vat to one side, probably Roman, that was always filled with water for the birds and often scattered with rose petals.

There was a white mishrabiyah across the big arched window that overlooked the road to Jerusalem and the Jordan Valley, to break the force of the afternoon sun, which instead left checkered patterns across the room in late afternoons, or was opened to let in the air from the cool and then deserted hills. At the beginning there were no lights to be seen at night outside those of the house and grounds. The nights were blissfully silent and balmy, redolent with the smell of the roses and jasmine, the rare night time calls of birds, or the sound of a fox or wolf calling in the nearby forest, which the dogs would answer with a salvo of their own, marking the territory they protected.

Nothing in the house was brought from abroad, except perhaps the dining room table and a side board from Germany where they both went when Wasfi was posted to the Jordanian embassy there at the very beginning . . . The flowers and trees were indigenous too, long before the advent of water-hungry foreign trees for the gardens of the rich.

But the books and music came from all over the world. Saadieyh's French classics bound in red, the Orientalist books Albert Hourani, Ali's godfather, would help her choose from Oxford bookshops, Gibbon's *Decline and Fall of the Roman Empire* . . .

It was paradise on earth as a child and remained achingly poignant in later years, even when Saadieyh, imprisoned by Alzheimer, no longer fully acknowledged her surroundings or us as she was lost in the Ottoman mists that grew year after year after Wasfi's assassination . . .

Sometimes I hear Saadieyh's favourite French song on the radio. She would sing along to it, enchanted . . . 'Si tu n'existais pas . . . ' I can hear her voice, and that of Wasfi, teasing her as he used to . . . [376]

It is very difficult to intrude on such memories. Only in silence can the reader marvel at how easily these Jabris, provoked by intolerable woe, can distil from happy memories such a wonderful state of nirvana. Ali was nowhere near as vocal about his as Diala is, but you could practically hear the nostalgia in his sighs. So dear was this house to him that a seemingly reasonable suggestion by Cecil Hourani, Albert's brother and an old friend of Saadieyh's as well, to develop it into a library for Arab architecture, or a retreat where artists and architects would come to visit and work, struck Ali as too much interference.[377]

Saadieyh's will was her last word on her nephew. Her instructions to turn the house into a family waqf and a museum for Wasfi made no mention of Ali. Had Saadieyh left him the house, as she had promised, it would have been an affirmation of kinship and family, a recognition that he was of her and belonged to her, an acknowledgment of his life-long obsessive need for security. That she did not was the proof he had dreaded of her distrust and abandonment. When he kept repeating, after her death, that 'all is lost now', he was referring to the loss of his meaning as a Jabri.

For seven years, the house was untouched – except for the concrete that was poured into the pool for some al Tall wedding. Ali never visited it again. Finally, in 2004, King Abdullah II, Hussein's son, brought it under the protection of the government, ordered its renovation, and designated it as the Wasfi al Tall Museum. The same old wheel had come full circle again: another Hashemite, another royal embrace, another rescue.

*   *   *

How Ali loved his Hashemites! How he swooned, all graciousness and gratitude for royal patronage and royal friendships! How he rhapsodised about royal personalities and royal kindness! In his Jordan diaries are laudatory draft letters and sweet thank you notes and humble requests and effusive asides, all tasty treats of Ali's peculiar deference to his Hashemites. But nothing, nothing, among the entries comes close to explaining Ali's story with them like his farewell letter to a dying Hussein.

On January 28, 1999, King Hussein ibn Talal of Jordan[378] was breathing the last of his life, an era of monarchical resilience in one of the region's more volatile Arab locales. 'What prayer might one offer to our king?' Ali's private letter began.

Your Majesty, Habibi (beloved), Sayedna (our master), when did I first meet you? You've been such an important part of my life! We must have even overlapped at Victoria College! (I was seven!). Then years passed, you acceded in 1952 the year Queen

Elizabeth was crowned as well . . . Perhaps saw you as an in-
sentient adolescent at Wasfi's house in 62 or 65 or 66. Those
still innocent years before irrevocable fall of 67 which you tried
to prevent when we lost Jerusalem, when Palestine was completely overrun, the year that finished my father in London for
whom you sent condolences to Kuwait. After Wasfi's death I
saw you more often, visiting sitt Saadieyh in Wasfi's house,
always gallant, always faithful, our monarch, whose aura could
not but be taken as a living national force. Evenings in Aqaba on
your days off. Your wonderful visit with Queen Noor after which
one couldn't throw your cigarette butts for days!! Prince Raad
was there with Prince Mir'ed. The years passed again as one
strove in one's own particular capacities to serve the country, a
culture almost in violative transition stretching for economic life-
lines sometimes had damaged cultural resources that I fought to
defend but which went against a certain progressive will to move
forwards which you yourself upheld . . . Without dwelling on
biographical details, perhaps my last significant encounter was
when HM Queen Noor requested a presentation for the Aqaba
palm shore development scheme – I was flustered & perhaps not
quite humble enough and I think you were neither convinced nor
moved to exert an arbitrative influence against the demise of what
I saw as a prime enclave of indigenous traditional Jordanian
genius developed environmentally over the centuries. I am so
sorry Sayedna that that moment could not sway you but even
more sorry that it was as if we took your complexly-directed
guidance of the country for granted and I can't bear to think of
being bereft of your captainship and your . . . emblem and guiding
hand that perhaps we have not sufficiently understood or
appreciated through the decades of your efforts at the helm.
'God bless the Jordanian family – may it ever flourish in your
name.'[379]

Where do I start in disentangling these florid emotions? A dash
of a reprimand inside a panegyric, a hint of reproof strangled by
fawning. Ululations of aristocratic credentials announce a noisy

symphony of reverence that drowns out the hum of gentle tut-tuts and muffles the courtier's entreaties for relevance.

Harsh? Not really. Ali's farewell to Hussein was all about the tension between what his heart felt and what his eyes saw and registered. After all, his studied rants about the pervasive face of the Jordanian *Mukhabarrat* (intelligence services), about the poverty of input and mediocrity of output that defined a whole society's expectations of itself, about the state's indifference towards history's bequests, inundate his Jordan diaries.

Tuesday night at Salomon Bar . . . having a quiet beer. This . . . mustache macho case eyeing me (mentally) later followed me to street jumped in cab with me! Pulled out wallet and demanded my passport. 'Mukhabarrat. Why you speak English?'

'Amel Halak Ajnabi' (pretending to be a foreigner).[380]

Only days earlier he was taking pictures in downtown Amman, near the Roman amphitheatre:

HUMAN CONDITION CONFISCATED FILM

#1 a reeking gutter by the municipality #2 the sign of the women's WC by the Philadelphia #3 the sign of the men's #4 a shot into the interior of the stairwell shaft with iron gates locked shut and the bottom sullenly reflective with urine #5 the battered iron railing curving foreshortened against backdrop of Town Hall #6 a mound of rubbish and gardener's cleanings pressed into a corner-supported pile #7 the gleaming gold of a huge brass crescent mosque . . . #8 a close up of the hand-beaten hammered golden metal in its curved double-horns disk, long slanting shadows traversing pavement fleeting with the shades of passersby and tread of Arab feet and then #8 ran into jammed non-flash right in the middle of the stinking gent's bog of the lavatories of the great mid center mosque where among leaking urinals and blocked Islamic (what's the archeological term correct for shit hole? I've forgotten) and prayers-to-be waiting for their turn in the stalls and attendants swabbing non-descript black pits and the shuffle of a silenced central crowd lurking among the processes of quiescent biology and the flash won't go and then in the entrance corridor in that pervasive alkaline aroma as I fiddle with the contraption and it won't work and that odd youth is gazing at me in that uniquely Middle Eastern intensity of non-identification so then suddenly I took a relief shot of 2 red motorcycle helmets on a pair of military uniforms with one funky brown neck against a background of Arabic script on blue shop front and then seconds later I am under arrest it's the military police.[381]

So wherefore Habibi Sayedna, Your Majesty, our monarch, captain of the ship, and all the rest?

Rula smiled as I read her the letter to Hussein. She was not surprised. 'That is what Ali was about: his ability to tolerate contradictions. Or maybe, for him, there was no contradiction. He was genuinely faithful to both realities'[382] – fealty to the Hashemites, eternal gratitude for their support, friendships with many among them and a defiant pen that took in the mistakes and raged against the disappointing performance. If you stick with Rula's opinion, you would be almost sure that Ali's personal loyalties did not co-opt his intellectual integrity. Had they done so, his letters, diaries and conversations would have glossed over the regime's shortcomings, and his many encounters with the family would not have featured open, if always tactful, disapproval. But step outside Rula's interpretation and you might wonder. Can a writer of such letters escape the label of sycophant? Remove the name Hussein and add in Nasser. Would the scribbler not be named a Nasserite? Is this not an apologia which demeans the scathing assaults that characterised Ali's every other private thought about Jordan?

In truth, it would have been impossible for Ali to be unenthusiastic about the Hashemites. His innate high regard for his own aristocratic roots, his personal connections with the family, his want of a royal pat on the back, his need of protection, his search for meaning, found plenty of space in a man so relaxed about the conflicts and contradictions between his many selves. Ultimately,

Ali, Saadieyh's nephew, found in the persons of the Hashemites, if not in their dominion, humaneness, decency, benevolence. Princess Wijdan was a fellow artist and a friend. Prince Raad and his wife Princess Majidah were dear friends.[383] Prince Talal and Princess Ghida were good acquaintances and so was Princess Alia, Hussein's eldest daughter. Prince Hassan, King Hussein's brother, and his wife Princess Sarvath were always very kind. Hussein and Noor were gracious, often accessible. Visits to the palace were not frequent but more than occasional. Invitations to receptions and weddings and dinners were not unusual.

And, well, yes, perhaps for Ali, there was a softness in Hussein, a mercifulness in him, that, for all his shortfalls, made it possible for Ali to love the man while disliking his realm. As I write these words, I think to myself how hollow this claim must sound to the dissenters who taste the humiliations and harassments, or to the deprived who live in that pitiless region that lies below the poverty line, or to the fragile who beg in vain for the state's protectiveness against society's oppressiveness. But would that we in the Arab world could live without the moral relativisms that separate the bad from the less bad, the downright nasty from the tolerably callous. Ali knew the grievances of those on the other side of the tracks, but he may have reasoned that Hussein, in the making of his people's regrettable state of affairs, was more overstretched father than active partner. A copout by an artist and a man who saw enough to know better, many of the Hashemites' detractors are sure to think. I wonder how Ali would have answered this one?

*   *   *

Rest your eyes a bit on this part: 'I was flustered & perhaps not quite humble enough and I think you were neither convinced nor moved to exert an arbitrative influence against the demise of what I saw as a prime enclave of indigenous traditional Jordanian genius developed environmentally over the centuries.' Fadi says 'this is pretty much Ali's saga in Jordan',[384] the part that caused just as much distress as Saadieyh, the one that doomed life after her to heart wrench, because, for all his allergies to commitments and responsibilities, Ali, soon after settling in Jordan, had finally found his calling. Towards the end, Ali may have looked like a lost man running into the walls of his labyrinth, but his beginnings in the country offered inroads into decades-old indecision. The youthful self-absorptions of an aspirant vagabond were subsiding and altruistic passions were starting to shape the profile of this artist.

> Unlike his great exegete Sartre, Genet cannot harness his insights as an artist for ideological and political ends. For Genet in the 'Screens' the final historical eventuality is not the social one of revolutionary victory but the personal and individual one of death, which both cancels and transfigures the sense of self with its burdens of guilt and rebellion.[385]

This take by Jack Kroll on Jean Genet's resistance to a friendship between his ideas and a broader purpose is quoted in Ali's 1971 journal. It mirrored Ali's ambivalence towards his own artistic intentions. But by the time he had reached Amman in 1978, Ali's uncertainty had finally begun to lower its guard. Everything in the Jordanian terrain, in the southern desert, in the Bedouin, in the ruins that illuminated the beauty of an antediluvian landscape like precious stones, in the helplessness of native habitats before the onrush of modern cityscapes, nudged him towards a path beyond brush and canvas. Conservation was a vocation that would bring him closer to architecture, a profession that had eluded him, and to an adored father whose example had always haunted him. Now he could think of himself as some sort of servant of a national cause, as a fellow urban planner.

The journals begin to veer away from visual renditions of modern anthropologies. The pencil instamatics of social realities become scant. Only the very personal interrupts discursions on archaeology, on urbanism in Islamic cities, on testimonies to Islam's commitment to restoration, on Jordan's inability to be sensitive and selective and tasteful in its uptake of modernity.

> I would have thought that despite the tremendous growth of the capital and all the boom-town phenomenology that I personally

have come to hate as a destructive growth pattern – destructive to all our inherent values and traditional visual kinship patterns – that we somehow still have the cozy elements of a closely-knit society where most people know each other and there is every reason to feel part of a distinct homogenous social structure that can share these decisions and take part actively in the consensus on what proportions our immediate environment should adopt between the future and the past.[386]

His notes are sentences in mid-thought, often scribblings from scholarly texts and lectures: on this page is Homsian-born[387] Roman Empress Julia Dumna (AD170–217), on that page Philip the Arab, Roman Emperor from AD244 to 249, followed by Edom and biblical Petra.[388] Incense trade routes jostle with caravan stations, Ashurbanipal, king of Assyria (668–627BC), shares a tiny space with Nineveh, home to his famous library.[389] Remarks linger over Muhammad ibn Ahmad Shams al-Din Muqqadisi's division of tenth century Bilad al Sham (the Levant) during the Byzantine Empire and swoop down on ibn Khaldun's disciple al Maqrizi (1364–1442), most probably in relation to Khitat, the historian's topographical map of Cairo.[390]

Time was spent in Iraq al Amir, west of Amman, where François and his French expedition were excavating and restoring Qasr al-Abd, the Tobiads' second-century Hellenistic palace;[391] in Wadi Rumm befriending the land and its main tribe, the Huweitat; in Petra, where he was first transfixed by the Madbah (sacrificial slab); in Pella (or Tabaqqat al Fahl), in the foothills of the north of the Jordan Valley, with the University of Sydney excavations team as they dug their way through layers of ruins stretching from the Neolithic period to the Islamic age.[392] His paintings were turning into fervent documentations of historical Jordan and of frail native environments on the brink of deletion. They stand today as a voluminous record of ancient relics and decapitated neighbourhoods. The ennui that ran through the diaries – one endless depressed diatribe – was absent from the artworks. The canvases are many, the hand's method beguilingly eclectic; in

Ali and Rifles. 1996. Courtesy of Rami Sajdi

some, like the black-and-white Timurid Khwaja Aghacha Mausoleum,[393] precise, chillingly real; in others, like Amman by Night,
mock-serious, sometimes even kitschy. There is no anger in them,
just passion at its most meticulous or decorative or socially con-
scious or wry. Beauty was his thing. Not the screaming kind, the
other one: that which lies shy and reticent in the humdrum and
ordinary – the very subtle colours on a derelict wall or stone as it
lives through the ephemeral light of the different hours of the day;
the haunting grace of a decaying grave; the busy cheesiness of a
driver and his taxi.[394]

Everyone wanted a painting by Ali, but there was no vindication
in society's embrace of him as a painter. The awe he found mildly
tolerable, almost beside the point; the panting eagerness he brushed
off as boorish. The exhibitions he hated as a glorified marketplace
of hagglers, the private sales he sought when desperate for financial
relief, the commissions he accepted only rarely, mostly for royalty or
embassies. 'Don't you dare call my works paintings,' he beseeched
Nuha, the first to exhibit him in Jordan. 'Every time he was called
upon to perform he felt like he was prostituting himself.'[395]

Most of the six solo exhibitions which he mounted over the

course of his twenty-four years in Jordan were halfway houses between pure painterly shows and expositions of his conservation schemes and would-be renovation projects. Once persuaded to partake in these public displays, he would turn his venues into a continuum between the actual painter in him and the wannabe preservationist.[396] At the National Gallery in 1983, Ali's interpretations of the Bilbeisi House's proposed restoration were just a few metres away from his Ibn Tulun Mosque series.[397] At the Darat al Funun Gallery, in 1995, works on the last shipyard in Aqaba inside lead the way to his treatments of Aqaba's threatened natural shorelines on the balcony.[398]

Even that near-indecipherable installation at Darat al Funun, in 1998, seemed fixated on how the past should have its place in the present, and the present in its future. Two walls facing each other took up the entire installation: on one were small recreations of the eight conceptual diagrams of Peter Eisenman's model for the Wexner Center for the Visual Arts in Columbus, Ohio; on the other were eight very old jars of incense traded by the Nabataeans.[399] In the corner was a computer that showed the different faces of the desert. Every time I look at pictures of the installation, all I can think of is Ali's escape from the actual artist in him to the wishful architect. I could be wrong, of course. Ali was silent about his setup, and there is no real literature on it. I had to search for clues anywhere I could find them. Friends drew a complete blank, and then I came across an essay written about Peter Eisenman by Hans Morgenthaler:

> He [Eisenman] remained committed to an architecture which emphasised meaning over form, but broadened his choice of expressive features. For him, architecture was no longer about aesthetics, but also about economics, politics, and history . . . he began to incorporate memory and history into designs. He took a stand against rationality, clarity, and purity in architectural form . . . Eisenman wanted his buildings to be narratives . . . [400]

This narrative, I imagine, would have resonated with Ali.

*   *   *

Ali wrote this about himself a few months before he died: 'Most concerned with the heritage of the past as well as its contemporary expression . . . he endeavours to achieve the safeguarding and highlighting of traditional environments, urban or country.'[401] The unobtainable, again! He let go of so much but not this one, this quest for which he was so temperamentally unsuited. There are talents, skills he had to have to persuade a hungry country of the merits of controlled tourism, to convince an impatient municipality of the benefits of careful, environmentally friendly development, to discourage a government from a rash leap into haphazard newness. He had none of them. For all his eloquence, 'when in the presence of officialdom Ali just could not articulate his thoughts and ideas; he would become discombobulated'.[402] In the company of even the most junior decision-makers, he would become flustered, unfocused. As an advocate, he was most things he should not have been: too nervous, overly emotional, annoyingly thin-skinned, almost always ready to be offended. There is not a single undertaking, private or public, during which Ali did not perceive constant indignities and betrayals.

You are received by the Director of Antiquities in His office and you proceed to touch on subjects outrageously neglected by the various governmental power factions, between antiquities, munici-palities and policy, etc. and the Director hardly lacking enlight-enment proceeds to deliver an almost savagely comprehensive analysis of the complex mesh of factors causing this insoluble inertia, after which I am shown out in a tense silence that means people like me simply waste his precious time. In recalling his exasperation, I am unimpressed: these remain sophistries only possibly as pretexts for inaction. How much more filth to accumulate in a society not without its aspirations for order? Now what should I do?[403] Write a polite note to Director apologising for having wasted his time on such irrelevant issues at the moment in the hope of salvaging a positive mental image in his mind for future projects. Or do I forget all this and play further procedures strictly by rules of chess? Or do I publish this in incognito form?[404]

This incident replayed itself with almost every official he met. He wanted it all his way, François remembers, in total sync with his vision, sensitive to his bizarrely elastic sense of time.[405] His particular genius wanted to be alone and such projects insisted on the relevance of others, on compromises with them, on strict delivery dates. It did not help him that he always shot down ideas with such precision and cut well-crafted holes in every initiative but rarely could point the way to a viable alternative. He seemed to have only one prescription for every proposed tourism scheme or renovation plan: 'Don't touch it.' He was 'in tears about any discussion on development in . . . Aqaba, in Petra . . . He preferred the world to stay still.'[406] Or, as Aysar suggests, Ali did have solutions but they 'were simply not acceptable . . . He refused to compromise with modernity . . . He wanted to preserve the heritage as he knows it. To him, this was the very environment that attracted tourists. Tourists come to see palm trees in Aqaba, not concrete.'[407] But by insisting on everything or nothing in a poor country anxious to exploit its scarce advantages, Ali effectively threw himself out of the game. If he did not walk out on the projects first, he was eventually 'surgically removed.'[408] Even on those rare assignments which he did own and complete, his state of near-hysteria in choosing the right stone, or the right tree, or the right cushion, in bringing the designs to perfect, authentic fruition, made the whole process mad, the end full of bitterness, the aftermath heavy with suspicions.

I am in a very overwrought, undermined, paranoid state feeling vulnerable, defenseless, unappreciated and exploited at the same time and without even the likelihood of being allowed or enabled to finish things in the proper harmonious and natural way which would be the only way for the whole project to be a success and a resonating ecological lesson instead of a mess shrapnelled at the end by viciously triumphant bureaucracies. Perhaps they – and even she [Princess Alia, the eldest daughter of King Hussein] all got sick in the end of too much naturalistic puristic romanticistic piety.[409] . . .

Isn't it time to call enough is enough? I am practically begging them to use my services but their total obliviousness and squalor is finally too much. I am not a gabi [collector] to run after their bills.[410]

This horse hospital in Petra, about which Ali was complaining, was a rare victory for him. The result was very impressive, but his nerves (and probably theirs) were a total wreck. There were other successes, like the Wadi Rumm reception tent commissioned by Tony Atallah[411] during his days at the Department of Tourism and Ali's creative contributions to the Jordanian stand at the Seville Exhibition in 1992, but they were too few and the toll on him too heavy. His library is crammed with detailed studies or catalogued commentaries on preservation sites or urban renewals that died or never came to life. The early twentieth-century Bilbeisi family house and the Philadelphia Hotel in downtown Amman, the aeons-old Arabian palm trees of Aqaba, the ransacked, hotel-sprinkled environment surrounding Nabataean Petra – these are but a few of the condemned properties or hassled localities for which Ali had written a eulogy.

> In full throes of demolition [the Bilbeisi house]. I didn't think I'd see such a thing or live such a day . . . workmen drilling and those features tumbling forth . . . and the windows finally at their hour of truth and no one there to save . . . finally Saadieyh's republican values came through to calm.[412]

You would have thought that after the first few of these disappointments Ali would have moved towards devotions less futile. His piles upon piles of criticisms and castigations over the course of two decades read like an excruciatingly slow, drip-drip, masochistic piece of melancholia. But he felt trapped by duty and location. He painted but he hated to sell his paintings, and he lived in a struggling society in which bread-and-butter issues made competing 'lofty' concerns appear bourgeois and unfeeling. And yet to have been satisfied with producing art for those who could afford it, when a land and its people faced 'interruption, dissonance, loss',[413] seemed fraudulent to him. 'I would like to be doing stuff that . . . does not sit on walls, have a price tag on it or end up in the homes of the rich,'[414] he explained once in a rare interview. History to Ali was always very personal. A record of things past, unearthed artifacts of bygone lives, offered tangible proof that names like his, families like his, people who have a feeble claim on the present, once defined it. For him, intact and harmonious physical environments were pivotal for a harried culture grappling with burning problems of marginalisation and disruption. They offered it a much-needed connection to a distinct identity. If sacrificed to immediate material gain, their footprints on a people's collective memory would be lost – forever. Such discontinuities were frightening to a man whose life never had enough anchors. That he kept insisting on such preservationist pursuits, although he was so obviously ill-equipped for them, finally reflected nothing more than his fidelity to his life-long passion for roots and history, and his newfound meaning in both. Let go of that, he thought, and you will have abandoned the things that give your life purpose.

Still, even to those closest to him, something about Ali's fractious relations with life smacked of the bizarre. They were real enough, but they appeared so self-inflicted. In his own eyes, he was a helpless victim of misfortune, an injured soul bullied by a fickle fate, a trapped bird pining for life outside its cage, a lonely champion of an honourable cause, an earnest, well-meaning Jabrian at the mercy of a sadistic aunt. Vintage Ali, we all thought. Prison doors wide-open, you could see him inside, frantic, tearful, pleading with the Gods for an exit. You call out to him to come to you, you walk in wanting to hold his hand, he looks at you, slightly annoyed, and then plunges into another round of moans and groans about life's jeers and disparagements. In this all-out war between him and his situation there were one or two truces. But his periodic surrenders were so awkward and so out of character that the consequences dithered somewhere between the distressingly appalling and the downright comical. And nowhere was there a worse capitulation than in his momentary siding with Saadieyh

when a man from a Christian family fell in love with Diala –
mortification and bawls, the oh-no-you-don't and this-can-never-
be from brother and aunt.

'How could you do this to your sister, Ali; you of all people,'
Raghida asked him.

This startling answer came back: 'Well, we are Jabris. We cannot
have a marriage with a Christian man.'

' "Oh, my God! How could you? How could you even say this?" I
kept repeating. He just sat there in silence.'[415]

Within a month, self-rebuke replaced this slip-up and repentant
spasms searched for solace.

For a while there, Ali even tried out Islam. The usual gestures,
like the *Basmalah* (In the Name of God the Merciful), which
graced the inner cover of so many of his diaries and prefaced every
announcement or anniversary of the death of a dear one, he had
embraced since Cairo. Ali was a superstitious man. He believed in
the evil eye, in otherworldly forces in cahoots with happenstance,
in the power of the I-Ching. It was easy to adopt the *Basmalah* as
one more petition to God to lighten up the karma. But in 1984, he
ventured further into the interiors of mosques and the insides of
Islamic practice. He probably thought piety would shorten the
distance between him and his Arab identity. After Hala's death,
he picked up the habit of prayer, learning from fellow believers in
the mosque the art of bending over and kneeling in submission.
There are drawings of prayer movements in that year's journal, a
brief how-to manual.[416] But this courtship was also very short-
lived. Apparently, the rituals of active belief put peculiar pressures
on his daily routine. At a dinner at Prince Talal and Princess
Ghida's house years after, Ali was asked how he felt about the
Hajj. A long pause . . . and then: 'I did become religious after my
mother's death. I began to pray five times a day. But then I was
having to make all my appointments around absolutions and
prayer time. I'd agree to see the carpenter before noon prayer, the
framer after afternoon prayers . . . After a while I thought I might
as well stay in my plastic *shibshibs* (slippers) and carry my gallon
[pail] of water around with me wherever I went.'[417]

This anecdote reminds me of that memorable Cairo letter to Antonia, of the mirth that often tickled his painful struggle with belonging:

I don't think I believe in God, but I believe in the anonymous unity of men, and I submit myself within this occasional obeisance to the power of the culture – 'my' culture, supposedly, but really I remain a dwarf Gulliver among millions, still unable to use a native toilet. I'll be really Arab when I can squat down on my flat arches to deliver my fat additions . . . [418]

The metaphor does the trick, but did Ali not know that, in this delicate balancing act at least, he was not the only confounded Arab?

Nothing worked for Ali, nothing helped him mend the rifts between him and his Jordanian fix – not the humour, not the white flags, not the strained accommodations with Saadieyh, the fleeting visits of love, the desert, the Ghor, the accolades, the love of friends. Some of his alienations as an Arab were ones that had long nested in each one of us, others were of a completely different order, confining him to a perennial state of exile.

*   *   *

François thinks Beirut could have been his way out. 'After his visit to Beirut, he said he could see himself there.'[419]

I saw Ali in Beirut on that one trip of his in 2001. He spent Christmas with me and my family. It took us years to convince him to make the crossing. He feared a repeat of his overnight stays in Syrian jails, but he finally made it in the company of Fadi and Rula, my brother and sister-in-law. He hung out at my new apartment, giving me ideas and pointers. I showed him where I was going to put his Umm Kalthoum. He liked it. He said nothing, as usual, about my other paintings. Ali never said anything about any Arab painter. He was always silent about Arab art, not a word, not even a grimace, never a nod. And then, two years after his death, a copy of this *Eastern Art Report* interview in October of 1990 reaches my hands:

AJ: . . . We are doing images on flats, while those revolutions have been performed 25 years ago. Conceptualism, minimalism, I don't know what. We've had goats sticking out of tyres, and our artists are still doing pictures on walls.

EAR: But this is a problem that artists from anywhere other than the mainstream are always going to face. They are either going to be accused of being derivative, endlessly derivative, or backward . . . How do you solve that problem?

AJ: You don't really. Take the international art festivals: The Arab world is simply not figuring in any of them.

EAR: But the Arab artists living abroad are getting attention.

AJ: Are they? But what kind of attention? From a tiny specialised audience!

EAR: In the British Museum's John Addis Islamic Gallery you have a couple of modern artists with works of modern calligraphy.

AJ: Well, the British Museum was wrong to include them.[420]

Typical Ali. No 'humm, I should see them'. No 'who are they, don't know them, I'll have to pay the museum a visit'; 'yes, maybe there are one or two exceptions'. Iraqi works by Ismail Fattah and Nuha Radi, or Egyptian ones by Adel Siwwi, did not provoke in him more than a smile. Only once did I find him in awe of another Arab artist. In 1983, Raghida, Nawal, Ali and I went to visit Iraq's Issam al Said.[421] That was the only time I witnessed Ali totally absorbed by another Arab painter. This may explain why he hid so many of his Jordanian paintings. Along with those buried Cairene paintings, Jordanian ones were found, some small, some much larger drawings. One or two nudes show up again, reminders that here as well Ali was not without physical love unforgettable enough to end up on paper. There is hip Amman by night drenched in fun and colour, cool Jordan by the pool at the Bisharat's farm in Mukheibeh down in the Jordan Valley. There is that cherry blossom tree.[422] The first time I saw it, for some reason, Yeats' perhaps much-abused *The Wind Among The Reeds* came to me.

Had I the heavens' embroidered cloths,
Enwrought with golden and silver light,
The blue and the dim and the dark cloths
Of night and light and the half-light,
I would spread the cloths under your feet:
But I, being poor, have only my dreams;
I have spread my dreams under your feet;
Tread softly because you tread on my dreams.

There is Joseph Cornell, of all people, and his assemblages. The influence of Max Ernst's series is there, so are the works – Medici Boy, Caliph of Baghdad, all titled and boxed in – Ali's pencilled collage of Cornell's collages. Why did he hide these? Maybe Ali did not take them seriously. Maybe they were another proof of the painter that he was and did not want to be. But their richness uncovers what the Jordan diaries' paucity suppresses: the light days, the spontaneity of Ali's prolific brush, the heated nights, the many faces of the painter that he was, the truth about this man and its many sisters.

*   *   *

This is coming to an end. I am losing steam. I stare at all the notes and copies of letters and books and diaries, and I ask myself, have I, have I managed to knit together the lives and characters bestrewn all over this Ali? Have I written enough, or have I barely scratched the surface of this man?

I often wonder what Ali felt those few seconds before he died. Did he think how ironic it was that even in death his life had to be so rich and yet so unkind? It would have been so like him to go so resigned and yet so knowing.

Little soul, gentle and drifting, guest and companion of my body, now you will dwell below the pallid places, stark and bare; there you will abandon your play of yore. But one moment still, let us gaze together on these familiar shores, on these objects which doubtless we shall not see again . . . Let us try, if we can, to enter into death with open eyes.[423]

Epilogue by Diala al Jabri

Oh my father, I am Yusuf
Oh father, my brothers neither love me nor want me in their midst
They assault me and cast stones and words at me
They want me to die so they can eulogise me
They closed the door of your house and left me outside
They expelled me from the field
Oh my father, they poisoned my grapes . . .

Mahmoud Darwish

To be born of idealist parents, little more than innocents themselves, is to be forever an innocent – *Le Petit Prince* of St Exupery,
between his lonely planets, including the one on which he watered
his sole flower. It is also to re-enact Exupery's *Vol de Nuit* and fly
uncharted over the desert at night, with only the glow from the
instrument panel and the stars to light the ebony night over the
Pharaoh's deserts as Ali did. He retained a childlike heart free of
cynicism throughout his life.

Our mother used to tell me how, after boarding school in
Jerusalem and then school in Switzerland (when Jiddo was in
exile), she began her American adventure driving across America,
swimming and riding on the Mellon estates with her friends and
then going to Berkeley before WWII broke out and she had to
come back to Jiddo's house in Aleppo. She made herself plain to
avoid unwanted suitors by putting a big floppy hat over her shiny
hair and playing dumb, once throwing the huge diamond ring of
one such filthy rich but otherwise unpalatable would-be fiancé
away and laughing as he threw himself on the floor after it. Our
father – then also a would-be fiancé – was out with her when he
stopped his car to help an elderly man pick up an overturned

basket of oranges, and that made all the difference. Ali always had that same kindness within him.

One winter after their marriage, Armenian refugees fleeing the Turks across the icy mountains sought sanctuary in Aleppo, where our father was the young mayor. He came home and asked our mother for all her jewels so that they could buy bedding for the refugees. Another time, when riots against the Jewish community in Aleppo were incited, our father led by example, standing in front of the age-old Jewish quarter to discourage the rioters and sending our mother to their Jewish neighbours. However, eventually suffocated by pressures and interference, they left Aleppo and set off across the Arab world to start anew away from the withered roots of centuries past, on the quest that their son would later bring to a conclusion: first to Jordan, when Ali was born in Jerusalem, and then to Beirut – our mother's real love and later one of Ali's – from which our father commuted to build Banyas harbour. He once took Ali on site with him and the heart-breakingly loving little boy he was then drew a sign saying Home Sweet Home and put it up on the wall of their shared room . . . He told me this story in the last few years of his life.

I still have the plan for a big house by the sea that Sheikh Fahd Al Sabah of Kuwait wanted to build – for the Arab idealist friend he had first met at AUB – next to his own. But Daddy never accepted any nationality other than Syrian or sought any property above what he thought he had in Aleppo. He really went to Kuwait to help build another country and carried developmental dreams and responsibilities he shared with his friends there, especially before the real black gold rush started, when everybody who could sell anything (physical or moral) flooded there from all over the world. He was an insider at first and then, when he no longer wanted to be among the thrusting hordes that surrounded power in the Gulf, he remained a friend till his early death. There is a story of Sheikha Lulwa, Fahd's first wife who adored daddy, once opening a cupboard to him and telling him: 'Abu Ali, khodh' (Father of Ali: take). Daddy looked in on shelves of spaghetti and gold ingots (the effervescent innocence of Kuwait in the early

1950s as retold to me by my mother) and gallantly and equally affectionately reached in for a box of spaghetti. Other stories tell of Hala – who they called *al nisra* (the falcon) – discreetly refusing diamond necklaces from other Sheikhs at an eye signal from our father. Eventually all I left Kuwait with – decades after my father and then my mother died – were thousands of loving memories of a turquoise Gulf and its people and photographs: among them one of Sheikh Fahd, inscribed *Min Abu Ali ila Abu Ali* from the father of Ali to the father of Ali, given in friendship and trust a few years before Sheikh Fahd's death. After our father's premature death, the decades my mother fought in Kuwait's arbitration courts trying to win some vestige of my father's rights came to nothing, but ruined her health and life and our inability to lead a family life in comfort, closer to Ali, rather than each battling on his or her own pitch.

All we attained were a whole wall full of my loving colour photographs of Kuwait, collaged with old sepia photographs of the historical Kuwait. I also have the jewel-toned sketch of a little black slave holding a parasol that Ali drew for me in childhood, hidden for decades until it came to rest with me here. There is Ali's childhood copy of *Alice in Wonderland* and his copy of the letters of the Marquise de Sevigné; a few books with Rugby labels; the kelim cushions and the Kutahiya tiles with 'In the name of God the Merciful and Compassionate' scripted on them in Arabic that Ali brought back from a happy trip to Turkey with Fadi and Rula. So much that was reminiscent of our roots was lost in our Beirut apartment, ransacked at the onset of war: Ali's childhood pictures, pictures of our parents in America, one of our mother pregnant with Ali looking into a mother of pearl mirror like the Giaconda, family antiques and memories, the opalines, the carpets, the first edition books in several languages, our grandfather's desk with its secret drawers for land accounts and other things; the Turkish silk tapestries embroidered with the tree of life in gold and silk hues, the gold swords from Al Saud, the Chinese vases from Aleppo where the Marcopoli family, descendants of Marco Polo, still lived, Aleppo having been on the ancient silk and trade routes to and from Venice and China . . . all are indirect stage settings for the roots of our narrative. I mention them not out of attachment to material objects but for their emotional and cultural significance – as vestiges of a rich and culturally diverse Arab world and to show how much Ali and I shared and belonged to that which was irretrievably lost – a burden we both carried in our different ways, trying to go on to build different associations and achievements and give significance to our so visibly ephemeral lives.

Some of Ali's words written to me once:

Friday evening a week after and almost a day after you have gone and life has certainly lost some balance with your absence and I ask people I appen (sic) to be with what brothers and sisters they have . . . so much time and energy is spent on just avoiding the issue or seeking chloroform in this lonely rough town where everything is recent or new or insincere – i.e. friendships not easy to come across and now that age where most interchange is surface as people are busy with their own trips . . .

Geez I feel like sludge. My eyes are peeled tomatoes, my stomach's crawling skin feels about to unwrinkle like a caterpillar and them mosquitoes keep me obsessed till the wee hours . . . on my floor bed with the door open and guttering candles as I continue with Plato across the little hall from your dark room which looks sweet and fresh and awaiting your return . . .

Saturday evening the thirteenth of September 1980

I want to write back to him: a letter in a bottle from a town with no sea . . .

I look out too for a light in your window every time I pass by the apartment under which the babes in bare-tummy leopard skin halter-ensembles you described still park their Daddy's cars for their nights out . . . it is always dark . . . We never found our father's masbaha (worry beads) after your murder, but our old friend Um Kalthoum is with me now. I am trying to forget what it felt like climbing those stairs, reading the Fatiha to myself (though not religious), knowing I was to find you gone. But I never will . . .

Since you left, the 'Coalition' entered Baghdad in 2003; it has been shattered systematically . . . sectarianism fanned from within has mushroomed into ethnic cleansing, insurgencies and women suicide bombers setting themselves off in crowded souks. The UN High Commissioner for Refugees has said the Iraqi refugee crisis is now the most 'significant population displacement' in the Middle East since 'Israel was established in 1948'. About 2 million Iraqis have fled, mostly to Syria and Jordan, and about 2.5 million more are displaced inside Iraq – conservative estimates of civilian dead range from 350,000 up to a million. Fire-breathing Robert Fisk told us that the 'minimum estimates for Iraqi dead mean that the civilians of Mesopotamia have suffered six or seven Dresdens or – more terrible still – two Hiroshimas'.

The USS *Cole* was deployed off the vulnerable coastal waters of Lebanon as it once had been off Yemen. Rafik al Hariri was assassinated not far from the St Georges, strangely enough on Valentine's Day 2005. Since then prominent Lebanese figures have been assassinated, one after the other, like clockwork oranges. Then there was Israel's onslaught into Lebanon in the summer of 2006. They are still trying to find and remove the cluster bombs the IDF sowed in the last few days before that 'expressly delayed' ceasefire. Lebanon leaderless – due to political gridlock between weakened factions for an everlasting time – is now at yet another dangerous juncture . . . we always stand at the precipice of loss.

They are drinking seas of blood in Gaza, the new big concentration camp of this century; remember how you tried to convey your agony at the first Intifada to a well-known but unmoved international journalist; how you feverishly began to work on your depictions of Afghanistan. Then we might leaf through our memories, long live Jordan, Iraq, Kuwait, Palestine, Syria, and Egypt . . . freedom on the electric edge of life. I am with you in spirit where you are overlooking the shrinking pristine wilderness outside Petra, overlooking the hills of Moab/Palestine, till we meet again . . . 'in this secure town, of figs and olives' . . . or any other realm, wherever you are . . . the Elysian fields perhaps??? Illusions perdues.

We are but bastards of history and time.

I am at a loss before my happy childhood picture between both Ali and Wasfi decades before all this. Those days truly were pure childhood perfection . . . each Damascene rose in the garden as big as a soup dish. Saadieyh was delightfully full of life, optimism, affection, attachment and compassion and Wasfi a stronghold of protective masculine presence, especially after my equally amazing father's death four years before him. They had been friends, the blond and idealistic man from Aleppo and the swarthy leader from Irbid, born of the memorable Jordanian poet, Arar. The house was always full of fascinating people and books and music. Honey came from the bees in the garden at the lower end of the estate; figs and grapes off the trees and the vine.

That was before Wasfi's assassination and the insidious, sad erosion of years of tranquillisers to face the solitude as she begged us to come to her, culminating in withdrawal into herself and aged decaying cells . . . a decline so heartbreaking to live beside. Contrast those first happy days to the Byzantine intrigues that eventually loomed around the damaged mind of an old woman yet full of *amour propre*. There is nothing worse than seeing someone you love disappear into themselves though the ailing physical self is still there. This immersed us in total dread of the awful ending of her death – the final loss of belonging, indeed Paradise Lost – leading up to the time before I went to find Ali, sensing that hell itself was behind those vacant, lit windows beaming evilly into the utter stillness and emptiness of the traditionally blessed and benevolent Ramadan night?

Ali was initiated into the legend of Um Kalthoum on a Ramadan night more than two decades ago in Cairo. Um Kalthoum's voice seduced his post Iftar evening, introducing Ali to her as he walked by his aunt Saadieyh's side, at a time when they were accomplices, strolling through the quiet downtown streets savouring the lull before the Ramadan night comes alive in Egypt. Her presence came upon them, entrancing both as her unmistakable voice rang out into the silence with her irreplaceable intonation of *'Aqbal Al Leil'*. The very meaning of the song ('Night has Come upon Us') marked the years ahead. Um Kalthoum and that song in particular became a theme, a heartthrob and a lullaby to us all.

Ali began a painting of her in his apartment back in Amman, Jordan, often listening to that song as we all did – together or apart – repeating the story of the 'awakening'. The painting and repainting went on for more than two decades. One would often go to bed saying goodnight to her with one face only to awake to her with a void in place of a face or the beginnings of another as Ali would have been driven back to her side at night.

Um Kalthoum's completed painting, after twenty years of daubing and redaubing, as Ali would say – until she became a member of the family – found unframed above a cupboard with the frame ready near by, was a witness to Ali's murder on November 28, 2002, thirty-one exact years after Wasfi's assassination in Cairo.

I think we grew up on grainy black and white cine footage of people in tears prostrating themselves at the feet of 'Al Sitt' on stages all over the Arab world and in Paris itself . . . Her audiences seemed to throb with emotion and she was the voice to a certain image of Egypt and a mirror of ourselves we chose to reflect upon . . . and then the years of disillusionment after Um Kalthoum and after Abdel Nasser . . . the scene we see today of riots in Arab countries not riven by combat . . . sectarianism, war, occupation, Palestine at 60 (or is it an Arab *espoir* that turns 60?) while Um Kalthoum is reborn into Said Mourad disco and *découpage à la Libanais* . . . yet still that voice defies classification . . .

Aqbal al Leil, *'al Bu'ud alamani al Sahr'* ('distance has taught me sleeplessness') . . . the motifs of a lost Arab world and its very resurgence . . . the secret of Um Kalthoum and Ali's immense heritage.

The threads are woven like an ethereal tapestry . . . A Ramadan night and a crescent moon across time from Cairo to Amman, from the voice of *Al Sayidah*[424], to the utter void of murder in a screenplay by Bunuel – *The Discreet Charm of the Bourgeoisie* – a surrealistic celluloid world where all is interrupted and all goes horribly wrong for the actors as if in a dream. What use are Ottoman relics and stage settings to us now; does one pitch headlong into oblivion carrying a Chinese vase, even if from Aleppo centuries ago?

Diala al Jabri
30 June 2008

Acknowledgement

To be the last of a line in the quicksand of the Middle East is a crushing responsibility. Before we vanish I had to place my hand in that of others to perpetuate the dream . . . to relay all that may grant immortality for Ali and for those he carried the blood of. It is in many ways a Faustian contract to entrust the enquiry, the judgement and the description to others.

One must express admiration for the searching gaze of Amal, who has wrought this rather exquisite – and only sometimes alien – crystal chandelier of narrative and documentation, sweeping with great wit and vision across the confusion of Arabism, and thanks to Ali's friends who have not allowed him to die. I have never known life without Ali, however far the physical distances between us sometimes and I am my brother's keeper. There is the fearful abyss Ali's absence and its circumstances have left, within the grander chasm of furies the Arab world now flounders in, but also the lingering essence of Jasmine and Damascene roses . . . the continuation of our Arabian nights . . . somewhere in Karbala and Najaf, decimated by state-of-the-art firepower, we still have mystic domes and minaret spires of belief, in Basra and on the remnants of Shatt Al Arab – from where the dhows would travel to India and Africa in the days before oil – there still are tall palm tree forests (though army helicopters sprayed them with Agent

Orange to flush out 'insurgents'), the Nile still flows through history, the desert castles still mark the old trade routes to Nejd and the Meccan pilgrimage. You are still in Petra where you used to escape in life.

Glossary

Alami, Musa (1897–1984): Musa Alami, of the Alamis of Jerusalem, was one of the Palestinian cause's most savvy advocates. In the early days of the Arab-Israeli conflict, his was a moderate voice and a sharp mind at a time of panic, confusion and tumult.

During the course of his public career, Alami, who studied law at Cambridge University, served as a key member of various Palestinian delegations formed to present the people's case to Western and Arab officialdom. A strong believer in the sway of public opinion, Alami, in the 1940s, persuaded the Arab League to establish a network of publicity offices in London, Washington DC, Jerusalem and Beirut. He also was instrumental in convincing the League to form the Arab Development Society (ADS) whose main mission was to help the Palestinian agricultural sector. Over the years, however, both endeavours caused Alami much frustration and ended in disappointment largely due to Arab governments' failure to honour their financial commitments.

Al Tall, Wasfi (1919–71): By the time of his assassination on November 28, 1971, al Tall, who was serving his third tenure as prime minister of Jordan, had emerged as one of his country's most hardline East Jordanian opponents of the Palestine Liberation Organisation (PLO). He was the victor in that finally violent showdown between the Hashemite monarchy and the movement in 1970. For that, and for his passion in fighting the fight, al Tall paid with his life.

The son of a Jordanian poet and a Kurdish mother, and born himself in Arabkir on the Turkish side of Kurdistan, al Tall started his career in the service of the Palestinian cause. An *AUBite* (a graduate of the American University of Beirut), al Tall, in 1946, worked for Musa Alami's Arab Office in Jerusalem, one

of four publicity offices financed by the Arab League and headed
by Alami. Soon thereafter, al Tall became Alami's permanent
secretary and right arm. Al Tall also volunteered for the Army of
Salvation (Arab funding for the offices was fast dwindling by that
time) which was created by the Arab League in 1947 to help the
Palestinians in their battle against Zionist forces.

After the 1948 Arab-Israeli war, al Tall worked briefly for Alami's
Constructive Enterprise, a project that promoted education and
agriculture, but his love affair with Saadieyh al Jabri, Mousa's
wife, brought the professional relationship between the two men to
an end. Wasfi married Saadieyh in 1951.

Al Tall's rise in the political hierarchy of the Jordanian regime
started in 1955, with the relatively modest but not altogether
peripheral position of Director of the Department of
Publications. From the start, he was ferociously antagonistic
towards Gamal Abdel Nasser, the President of Egypt, and deeply
indisposed to his particular brand of Arab nationalism. In 1959,
al Tall's propaganda war against Nasserism, from his pulpit as
Director of the Broadcasting System, was notable for a rhetorical
fire no less searing than Nasser's own best lobs against Jordan.
His impeccable pro-Hashemite credentials recommending him,
he was, by now, on the rim of the King's inner circle. In 1962,
after several political and diplomatic postings, the last of which
was a short stint as ambassador to Iraq, al Tall was at the centre
of it: at the age of forty-three, he was appointed prime minister of
Jordan.

Of all the prime ministers who served under King Hussein of
Jordan, and there were many, al Tall came closest in charisma,
influence and popularity among East Jordanians to Hussein. In
his bold and often blunt politics, however, he stood miles apart
from his infinitely more diplomatic and cautious monarch.

Aqaba: Situated in the extreme south of Jordan, Aqaba, referred to
by the tenth century geographer Muqaddissi as 'the port of
Palestine on the China sea', is the country's only outlet to the sea –
a welcome gift of the British Mandate which incorporated it into

Transjordan in 1925, four years after the birth of the Hashemite
Emirate itself.

Archaeological excavations in this ancient city have unearthed
evidence of human settlement as far back as the fourth millennium
BC. Aqaba thrived under the Nabataeans, was a significant trading
post for the Romans and boasts one of the oldest churches known
to man (*c.* 290AD). Samples of pre-Ottoman Islamic and crusader
handiwork include excavated sites along the waterfront route,
which show an example of early Islamic town planning; the
Crusaders' Castle on the off-shore Island of Far'oun (in Egyptian
territorial waters), which was captured by the Ayyubids; and the
Aqaba Fort rebuilt by the Mamluks. But for nearly four hundred
years, from the times of the Ottomans onwards, Aqaba, so named
by the Mamluks but known for centuries before them as the port
city of Ayla, lived simply and obscurely as a tiny, out-of-the-way
fishing village.

Aqaba has an exalted place in the chronicles of the Great Arab
Revolt. In 1917, Prince Feisal ibn al Hussein's Arab-led forces,
accompanied by T. E. Lawrence, seized it from the Turks. The
port, which had posed a potential threat to the British-controlled
Suez Canal, was thus rendered safe, helping open up supply lines
to British units positioned in Transjordan and Palestine.

Arab Revolt (1916): The Revolt was declared by Hashemite
Hussein ibn Ali, the Sharif of Mecca and ruler of Hijaz.
Increasingly disenchanted with the secular policies and Turkish
orientation of the Young Turks – the ascendant coalition of
reforming Turkish officers and functionaries – Hussein decided,
after an exchange of letters with Sir Henry McMahon, the British
High Commissioner in Cairo, to join hands with the British against
the Ottomans, in the hope of securing for himself an Arab Kingdom that encompassed the Arabian Peninsula, Mesopotamia and
Syria, including the Mediterranean port of Alexandretta (Isken-
derun) in southern Turkey.

The correspondence between Sharif Hussein and McMahon,
commonly referred to as the McMahon Pledge, occupies centre

stage in the controversial history of British diplomacy in the Arab East. In his letters to McMahon, the Sharif, who was in contact with nationalist secret societies al-Fatat and al-Ahad as well as various nationalist figures, articulated Arab demands for the establishment of an independent state. McMahon's response, rich with artfully vague diplomatic speak, gave assurances to Hussein of British support for Arab independence, provided that such assurances did not conflict with the interests of France and were mindful of Britain's own arrangements in and plans for Mesopotamia. From the geographical space delineated by Hussein, the McMahon letters excluded Alexandretta and the areas to the west of the districts of the Syrian interior – Damascus, Homs, Hama and Aleppo – which the British apparently did not deem sufficiently Arab. McMahon also indicated in his letter that British interest in Baghdad and Basra had to be safeguarded through 'special administrative arrangements'.

It is widely acknowledged among scholars that the Sykes-Picot Agreement of 1916 and the Balfour Declaration of 1917 – the first essentially conceding Syria and Lebanon to the French, the second endorsing the establishment of a Jewish national home in Palestine – made the fulfilment of the McMahon Pledge to Hussein practically impossible.

The importance of the Arab Revolt itself to the Allied Armies' strategy in the East has been much debated, but there is a consensus of opinion that, at a minimum, sabotage activities along the Hijaz railway and successful raids on the port of Aqaba and other locations important to field Marshal Edmund Allenby's Egyptian Expeditionary Force were effective in sapping the energies of the Ottoman army and drawing it away from the strategically pivotal Suez Canal.

Cavafy, P Constantine (1863–1933): Cavafy is recognised today as one of the twentieth century's most influential poets. He described himself as an 'historical poet', and was passionately committed to Hellenism, recreating in his historical poems episodes of life in an ancient East that offered vivid expressions of it.

Cavafy's city, Alexandria, real and mythical, was as significant to his verse as it was to his life. In youth, his relationship with the city was turbulent and often painful, but as he settled into midlife, he became increasingly devoted to the Mediterranean city where he was born. Except for an eight-year interruption spent in England (1872–77) and Constantinople (1882–85), Cavafy lived all his life in Alexandria.

This Greek poet, who worked for close to three decades as a clerk in the Water Irrigation Department in the Public Works Ministry of Egypt, never sold his poems (a collected edition was first published posthumously in 1935), but did privately print and distribute a few of them to a select group of readers and friends, E. M. Forster among them.

It should be noted for the purposes of this memoir, that Marguerite Yourcenar, who translated Cavafy's poems into French, and Lawrence Durrell, were ardent admirers of his.

City of the Dead, Cairo: The City of the Dead, which is located on the edge of Cairo's medieval Islamic city, boasts some of Cairo's finest Islamic shrines and mosques. This burial place was created by Amr ibn al Ass, the Arab conqueror of Egypt (639–641AD), to accommodate his newly established capital, al Fustat. The gravesites in the City of the Dead cater to the dead and their living relatives, typically incorporating a courtyard and rooms to permit extended visits with the deceased.

By the 1930s, the City of the Dead had already begun to offer long-term residence to Egypt's underclass. In the ensuing decades, it became a near-permanent home to rural migrants and poor Cairenes desperate for housing in a city suffering from increasingly severe housing shortages. Today, the City is a vast urban expanse.

Curzon, George Nathaniel Marquess (1859–1925): Lord Curzon was one of the British Empire's chief diplomats in the latter part of the ninteenth and early part of the twentieth century. He was Viceroy of India between 1898 and 1905 and served on the

Eastern Committee of the War Cabinet during WWI, capping his career as British Foreign Secretary between 1919 and 1924.

Fairouz (*c.*1935): Although Lebanon's Fairouz never quite reached the regional heights of Egypt's Umm Kalthoum, she easily established herself as her country's premier singer. In her heyday in the 1960s and 1970s, Fairouz often blended love ballads with patriotic songs, crying over the loss of Arab land as she would over personal heartbreak.

Feisal ibn al Hussein I, King of Iraq (1885–1933): Feisal was the third son of Sharif Hussein ibn Ali. Between 1916 and 1918, he led the Arab Revolt against Ottoman rule, coordinating his military campaign closely with the Allied Armies' assault on the Ottoman army.

In 1918, very soon after the surrender of Turkish troops in Damascus, Feisal formed a provisional government that presumed to administer the whole of natural Syria, including Palestine and Lebanon. In January 1919, he went to the Paris Peace Conference to garner support for an independent Hashemite Syrian state, but his efforts met with formidable resistance from England and France: the French considered Syria and Lebanon its spheres of influence, as agreed with the British in the 1916 Sykes-Picot Agreement, and the British were careful not to upset arrangements concluded with the French and promises made to the Zionists to help establish a 'Jewish home' in Palestine.

In the ensuing months, while trying to create a firm foothold in Syria to preempt the advent of the French Mandate, Feisal embarked on a series of unsuccessful initiatives designed to reconcile French interests with his and those of the anti-French Syrian nationalists. In 1919, he established the Syrian National Congress, a parliamentary body, with the purpose of expanding and strengthening the institutional structures of his reign. In February 1920, the Congress proclaimed Feisal constitutional King of an independent 'Syria with all its natural boundaries', but in the end, Feisal and his supporters were no match for the French. On July 24, 1920, only five months after he was crowned

King, the Syrian army was routed by French troops in the Battle of Maysaloun. A few days after, Feisal left Syria for good.

In 1921, England's Cairo Conference drew the final political map of the British Mandate in the Near East and made Feisal king of Iraq. A referendum gave the new monarch a near unanimous popular vote and approved the establishment of a constitutional monarchy. However, notwithstanding Feisal's close alliance with England, his policies were often at odds with British commands and interests, leading Winston Churchill to rail against Feisal as an ingrate. In Hanna Batatu's words: 'though a creation of the English, the Hashemite monarchy was, in the first two decades of its life, animated by a spirit inherently antithetical to theirs.' (See 'The Diversity of Iraqis, the Incohesiveness of their Society and their Progress in the Monarchical Period Toward a Consolidated Political Structure', in *The Modern Middle East*, p. 512.)

In spite of Feisal's best efforts to implant deep roots for his family in Iraq, Hashemite hold on the country proved very turbulent and ultimately very brief, ending, in 1958, in a violent *coup d'état*.

French and British Mandates in the Arab East: The mandate system was created in 1919, under Article 22 of the Covenant of the League of Nations. The mandate's ostensible mission was to help the newly formed Arab states, carved out of a defeated Ottoman Empire, towards self-rule. In reality, it reflected long-standing British and French colonial interests in the region. The French assumed the mandate for Lebanon and Syria, the British for Iraq, Palestine and Trans-Jordan.

While the British sank inexorably into the morass that would very quickly become the Palestinian-Israeli dilemma and got busy moulding out of different Mesopotamian provinces a unified Iraq, the French spent the duration of their tenure breaking up and reattaching different parts of Syria, embarking upon a series of policies designed to dilute nationalist sentiment and encourage the parochial tendencies of the country's minorities. In 1920, they launched Greater Lebanon as a separate nation, adding to Mount Lebanon the cities of Tripoli, Beirut, Sidon, Tyre, the surrounding

southern terrain and the Bekaa Valley. They also set up Damascus
and Aleppo as two separate states, thereby partitioning an already
emasculated Syria. While the cities of Hama and Homs were
joined to the Damascene state, Alexandretta, which formally
remained part of the Aleppine state, was accorded considerable
autonomy. In 1922, they designated Jabal Druze (the Druze
Mountain) a separate entity and declared the Alawite region an
independent state. A federation encompassing the three states of
Damascus, Aleppo and the Alawite region was then established,
only to be dissolved again in 1924, when Damascus was merged
with Aleppo and the Alawite region was kept separate. In 1936,
they pulled the four entities together under one Syrian banner
but, in 1939, reestablished Jabal al Druze and the Alawite area as
separate units. Finally, in 1942, the four entities were regrouped
again as part of the Syrian state (see P. Khoury, *The French
Mandate*, pp. 58–9).

Full-fledged negotiations between Syria's National Bloc and the
French government commenced in 1936, culminating in a treaty
of independence that the French Chamber of Deputies did not
ratify. Syria finally won independence eight years later, in 1944,
but French troops did not fully evacuate the country till 1946.

Hussein ibn Ali, Sharif of Mecca (1853–1931): He was a direct
descendant of the Prophet Mohammad, through the prophet's
grandson Hassan, and the last of a very long line of Hashemite
custodians of Mecca which began towards the end of the twelfth
century.

Sharif Hussein belonged to the Aouni branch of the Hashemite
family, which historically competed for influence in the Hijaz with
the Zaidi line. His father never became Emir of Mecca, but he
himself assumed that mantle in 1908, having been appointed to
the position by the Ottoman Sultan Abdul Hamid II, to whose
realm the entire Hijaz belonged. But the ascension of this
ambitious Sharif to arguably the most prestigious post in Islam
was not without intrigue. His tepid enthusiasm for his uncle
Aoun al Rafiq's (1882–1905) incumbency forced him to take up

residence for fifteen years in Istanbul as the 'guest' of the Sultan. His own assumption of the custodianship, in 1908, was not without its tricky moments, for he was not the only contender for the job. Sharif Ali Haidar, a Zaidi, fought for the appointment as well. It appears that Ali was the preferred choice of the Young Turks, the clique of officers and officials who had just forced Abdul Hamid to accept a new constitution, but the Sultan managed to place Hussein at the helm of Mecca.

Therefore there was no twist of irony in Hussein's volte-face towards the Ottomans in 1916, when he declared the Great Arab Revolt against the Empire and proclaimed himself king of Hijaz. In rising up against the Ottomans, Hussein was expressing his chagrin with the Young Turks as much as he was pursuing his own longstanding political ambitions.

But those ambitions were never realised. After the war, the terms of the Paris Peace Conference and the mandate system sanctioned later by the League of Nations rendered the establishment of a Hashemite Arab kingdom unachievable. Hussein accused the British of betraying promises made in the wartime Hussein-McMahon correspondence and rejected the Versailles Treaty, a stance which contributed much to England's growing preference for Hussein's longtime rival Abd al Aziz ibn Saud of the Al Sauds of Nejd in central Saudi Arabia. In March 1924, when the Turkish Parliament abolished the Ottoman Caliphate, Hussein declared himself Caliph (leader of all the Muslims) but his position against ibn Saud had grown palpably weaker. Defeated in battle, he was forced to abdicate to his son Ali, in October of the same year, and went into exile in Cyprus. Ali's own beleaguered reign lasted eleven months. In December 1925, he too abdicated, leaving Sultan Abdul Aziz ibn Saud uncontested master of the land. The triumphant ibn Saud then proceeded to unite the various tribes and regions of Arabia under his realm, finally founding, in 1932, the kingdom Saudi Arabia.

Shortly before his death in 1931, Hussein settled in Trans-Jordan. He was buried in Jerusalem.

Hussein ibn Talal, King of Jordan (1935–99): Hussein's great grandfather was Sharif Hussein ibn Ali, and his grandfather was Abdullah ibn al Hussein, founder of the Hashemite Emirate of Transjordan in 1921, which became the Hashemite kingdom of Jordan in 1946.

After the assassination of Abdullah in Jerusalem, in 1951, Talal, Hussein's father, ascended the throne, but illness and the British brought his rule to a swift end, forcing the country into the temporary care of regents until his eldest son could come of age. Hussein became king in 1953, during a very stormy decade that nearly wrecked his reign. His country's resource-poor landscape was peppered with hundreds of thousands of Palestinian refugees (the saddest evidence of the 1948 Arab defeat), the region itself was shaping up as a major Cold War arena and many among Jordan's political elite were just as unenthusiastic about him as they were about his family. More ominously, Egypt under Gamal Abdel Nasser, the Arab world's rising strongman, was fast-becoming a main agitator against the young Hashemite monarch.

Throughout his forty-seven-year tenure, Hussein would be viewed by his enemies as the latest in a line of Hashemites who had colluded with the Zionists and were beholden to their Western patrons. He survived many assassination attempts and a PLO challenge, in 1969–70, which came close to costing him his throne. But by the time he died in 1999, after a long fight with cancer, he had become the region's most enduring patriarch, a master politician – those who loved him, and many besides, could claim with ease – who relied much more on political skill than brutality in managing the affairs of state and transforming Hashemite Jordan from a political question mark into a solid fact.

King Hussein married Lisa Halabi (Queen Noor) in 1978.

Irslan, Shakib, Prince (1869–1946): Irslan, from the Shouf Mountain of Lebanon, hailed from one of the Levant's most prominent Druze families. He was a polemicist and, before the fall of the Ottoman Empire in 1918, a passionate advocate of pan-Islamism under its tutelage. He was wary of Arab Nationalism and opposed to its secular orientation, believing that a resurgent and reformed Ottoman state was the Muslims' only hope of escaping Western domination. Even after the demise of the Ottomans, Irslan continued to call for Arab independence under an Islamic banner.

In the early 1920s, Irslan co-founded and became secretary of the Syro-Palestinian Congress, which was established by a number of notables to argue the Arab case against the mandate system before the League of Nations in Geneva. Irslan and Ihsan al Jabri, both of whom resided in Geneva in the 1920s and 1930s (al Jabri until 1936) became members of the Permanent European Delegation charged with representing the Syrian and Palestinian cases before the international body.

Lahham, Duraid (1934–): For a while, no political dissident, no social critic, no actor or comedian, came close to Lahham in giving eloquent vent to the Arab world's social maladies and political haplessness. In the 1960s and 1970s, through the seemingly clownish character of his Ghawwar al Tawsheh, a merrymaking Syrian prankster, Lahham painted a scathing satire of life in Arab society.

Ghawwar was popular enough by the mid-1960s but became a star in 1971, thanks largely to his very successful series, *Sahh al Nawm*,[425] which first aired on television in that year. But Lahham can take only part of the credit for Ghawwar's success. From the start of his acting career in 1960, Lahham was the wisecracking half of the acting duo Ghawwar and Husni al Barazan (the late Nihad Qa'li). If it were not for the overweight Husni's very well played sucker, Ghawwar's machinations might not have been as sidesplitting.

It was also thanks to the late and brilliant Mohammad al Maghout, one of the Arab world's most talented playwrights, that Lahham's two plays, *Day'it Tishrine* (October Village, 1974) and *Kassak Ya Watan* (Cheers, Oh Nation, 1978), were such exquisite renditions on the Arab-Israeli conflict.

Lawrence, T. E. (1888–1935): Ned, as Thomas Edward Lawrence was nicknamed, was the second of five illegitimate sons to Thomas Chapman and Sara Junner, who opted to live a non-matrimonial life together when the first Mrs Chapman refused to grant her husband a divorce.

Lawrence's youth was spent in Oxford, his university days at Oxford's Jesus College. His first encounter with the Near East was in 1909, when he was still at university. Interested in crusader castles, he embarked on a summer trip to Syria, covering a thousand miles on foot and studying the thirty-six castles which provided him with the essential material for his thesis on 'The Influence of the Crusades on European Military Architecture to the End of the Twelfth Century'. In 1910, he graduated with a first class degree in history.

Lawrence went back to the Middle East in 1911 as an apprentice archaeologist. He joined D. G. Hogarth (a British archaeologist with whom Lawrence had already formed an acquaintance at Oxford and who would become a mentor to him) on a dig in Carchemish in northern Syria. By 1914, Lawrence's familiarity with the language and terrain of the area made him very useful to the British Empire. He and Leonard Wolley, a fellow archaeologist, were hired to camouflage a military intelligence survey of the Sinai desert with an archaeological purpose.

After the outbreak of the war, Lawrence's work for his country began in earnest. In December 1914, he was dispatched to Cairo to help establish a much needed Military Intelligence Department. By 1916, he was on the side of Feisal ibn al Hussein and his Arab forces to help direct their sabotage activities against the Ottoman army.

In the post-war settlements period, Lawrence, in typical form, acted as both a confidant to Feisal and an agent of empire. In 1919, he participated in the Paris Peace Conference as a member of Feisal's delegation, in the hope that the prince would be able to extricate Syria, with British acquiescence, from the tutelage of the French, to whom Lawrence was particularly allergic. However, neither he nor Feisal had the wherewithal to overcome England's reticence to alter in any measurable way the terms of the 1916 Sykes-Picot Agreement. In 1921, Lawrence was enlisted as an adviser to Winston Churchill, then Colonial Secretary, during the Cairo Conference, which was convened to put the final touches on the British Mandate's political setup in the Near East. It was this map that placed Hashemite Feisal and Abdullah in Iraq and Trans-Jordan, respectively, an accomplishment Lawrence considered principally his own.

After several petitions, Lawrence was finally accepted into the Royal Air Force in 1925, but fame and controversy continued to intrude on his RAF service and life. The publication of *The Seven Pillars of Wisdom* during those years solidified his celebrity status and rendered his efforts to live a quiet, withdrawn life all the more difficult. But Lawrence stayed in the RAF till 1935, a few weeks before his death in a motorcycle accident.

Lawrence's *The Seven Pillars of Wisdom*, a fascinating account of a war effort that blends character studies and autobiography with military strategy and political and cultural commentary, is his most celebrated literary achievement, but it is not the only one. Along with a couple of translated works, Lawrence wrote *The Mint*, a memoir of his years at the Royal Air Force, which was published posthumously.

Ma'an: Ma'an, which ranks today as one of Jordan's poorest cities, was part of the Hijaz before the British annexed it to the nascent Emirate of Transjordan in 1925. Its serious susceptibility to Islamic fundamentalist currents has given it a weight among Jordanian towns that far outstrips its tiny size.

The history of Ma'an stretches back to the Sabaeans (the people of ancient Saba in south Arabia). Thanks to Lawrence of Arabia, this once active pilgrim stop should be known to quite a few outside of Jordan as one of the stations on the Hijaz railway (which linked Damascus with Medina and Mecca) that were targeted and captured as part of the Arab armies' efforts to disrupt Turkish supply lines in WWI.

Ottoman Empire (1281–1922): By the fifteenth century, the Ottoman dynasty, founded by Osman I, was already presiding over an expanding empire from their capital at Constantinople (Istanbul).

On the eastern front, by 1517 the Ottomans were in control of the Arab region. However, the Safavids of Persia continued to fend off their encroachments well into the seventeenth century (finally losing Baghdad in 1638 to Murad IV), when, ironically, the Ottomans were already in decline.

The waning of the Ottoman Empire was painstakingly slow, effectively starting in the latter part of the seventeenth century and officially ending with the Treaty of Sèvres in 1920.

Palestine Liberation Organisation (PLO): In 1964, the Arab League established the PLO in recognition of the Palestinian people's right to their own liberation movement in the fight for statehood. Regional powers, Nasser's Egypt foremost among them, sponsored the move to catch up with the rising tide of Palestinian nationalism and to control its tools of expression.

Originally, the aim of the PLO, which brought together different Palestinian factions under one umbrella, was to liberate the whole of Palestine, but eventually the movement recognised the right of Israel to exist and accepted a two-state solution.

Ahmad Shukeiri (1964–1967) and Yahya Hummuda (1967–69) headed the organisation before Yasser Arafat, the leader of Fatah (the strongest among Palestinian guerrilla groups) won the chairmanship in the Palestine Congress meeting of February 1969.

Petra: Petra, in the south of Jordan, was the capital of the Nabataean Kingdom which began to flourish in the second century BC. During its apex, Petra thrived as a trading city strategically located on the southern Arabia incense, silk and spice trade routes that connected China and India with the Mediterranean. After its annexation by the Roman Empire in 106AD, Petra suffered gradual decline, largely due to the rise of maritime trade and the ascendance of the city of Bosra in present-day Syria.

Today, the 'rock city', which was rediscovered in 1812 by the Swiss explorer J. L. Burckhardt, is considered one of the most spellbinding historical sites in the world.

Saladin (1137–93): He was chosen by Dante as one of the 'virtuous non-Christians' to be included in Limbo, alongside the likes of Plato, Socrates and Ibn Rushd (Averroes), and whenever medieval Europe spoke or wrote of him it was almost always with deep respect, even veneration.

Founder of the Ayyubid dynasty (1174–1260) and sultan of lands much vaster than Egypt, where his Sultanate began, Saladin was born in Tikrit to a Kurdish family with strong links to the Seljuk Atabegs (governors) of Northern Iraq and Syria, who, under Imad al Din Zengi, built their own Zengid dynastic house in the twelfth century.

Saladin first went to Egypt in the company of his warring uncle Shirkuh, lieutenant to Nur al Din, son of Imad al Din and ruler of Aleppo and Damascus. During the 1160s, Shirkuh was dispatched to Egypt at the head of a series of campaigns in support of one Fatimid faction against another. In 1169, having subdued all camps within the Fatimid family, Shirkuh became vizier of Egypt, the position to which his nephew acceded upon his uncle's death in the same year.

By the time Nur al Din died in 1174, Saladin's ambitions had become too threatening to the Zengid ruler. He was already dominant in the Hijaz, Gaza and Ayla (1170) and had already deposed the last Fatimid Caliph (1171), thereby bringing Shiite Egypt to an end and re-imposing Sunni dominance in an East long pulled apart by Abbasid and Fatimid rivalry and debilitating divisions within an Islamic community run by all manner of competing major and minor dynasties. In fact, Saladin could not manage his finally successful assault against Jerusalem, in 1187's Battle of Hattin, before doing away with the last of the Zengids and bringing Syria and Northern Iraq under his sway (Damascus in 1174, Aleppo and Mosul in 1176).

The one feat for which Arabs and Muslims often hail Saladin

is that of conquering Jerusalem and wresting it from Crusader hands. However, the saviour of Jerusalem was not immediately and always victorious against his Crusader adversaries. In 1177, Saladin was defeated at the Battle of Montgisard by the forces of Jerusalem's Baldwin IV, the Knights Templar and Raynald of Chatillon. And after the Battle of Hattin, the city of Tyre, under Conrad of Montferrat, twice resisted Saladin's sieges, before King Richard I's own forces dealt the formidable Ayyubid a serious blow, in 1191, at the Battle of Arsuf. Jerusalem itself, however, remained in Arab hands.

The Ayyubids lasted in Egypt until 1250, and in Syria until 1260, although small Ayyubid realms lasted in certain pockets of Syria well into the fourteenth century. It was the Mamluks, the Ayyubids' own warrior slaves, who brought Saladin's dynasty to an end.

San Remo Conference (1920): The conference, which was held by the Allied Supreme Council (France, Great Britain, Italy, Greece, Belgium, and Japan) in Italy in April 1920, officially endorsed terms agreed in the Paris Peace Conference of 1919. It was in San Remo that the *Class A* mandates in the former Arab provinces of the Ottoman Empire were assigned to France and Britain. The mandates went further than the Sykes-Picot Agreement, giving France the whole of Syria and Lebanon, while assigning Palestine (including Transjordan) and Iraq to Britain.

Sykes Picot Agreement (1916): The agreement was the culmin-ation of secret negotiations between the French Francois-Georges Picot and the British Mark Sykes to resolve the two countries' competing interests in the Arab provinces of the Ottoman Empire.

The agreement divided the provinces into three main areas:

- *The Blue Area* under direct French control: the north Syria littoral reaching down to the gates of Acre beyond Beirut.
- *The Red Area* under British control: Basra and Baghdad.
- *Area A* comprising the French sphere of influence: The Syrian

interior (Damascus, Aleppo, Hama and Homs) and Mosul in northern Mesopotamia.

- *Area B* comprising the British sphere of influence: Jordan and Palestine, excluding Jerusalem.
- *Areas to be administered by an international body*: Jerusalem and the Holy places.

Weizmann, Chaim (Haim) (1874–1952): In the critical years of the early twentieth century, Weizmann, born in Belarus and a scientist by training, was one of the Zionist movement's most able activists. He became a British citizen in 1910, and his persistence, not to mention very nimble negotiating style, helped persuade the British government to issue the famous 1917 Balfour Declaration endorsing the formation of a 'Jewish national home' in Palestine. He served twice as president of the World Jewish Organisation and became the Jewish state's first president in 1948. Ezer Weizman, one of Israel's most capable military and political leaders and its president from 1993 to 2000, was the nephew of Chaim Weizmann.

Weizmann, in his own scientific field of chemistry, is also known as the 'father of industrial fermentation'.

Bibliography

Ahmed, Leila, *Women and Gender in Islam*, New Haven, Yale University Press, 1992

Ajami, Fuad, *The Arab Predicament*, Cambridge, Cambridge University Press, 1992

Al Ayashi, Ghaleb, *Tarikh Souria Al Sisyassi (The History of Political Syria)*, Beirut, Ashkar Ikhwan Printers, 1955

Al Hakim, Yousuf, *Souriyya wa al'A'hd al Feisali (Syria and The Era of Feisal)*, Beirut, Dar An-Nahar, 1986

Al-Jundi, Ahmad, *Fi Thikra Saaddallah al Jabri* (In Memory of Saadallah al Jabri), Damascus, Talas Publishing, 1948

Al-Khani, Abdullah, *Jihad Shukri al Quwwatli fi Sabil Al-Istiqlal wa al Wihdah* (The Struggle of Shukri Quwwatli for Independence and Unification), Beirut, Dar An-Nafa'es, 2003

Al Nounou, Mouti', *Mann Ightal al Wihdah al Masriyya al Souriyya?* (Who Assassinated the Egyptian-Syrian Union?), Beirut, Ouwaidat Publishing, 2004

Altounyan, Taqui, *Chimes From a Wooden Bell*, London, I. B. Tauris & Co. Ltd, 1990

Arar, Ziad Mansour, *Tarikh Umma fi Hayat Rajul, Arba' Sanawat fi al A'ahd al Watani, August 17, 1943–1947* (The History of a Nation in the Life of a Man: Four Years in the Nationalist Era), Beirut, Dar Al Ahad, 1947

Azm, Khaled, *Mudhakarat Khaled Azm (The Memoirs of Khaled Azm)*, Beirut, Dar Al Muttahidah Publishing, 2003. Volumes: 3

Baker, Randall, *King Husain and the Kingdom of Hejaz*, Cambridge, England, The Oleander Press, 1979

Batatu, Hanna, *Syria's Peasantry, the Descendants of Its Lesser Notables, and Their Politics*, New Jersey, Princeton University Press, 1999

Cleveland, William, *Islam Against The West: Shakib Arslan and The Campaign for Islamic Nationalism*, Texas, University of Texas Press, 1985

Copeland, Miles, The *Game of Nations*, New York, Simon and Schuster, 1969

Cooper, Mark, *The Transformation of Egypt*, Baltimore, The Johns Hopkins University Press, 1982

Di Lampedusa, Giuseppe, Tomasi, *The Leopard*, London, The Harvill Press, Random House, 1996

Djait, Hichem, *Europe and Islam*, Berkeley, California, University of California Press, 1985

Durrell, Lawrence, *Alexandria Quartet*, US, Penguin Books, 1991

Eldem Edhem; Goffman; Matsers, Bruce, *The Ottoman City between East and West. Aleppo, Izmir, and Istanbul*, Cambridge, Cambridge University Press, 1999

Fedden, Robin, *English Travelers in The Near East*, London, Longmans, Green & Co for the British Council and The National Book League, 1958

Fletcher, Richard, *The Cross and the Crescent*, New York, Penguin, 2003

Forster, E. M. *Alexandria, A History and A Guide*, New York, Oxford University Press, 1986

Furlonge, Geoffrey, *Palestine is My Country: The Story of Musa Alami*, Great Britain, Butler and Tanner Ltd, 1969

Graves, Robert; Hart, Liddell, *T. E. Lawrence, Letters to his Biographers*, London, Cassell & Company Ltd, 1938

Gordon, Joel, *Nasser's Blessed Movement*, Cairo, American University Press, 1992

Haag, Michael, *Alexandria, City of Memory*, New Haven, Yale University Press, 2004

Hirst, Anthony & Silk, Michael ed. *Alexandria Real and Imagined*, Hampshire, Ashgate Publishing Limited, 2004

Hopwood, Derek (Editor), *Studies in Arab History*, London, The Macmillan Press Ltd, 1990

Hourani, Albert, *A History of the Arab Peoples*, Cambridge, Massachusetts, Belknap Press of Harvard University Press, 1991

Hourani, Albert; Philip S. Khoury; Mary C. Wilson, *The Modern Middle East*, London, I. B. Tauris & Co Ltd, 1993

Irslan, Adel, *Mudhakarat al Amir Adel Irslan* (The Memoirs of Prince Adel Irslan), Beirut, Dar al Taqadumiyyah Publishing, 1983, Volumes: 3

Irslan, Shakib, *A Memoir*, Beirut, Dar Al Taliqah, 1969

Kazin, Alfred, *Contemporaries*, Boston, Little Brown, 1962

Khalidi, Rashid; Lisa Anderson; Mohammad Muslih; Reeva S. Simon, *The Origins of Arab Nationalism*, New York, Columbia University Press, 1991

Khoury, S Philip, *Syria and The French Mandate: The Politics of Arab Nationalism, 1920–1945*, London, I. B. Tauris & Co, Ltd, 1987

Khoury, S Philip, *Urban Notables and Arab Nationalism: The Politics of Damascus, 1860–1920*, Cambridge, Cambridge University Press, 1983

Keeley, Edward, *Cavafy's Alexandria*, Princeton, Princeton University Press, 1976

Lawrence, T. E. *The Seven Pillars of Wisdom: A Triumph*, New York, Anchor Books, 1991

Mack, E. John, *A Prince of Our Disorder*, Cambridge, Massachusetts, Harvard University Press, 1998

Marcus, Abraham, *The Middle East on the Eve of Modernity: Aleppo in the Eighteenth Century*, New York, Columbia University Press, 1989

Massad, Joseph A., *Colonial Effects: The Making of National Identity in Jordan*, New York, Columbia University Press, 2001

McGilvary, Margaret, *The Dawn of a New Era in Syria*, United Kingdom, Garnet Publishing, 2001

Meriwether, Margaret L., *The Kin Who Count: Family and Society in Ottoman Aleppo, 1770–1840*, Texas, University of Texas Press, 1999

Meriwether, Margaret L. & Tucker, Judith, *A Social History of Women and Gender in the Middle East*, Colorado, Westview Press, 1999

Morray, David, *An Ayyubid Notable & His World: Ibn Al-Adim & Aleppo as Portrayed in His Biographical Dictionary of People Associated with the City*, Leiden, E. J. Brill, 1994

Moss, Robert Tewdwr, *Cleopatra's Wedding Present: Travels Through Syria*, Wisconsin, The University of Wisconsin Press, 1997

Mousa, Suleiman, *T. E. Lawrence: An Arab View*, London, Oxford University Press, 1966

Petras, James, *Critical Perspectives on Imperialism and Social Class in the Third World*, New York, Monthly Review Press, 1978

Qassmieyyeh, Khieryyeh, *Al Raeel Al Arabi Al Awwal: Hayyat Wa Awraq Nabih and Adel Al Azmah (The first Arab Generation: The Lives and Papers of Nabih and Adel al Azmah)*, London, Riad El-Rayyes Books, 1991

Rodenbeck, Max, *Cairo, The City Victorious*, New York, Vintage Books, 2000

Rogan, Eugene L, Avi Shlaim, *The War for Palestine: Rewriting the History of 1948*, Cambridge, Cambridge University Press, 2001

Roolvink, R., *Historical Atlas of the Muslim People*, Amsterdam, Djambatan, 1957

Said, Edward, *Reflections on Exile, and Other Essays*, Massachusetts, Harvard University Press, 2002

Said, Edward, *Orientalism*, New York, Vintage Books, Random House, 1994

Seale, Patrick, *The Struggle for Syria: A Study of Post-war Arab Politics, 1948–1958*, London, I. B. Tauris, 1965

Seale, Patrick, *Assad*, London, I. B. Tauris, 1988

Shahid, Husseini, Serene, *Jerusalem Memories*, Beirut, Nawfal Group SARL, 1999

Shlaim, Avi, *The Iron Wall*, New York, W. W. Norton & Company, Ltd, 2000

Tabbaa, Yasser, *Constructions of Power and Piety in Medieval Aleppo*, Pennsylvania, Pennsylvania State University Press, 1992

Tachua, Frank, *Political Elites and Political Developments in the Middle East*, Cambridge, Massachusetts, Schenkman Publishing Inc, 1975

Thomson, Elizabeth, *Colonial Citizens, Republican Rights, Paternal Privilege, and Gender in French Syria and Lebanon*, New York, Columbia Press, 2000

Wallach, Janet, *Desert Queen*, New York, Anchor Books, 1999

Waterbury, John, *The Egypt of Nasser and Sadat*, New Jersey, Princeton University Press, 1983

Weeden, Lisa, *Ambiguities of Domination*, Chicago, University of Chicago Press, 1999

Westgate, Bruce, *The Arab Bureau: British Policy in the Middle East, 1926–1920*, Pennsylvania, The Pennsylvania State University Press, 1992

Wilson, Jeremy, *Lawrence of Arabia*, London, Heinemann, 1989

Woodward, Peter, *Nasser*, New York, Longman Limited, 1997

Yourcenar, Marguerite, *Memoirs of Hadrian*, London, Penguin Books, 1986

Zeine, Zeine, *The Struggle for Arab Independence: Western Diplomacy & the Rise & Fall of Faisal's Kingdom in Syria*, New York, Caravan Books, 1977

JOURNALS

Kermani, Navid, 'Silent Sirens', Commentary, *Times Literary Supplement*, October 1, 2004, pp. 12–15

Lawrence, T. E. 'Syria: The Raw Material'. The British National Archives. Ref: FO 882/26–247482. 1915, pp. 107–14

Sontag, Susan. 'Notes on Camp'. 1964, pp. 1–10

Watenpaugh, Keith. 'Middle-class Modernity and the Persistence of the Politics of Notables in Inter-war Syria'. *International Journal of Middle East Studies*, (35) 2003, pp. 257–86

NEWSPAPERS

Syria

'He Lived Honourably and Died Honourably'. *Al Ayyam Newspaper* (front-page tribute), June 22, 1947

'Will Saadallah al Jabri Marry Empress Fawziah or a Princess from the King's Household?' *Al Ayyam Newspaper*, January 1, 1947

'Interview with Saadallah al Jabri'. *Al Ayyam Newspaper*, December 23, 1936

Rayyess, Naguib. 'The Man We Are Eulogising Today Wanted to Build a State'. *Al Qabas Newspaper* (front-page tribute), April 6, 1948

'During the Reign of Saadallah al Jabri's Cabinet'. *Al Sabah Newspaper*, April 9, 1939

Lebanon

Mrowa, Kamel. 'An Example . . . in Saadallah al Jabri'. *Al Hayat Newspaper* (front-page tribute), June 25, 1947

Jordan

Dougherty, Pam. 'What Kind of Future Do We Leave Our Children?' *The Jerusalem Star Newspaper*, June 16, 1983

Ne'matt, Salamet. 'Gifts Left By Time'. *The Jordan Times Newspaper*, July 1, 1995

Sayyegh, George. 'Impressionism and Expressionism in the Works of Ali al Jabri'. *Al Dustur Newspaper*, June 22, 1983

USA

Rothstein, Edward. 'Shelf Life; Serendipitous History of the Gift of a Word'. Rev. of *The Travels and Adventures of Serendipity*, by Robert K. Merton and Elinor Barber. *New York Times*, January 31, 2004

Cohen, Roger. 'A Blood Bond Brings 2 Allies Together Again'. *The International Herald Tribune*, March 12, 2005, p. 2

LECTURES

Morgenthaler, Hans. 'Peter Eisenman's Realist Architecture', The Stanford Presidential Lectures and Symposia in the Humanities and Arts, 1998, p. 1

Tueni, Ghassan. 'Azamt al Hukum Ba'd al Nakssah' (The Crisis in the System after the Relapse). *An Nahar file*, II. 1967, pp. 1–46

MAGAZINES

'Interview: Ali al Jabri, The Pain of Painters with Causes'. *Eastern Art Report*, October 1990, pp. 20, 21 & 31

Kroll, Jack. 'Genet's Algerian Epic'. *Newsweek Magazine*, December 12, 1971, p. 58

DIARIES

Saadallah al-Jabri 1936 Diaries. Not published. Dar Al Sayyad (Al Saayad Publishing House, Lebanon)

Saadallah al-Jabri 1929 Diaries. Not published. Markiz al Abhath al Wathaiqiyyah (Center for Historical Documents), Damascus, Syria

Ali al Jabri Diaries, 1970–2002: The Ali al Jabri Foundation

LETTERS

The Gertrude Bell Archives at Robinson Library, Newcastle University, England

Ali al Jabri's letters to Diala and Hala al Jabri: Diala al Jabri

Ali al Jabri letters to Antonia Gaunt: Antonia Gaunt

Ali al Jabri letters to Saadieyh al Tall and Wasfi al Tall: Diala al Jabri

Ali al Jabri's letters to Ronald Cohen: Ronald Cohen

Ali al Jabri letters to Allan Walrond: Allan Walrond

Ali al Jabri letters to Beth Regardz: Beth Regardz

Other family letters: Diala al Jabri

REPORTS

Criminal Case number 1063/2003 Investigation Report: The Murder of Ali Majddedine al Jabri

INTERVIEWS

London, England

Antonia Gaunt: October 1, 2003 & January 31, & February 1, 2004

Kate Cliffe: January 26, 2004

Rick Watson: January 30, 2004 & 24 May 2004

Diana Buirski: January 31, 2004, 1 February 2004

Frank Drake: January 31, 2004

Allan Walrond: February 1, 2004 & May 19, 2004

Ronnie Cohen: February 1, 2004 & May 26, 2004

Sara Waterson: Series of e-mails during the course of 2004 & 2005: January 21, 22, 23 & 25, 2004; February 23, 26 & 27, 2004; March 1 & 4, 2004; June 16, 2004; July 13, 2004; November 14, 2004: January 13 & 14, 2005

Raghida Ghandour: May 13, 2005

John Dollar: June 8, 2005

Julia Hornak: Correspondence, July 20, 2005

Sir Morris Laing: Correspondence, March 2, 2004

Amman, Jordan

Diala Jabri: June 3, June 5, June 7 & November 8, 2003; March 9, March 10 & August 29, 2004

Rula Atallah Ghandour: November 28, 2004

Widad Kawwar: November 30, 2004

Essa Halabi: December 1, 2004

Hazem Malhas: December 1, 2004; June 25, 2005 (conducted in Beirut)

Salwa Dajani: June 14, 2004

Fadwa Salah: July 1, 2004

Fadi Ghandour: December 10, 2004

Nawal Abdullah: December 11, 2004

Nuha Batchon: December 12, 2004

Jaffar Toukan: January 19, 2005

Aysar Akrawi: January 22, 2005

Rami Sajdi: February 24, 2005

Tony Atallah: February 23, 2005

Khaldun Husari: May 15, 200

Luxor, Egypt

François Larche: April 10, 2004 & April 11, 2004

Aleppo, Syria

Alia Jabri: October 18, 2004

Joumana Geurani: April 22, 2005

Beirut, Lebanon

Sheikha Eltaf Al Sabah: July 15, 2004

Suhail Bisharat: July 26, 2004; June 26, 2005

Cecil Hourani: February 5, 2005

Bahija al Solh al Asaad: August 4, 2005
Khaldun Kikhia: August 9, 2005

CORRESPONDENCE

The United States

Beth Regardz: August 1, 2004; March 5, 2005
Ann Miller: March 12 & 14, 2005
Michael Moore: January 19, 2005

Notes to the Text

1 Ali al Jabri 2002 diary. Entry: January 19.

2 Ali al Jabri 1998 diary. Entry: July 10.

3 Interviews with Salwa Dajani (June 14, 2004); Fadwa Salah (July 1, 2004); Nuha Batchon (December 12, 2004.)

4 Ali al Jabri 2002 diary. Entry: February 1–2.

5 Interview with Antonia Gaunt, September 27, 2003.

6 Ali al Jabri 1971 diary. Entry: December 19.

7 Joseph Massad, *Colonial Effects, the Making of National Identity of Jordan* (New York: Columbia University Press, 2001), p. 245. At the time of the September strike, al Tall was one of King Hussein's closest advisers but he had not yet been appointed prime minister. That actually took place on October 28, 1970.

8 Cited in Asher Susser's *On Both Banks of the Jordan* (Oregon: Frank Kass, 1994), p. 152. The full quote reads as follows: 'We shall . . . purge the ranks – all the ranks – of those professional criminals who pose as fida'yyun (guerilla fighters), to save fida'i action itself from the evil designs against it.'

9 Massad, *Colonial Effects*, p. 247.

10 Letter to Saadieyh and Wasfi al Tall, November 29, 1970.

11 Cited in Asher Susser's *On Both Banks of the Jordan* (Oregon, Frank Kass, 1994), p. 170.

12 Ibid., p. 168. It should be mentioned that Saadieyh refuted this account to Diala.

13 Interview with Fadwa Salah, July 1, 2004.

14 Ali al Jabri December 1971 diary. Ali's journal entries, for the most part, were left unedited.

15 Interview with Diala Jabri (June 3, 2003); Nawal al Abdullah Kattan (December 11, 2004); Salwa Dajani (June 14, 2004); Fadwa Salah (July 1, 2004).

16 Letter from Ali al Jabri to Diala al Jabri on June 13, 1975.

17 Ali al Jabri 1973 diary. Entry: June 9.

18 Unsent letter from Ali al Jabri to Diney Buirski, most probably written sometime in late 1968 or 1969.

19 All the excerpts are my translations from French, the language in which Saadieyh and Ali corresponded.

20 Interview with Diala al Jabri, June 3, 2003.

21 Ibid.

22 Diala al Jabri correspondence, July 12, 2004.

23 Interview with Diala al Jabri, June 7, 2003.

24 Ali al Jabri 1980 diary. Entry: September 29.

25 Letter from Hala al Jabri to Saadieyh al Tall, April 25, 1974.

26 Letters from Diala al Jabri to Saadieyh, March 4, 1973, March 25, 1974, April 20, 1977.

27 Correspondence with Diala al Jabri , July 12, 2004; interview on March 9, 2004.

28 Ali al Jabri letter to Diala al Jabri, April 17, 1975.

29 Letter from Ali al Jabri to Ronnie Cohen, July 22, 2001.

30 Dr George Sayyegh, 'Impressionism and Expressionism in the Works of Ali al Jabri', *Al Dustur Newspaper*, June 22, 1983.

31 Edmund Keeley, *Cavafy's Alexandria* (New Jersey: Princeton University Press, 1996), pp. 19–23.

32 Ali al Jabri 2002 diary. Entry: June 19.

33 From an Ali al Jabri letter to Ronnie Cohen, July 22, 2001.

34 Ali al Jabri 1999 diary. Entry: July 2.

35 Ali al Jabri 1985 diary. Entry: August 15–16.

36 Ali al Jabri 1995 diary. Entry: July 14.

37 Letter to Ronnie Cohen, December 12, 1998.

38 Ali al Jabri 1979 diary. Entry: August.

39 Interview with Rula Atallah Ghandour, November 28, 2004.

40 From Ali's letter to the organisers of the Disorientation Project in the House of World Culture in Berlin, held in February 2003. The letter was published in the Disorientation Volume, p. 110.

41 Ibid.

42 Interviews with Fadi Ghandour (December 10, 2004); Hazem Malhas (December 1, 2004); Rula Atallah Ghandour (November 28, 2004).

43 Interview with Essa Halabi, December 1, 2004.

44 Interview with Fadi Ghandour, December 10, 2004.

45 Interview with Allan Walrond, May 19, 2004.

46 Ali al Jabri 1977 diary. Entry: April 12.

47 Both Ali (in his diaries) and Diala (in her interviews) mention that Hala and Majddedine obtained postgraduate degrees from US universities, the former from Berkeley, the latter from a university in Michigan. The author's own research to date has been able to confirm Hala's undergraduate degree from Vassar and Majddedine's engineering diploma from Robert College in Turkey.

48 Abba Eban (1915–2002) was one of Israel's most talented diplomats. He became representative to the UN in 1948, ambassador to Washington DC in 1950, an elected member of the Knesset in 1959, and joined more than one Labour cabinet as Minister without Portfolio (1959), Education and Culture Minister (1960–1963), Deputy Prime Minister (1963–1966) and Minister of Foreign Affairs (1966–1974).

49 Ali al Jabri diary. Entry: December 1971.

50 Ibid.

51 Correspondence with Beth Regardz, August 1, 2004.

52 Interview with Aysar Akrawi, January 22, 2005.

53 Interview with François Larche, April 10, 2004.

54 Interview with Fadi Ghandour, December 10, 2004.

55 Margaret Meriwether, *The Kin Who Count: Family And Society In Ottoman Aleppo, 1770–1840* (Texas: University of Texas Press, 1999), pp. 52 & 82.

56 Abraham Marcus in his *The Middle East On The Eve Of Modernity. Aleppo in the Eighteenth Century* (New York: Columbia University Press, 1989) states on p. 61 that Ashrafs' 'ranks swelled in the eighteenth century as ambitious men bribed their way into membership with the aid of fraudulent genealogies.'

57 Ibid., p. 62.

58 Meriwether, *The Kin Who Count*, p. 82–4.

59 Arab Awakening was first coined by George Antonius in his celebrated 1938 book which championed Arab nationalism and argued that its origins could be traced to the mid-nineteenth century.

60 Interview with Antonia Gaunt, January 31, 2004.

61 Letter from Ali al Jabri to Antonia Gaunt, July–August, 1977.

62 Ali al Jabri 1977 diary. Entry: September.

63 Letter from Ali al Jabri to Antonia Gaunt, April 15, 1977. In 'Cairo', in *The Modern Middle East* (ed. Albert Hourani, Philip Khoury & Mary Wilson. London: I. B. Tauris & Co Ltd, 1993), Andre Raymond writes about the cities of the dead which Ali describes: 'finding no space towards the east available for urban expansion, the human tide which has submerged the city has progressively colonised the cities of the dead of Qaitbay and Qarafa, where the tombs were built like real houses, set out in an organised network of roads' (p. 328).

64 Ali al Jabri 1979 diary. Entry: January 16.

65 Interview with Allan Walrond, February 1, 2004.

66 Interview with Hazem Malhas, December 1, 2004.

67 T. E Lawrence, *The Seven Pillars of Wisdom. A Triumph* (New York: Anchor Books, 1991), p. 30.

68 Ibid., p. 24.

69 Ali al Jabri 1980 diary. Entry: April: 5. These words by Lawrence appear on p. 38 in the original *Pillars*. But the quote in Ali's diary has been altered somewhat. Lawrence, in the *Pillars*, states, 'They were a dogmatic people, despising doubt, our modern crown of thorns. They did not understand our metaphysical difficulties, our introspective questionings. They knew truth and untruth, belief and unbelief, without our hesitating retinue of finer shades . . . Their imaginations were vivid, but not creative. There was so little Arab art in Asia . . . '

70 Interview with Raghida Ghandour, May 13, 2005.

71 Interview with Ronnie Cohen, May 26, 2004, & Raghida Ghandour, May 13, 2005.

72 Ali al Jabri 1977 diary. Entry: February.

73 Ali al Jabri September–November 1974 diary.

74 Interview with Diala al Jabri, June 3, 2003.

75 Madaba and Karak, two cities with a vividly rich Christian past, are both to the south of Amman. Ja'afar al Tayyar is an intriguing choice by Ali. Al Tayyar, the cousin of Mohammad and brother of Ali ibn abi Taleb, is one of Islam's most celebrated martyrs. He was killed in 629, in the battle of Mu'ta (south of Karak), the first face-off between the forces of the Prophet Mohammad and the Byzantines. But perhaps equally significant is Tayyar's connection to Ali ibn abi Talib, the fourth and last of the immediate successors of the Prophet, al Khulafa' al Rashidun, or the Rightly Guided Caliphs. Both Ja'afar and Ali belonged to Ahl al Beit, the House of Mohammad, to which the Hashemites themselves belong. Ali (d. 661), who was married to the Prophet's daughter Fatima, and his two sons, Hassan (d. 669) and Hussein (d. 680), are also Shiism's first three Imams and are considered by Shiites as the rightful political heirs of Mohammad. Ali and Hussein were slain in modern-day Iraq; Ali while praying in Kufa, Hussein in battle at Karbala. Hassan, it is suspected, was poisoned by his wife Ja'ada.

76 Letter from Ali al Jabri to Antonia Gaunt, January 14, 1979.

77 Ibid.

78 Lawrence, *SPW*, p. 351.

79 Letter from Ali al Jabri to Antonia Gaunt, January 14, 1979.

80 Interview with John Dollar, June 8, 2005.

81 Ali al Jabri 1979 diary. Entry: January 19.

82 Interview with John Dollar, June 8, 2005.

83 Lawrence, *SPW*, p. 351.

84 Ibid., p. 375.

85 Letter from Ali al Jabri to Antonia Gaunt, January 14, 1979.

86 Lawrence, *SPW*, p. 638.

87 Ibid., p. 102.

88 Letter to Ronnie Cohen, May 20, 1977.

89 Ironically, this Jordanian Badia uniform was a British concoction. It was the design of John Glubb Pasha, the British head of the Arab Legions, Jordan's army, for twenty-six years

until his dismissal by King Hussein in 1956 (Massad, *Colonial Effects*, p. 120).

90 Jeremy Wilson, *Lawrence of Arabia* (London: Heinemann, 1989), p. 95.

91 Lawrence, *SPW*, Dedication at the beginning of the book.

92 Lawrence, *SPW*, pp. 29–30.

93 Ibid., p. 564.

94 In his biography of Lawrence, John E. Mack attributes Lawrence's total lack of interest in sex to puritanism rather than asexuality: 'The evidence certainly does not support the view that Lawrence was "asexual", but rather that his early development brought about a deep need to reject and devalue all intimacy between sexes, and gave rise to intense fears and inhibitions that prevented action'. (John. E. Mack, *A Prince of Our Disorder*. Cambridge: Harvard University Press, 1998), pp. 420–1

95 Lawrence, *SPW*, p. 564.

96 For the rape incident, see *SPW* pp. 443–7. Much has been written about Lawrence's rape in Deraa by Turkish soldiers attempting to break him for the benefit of their pederast officer, a certain Hajim Bey. Of special interest to Lawrence's many biographers was the rape as a signifier of Lawrence's homosexuality, since he did admit to feeling sexual pleasure during the incident ('I remembered smiling idly at him, for a delicious warmth, probably sexual, was swelling through me . . . '). In the Oxford text version, Lawrence also wrote that in the aftermath of the assault he was 'feeling very ill . . . Probably it had been the breaking of the spirit by that frenzied nerve-shattering pain which had degraded me to beast level when it made me grovel to it, and which had journeyed with me since, fascination and terror and morbid desire, lascivious and vicious perhaps, but like the striving of a moth towards its flame.' (Cited in Mack's *A Prince of Our Disorder*, p. 231.) Of his appreciation for the male physique, Lawrence once wrote that 'I take no pleasure in women. I have never thought twice or even once of the shape of a woman: but men's bodies, in repose or in movement – especially the former, appeal to me directly and very generally.' (Cited in John E. Mack's *A Prince of Our Disorder*, p. 425.)

97 Wilson, *LOA*, p. 673.

98 Lawrence, *SPW*, p. 47.

99 T. E. Lawrence, 'Syria the Raw Materials' (1915), p. 112. FO/882/26. The rest of the quote reads as follows: 'Their wish is to be left alone to busy themselves with others' affairs. From childhood they are lawless, obeying their fathers only as long as they fear to be beaten, and their government later for the same reason: yet there are few races with a greater respect than the upland Syrian for customary law.'

100 Wilson, *LOA*, p. 544. A letter to G. J. Kidston, 1919; footnote 6 on p. 1100.

101 Lawrence, *SPW*, p. 58–9.

102 Ibid., p. 337.

103 Wilson, *LOA*, p. 248. Wilson contends that Lawrence wrote these words with the specific intent of competing against the India Colonial Office's proposition for the East, which aggressively argued against a Hashemite deal.

104 Ali al Jabri 2000 diary. Entry: March 21.

105 Ali al Jabri 1977 diary. Entry: April 21, 1977.

106 Letter from Ali al Jabri to Antonia Gaunt, July–August, 1977.

107 Ali al Jabri 1984 diary. Entry: June 22.

108 Wilson, *LOA*, p. 524. This is quoted from a 1918 letter to his friend V. W. Richards.

109 Lawrence, *SPW*, pp. 31–2.

110 Wilson, *LOA*, p. 95. The full quote reads as follows: 'The perfectly hopeless vulgarity of the half-Europeanised Arab is appalling. Better a thousand times the Arab untouched. The foreigners come out here always to teach, whereas they had better learn, for in everything but wits and knowledge the Arab is generally better man of the two.'

111 Edward Said, *Reflections on Exile, and Other Essays* (Cambridge, Massachusetts: Harvard University Press, 2002), p. 33.

112 Ibid., p. 32.

113 Wilson, *LOA*, p. 184. Lawrence stated this in an early 1915

report for the Arab Bulletin: 'Syria: the Raw Material' (AB, no. 44. 12.3.1917), p. 110. The *Pillars* echoes this perspective.

114 Lawrence, *SPW*, pp. 334–5, & Wilson, *LAO*, p. 185. These words also appeared on page 111 in Lawrence's report for the Arab Bulletin in early 1915, 'Syria the Raw Materials'.

115 Cited in Wilson, *LOA*, p. 100.

116 Lawrence, *SPW*, p. 219.

117 Edhem Eldem, Daniel Goffman, and Bruce Masters. *The Ottoman City between East and West, Aleppo, Izmir, and Istanbul* (Cambridge: Cambridge University Press, 1999), quoted from Masters section on Aleppo, p. 19.

118 David Morray, *An Ayyubid Notable & His World: Ibn Al-Adim & Aleppo as Portrayed in His Biographical Dictionary of People Associated With the City* (Leiden: E. J. Brill, 1994), pp. 2–6.

119 Philip Khoury, *Syria and The French Mandate. The Politics of Arab Nationalism, 1920–1945* (London: I. B. Tauris & Co, Ltd, 1987), pp. 28–37. Philippe Berthelot (1866–1934) joined the French Foreign Office in 1904. He was General Secretary of the Quai d'Orsay from 1920 to 1922 and from 1925 to 1932. Alexandre Millerand (1859–1943) was France's War Minister from 1912 to 1913 and from 1914 to 1915. He became Prime Minister in 1920 and ascended to the presidency nine months later. He was a member of the senate from 1925 to 1940.

120 Ali al Jabri 1983 diary. Entry: Late June or early July.

121 Umran Amman Al Qadeemah. Booklet produced by Mohammad Rafee', Amman, 2002. Handassah Magazine, produced by The Engineering Federation of Aleppo. Seventh year, 23rd edition, 2001. Interview with Diala Jabri, June 3, 2003. Ali December 1971 diary.

122 Draft letter from Ihsan al Jabri to King Khaled and Prince Fahd ibn Abd al Aziz of Saudi Arabia. Letter not dated, but it must have been written sometime between 1975 and 1977, during Khaled's short reign as King. Cleveland, *Islam Against the West*, p. 50.

123 Rashid Khalidi in his 'Ottomanism and Arabism in Syria Before 1914', in *The Origins of Arab Nationalism* (New York: Columbia

University Press, 1991), names Nafe as one of thirteen Arab representatives in the Mabou'than who began to veer towards Arabism as a response to the 'more intensely' Turkish Committee of Union and Progress (CUP) (p. 54 & 59).

124 Master, *The Ottoman City*, p. 76. The other notables included Hussam al Din al Qudsi and Kawakibi.

125 Interview with Alia al Jabri, October 18, 2004. Saadallah Jabri 1929 diary.

126 Interview with Sheikha Eltaf al Sabah, July 15, 2004; interview with Diala al Jabri, June 3, 2003.

127 Wilson, *LOA*, pp. 472–3 (excerpts from a report Lawrence wrote about Syrian exile groups).

128 Ibid., p. 472.

129 Henri de Jouvenel was High Commissioner of the French Mandate in Syria in 1925–6.

130 The Gertrude Bell Archives at Robinson Library, Newcastle University, England. Letter is dated February 1, 1926.

131 Khoury, *The French Mandate*, p. 125.

132 In February 1920, the National Syrian Congress elected Feisal King. He was crowned in an official ceremony on March 8, 1920.

133 For more on the backgrounds of Syrian notables, see Philip Khoury's *Urban Notables and Arab Nationalism*.

134 At the end of WWI, geographical Syria embraced today's states of Syria, Jordan, Palestine and Lebanon. The partitioning of the Levant was first agreed between Britain and France under the Sykes–Picot Agreement of 1916, and then refined and finalised in the 1920 San Remo Conference, which assigned class A mandates in the Arab provinces to England and France.

135 Yousuf al Hakim, *Souriyya wa al A'hd al Feisali* (Beirut: Dar An-Nahar, 1986), p. 92.

136 Elizabeth Thompson, *Colonial Citizens, Republican Rights, Paternal Privilege, And Gender in French Syria and Lebanon* (New York: Columbia Press, 2000), p. 119.

137 Cited in Wilson, *LOA*, p. 589.

138 Cited in Zeine Zeine's *The Struggle for Arab Independence. Western Diplomacy & the Rise & Fall of Faisal's Kingdom in Syria* (New York: Caravan Books, 1977), p. 57. Footnote no 38.

139 Cited in Wilson, *LOA*, p. 196. Not surprisingly, Hashemite assertions were regarded as no less laughable by the French. Commenting on Feisal's manoeuvres in Syria during his brief reign as king, Maurice Barres, a member of the French Academy and a Chamber deputy, said, 'Feisal's comedy has gone far enough. No nation other than France possesses in so high a degree the particular kind of friendship and genius which is required to deal with the Arabs.' Cited in Zeine Zeine's *The Struggle for Arab Independence*, p. 110.

140 Lawrence, *SPW*, p. 565.

141 Robert Graves & Liddell Hart, *T. E. Lawrence, Letters to his Biographers* (London: Cassell & Company Ltd, 1938), T. E. Lawrence notes to Graves, p. 113.

142 Shortly before his death, Hussein joined his son king Abdullah in Trans-Jordan.

143 Graves & Hart, *Letters*, pp. 113 & 114.

144 Cited in Wilson, *LOA*, p. 806. Letter to Mrs Bernard Shaw.

145 Serene Hussein Shahid, *Jerusalem Memories* (Beirut: Naufal Group Ltd, 2000), p. 37; interview with Diala Jabri, June 3, 2003; interview with Alia al Jabri, October 18, 2004.

146 Interview with Joumana Geurani, the great niece of Subheiyeh Guerani, April 22, 2005. This is confirmed by two other sources close to the Jabris who asked to remain anonymous.

147 Term used by William Cleveland in *Islam Against The West. Shakib Arslan and the Campaign for Islamic Nationalism* (Texas: University of Texas Press, 1985), p. 22 (under picture of Irslan).

148 William Cleveland in his *Islam Against the West* concludes:

At a time of land reform, educational expansion, and tentative, state socialism, those whose aim had been to preserve an ordered aristocratic system were dismissed as socially insensitive . . . Once the reins of government passed to upwardly mobile reform-minded army officers, men of Arslan's background and attitude lost their mystique and came to be reproached generally, as he and al-Jabri once were specifically, for their Ottoman atavism, their Turkish manners, and their politique de façon Hamidienne. (p. 162)

149 Interview with Widad Kawwar, November 30, 2004.

150 Furlong, Geoffrey, *Palestine is My Country, The Story of Musa Alami* (Great Britain: Butler and Tanner Ltd, 1969), p. 87. Interview with Cecil Hourani, February 5, 2005.

151 Shahid, *Memories*, p. 42.

152 Diala al Jabri correspondence, July 16, 2005; interview with Diala, June 5, 2003.

153 Interview with Joumana Geurani, April 22, 2005.

154 Shahid, *Memories*, p. 43.

155 On her mother's deterioration, Diala wrote to the author that 'she valiantly fought court cases for our rights . . . Won some, lost some. Drained by the years. The Kuwaiti courts killed lesser men.' (March 20, 2008)

156 Saadallah al Jabri 1936 diary. Entry: July 19.

157 In addition to the family letters and Serene Shahid's chapter on Hala in *Jerusalem Memories*, Hala's impressionistic portrait has been constructed from the collective descriptions of Diala al Jabri, Salwa Dajani, Fadwa Salah, Khaldun Husari, Cecil Hourani, Khaldun Kikhia, Bahija al Solh al Asaad, Sir Morris Laing, Sheikha Altaf al Sabah, Ali's own comments to Antonia Guant, Allan Walrond, John Dollar and Raghida Ghandour. See Interviews, pp. 118–19.

158 The term Syrian here refers to inhabitants of geographical Syria, and not 'citizens' of Syria as a nation-state, which did not exist at that time. Under the Mandate system, in August 1920, Syria was partitioned into separate units under French and British tutelage, and Greater Lebanon was proclaimed. To Mount Lebanon, mostly Christian, was added Tripoli, Sidon, Tyre, the surrounding areas that had previously fallen under these cities' administration, Beirut, and the Bekaa' Valley. See Philip Khoury's *Syria And The French Mandate*, pp. 57–8.

159 Interviews with Salwa Dajani (June 14, 2004); Cecil Hourani (February 5, 2005).

160 Interview with Diala al Jabri, June 3, 2003.

161 Giuseppe Tomasi di Lampedusa, *The Leopard* (London: The Harvill Press Random House, 1996), pp. 124–5.

162 Interview with Hazem Malhas, December 1, 2004.

163 Ali al Jabri 1985 diary. Entry: April 17.

164 Interestingly, the Jabris brought to mind *Il Gattopardo* to quite a few people who knew them or came to study them. Raghida Ghandour (May 13, 2005) was one good friend who made references to the novel when talking about Ali. Keith Watenpaugh, in his 'Middle-class Modernity and the Persistence of the Politics of Notables in Inter-war Syria', *International Journal of Middle East Studies*, (35) 2003, quotes Tancredi in Lampedusa's tale, p. 267.

165 Saadallah al-Jabri 1936 Diaries. Entry: June 23, Paris.

166 Ibid., entry: September 22, in transit to Turkey from Paris.

167 Ibid., entry: June 8, Paris.

168 Ibid., entry: August 3. Hashim Atassi (1875–1960), of the al Atassis of Homs, was three-time president of Syria: 1936–1939; 1949–1951; 1954–1955. Atassi was also one of the founders of the National Bloc, the organisation that, in 1927, brought Syria's main nationalist leaders under one umbrella.

169 Ibid., entry: September 3, Paris.

170 Ibid., entry in February, sometime between the 15th and the 19th, Syria.

171 Saadallah al Jabri, 'He Lived Honourably and Died Honourably', *al Ayyam Newspaper*, June 22, 1947, front page. Khoury, *The French Mandate*, p. 125.

172 Saadallah's 1929 dairy is replete with references to money difficulties. Also, Keith Watenpaugh, in 'Middle-class Modernity and the Persistence of the Politics of Notables in Inter-war Syria', refers to this same diary in alluding to Saadallah's financial problems (p. 263).

173 Others not mentioned here are: Ahmad Rajai', Dia', Ihsan.

174 Saadallah al-Jabri 1929 diary. Entry: February 16.

175 'Will Mr Saadallah al Jabri Marry Empress Fawzieh or A Princess from The King's Household', *al Ayyam Newspaper*, January 1, 1947.

176 Amir Adel Irslan, *Mudhakarat al Amir Adel Irslan* (Beirut: Dar al Taqadumiayyah Publishing, 1983), II, p. 676 (my translation). The entry in Irslan's diary is dated January 4, 1947.

177 Interview with Khaldoun Kikhia, August 9, 2005.

178 Saadallah Jabri in a front-page interview with *al Ayyam Newspaper*, 'Interview with Saadallah al Jabri', December 23, 1936.

179 There is a consensus that Saadallah was one of the earlier converts to Arabism if not Arab nationalism (see pp. 61–2 in Rashid Khalidi's *The Origins of Arab Nationalism* for definitions). However, Keith Watenpaugh, in his 'Middle Class Modernity', suggests that Saadallah may not have been as ardent a nationalist in his earlier years as is commonly believed – 'he probably saw himself as an Ottoman while a student in the capital and in the army' – but he does concede that Saadallah was one of the first notables to 'embrace a nationalist ideology' (p. 265).

180 Saadallah held several prominent positions both before and after the independence of Syria in 1946: Minister of Interior and Foreign Affairs (1936–1939); Prime Minister (August 19, 1943–October 14, 1944 and October 1, 1945–December 16, 1946); Speaker of Parliament (November 1944–October 1945).

181 Patrick Seale, *The Struggle for Syria. A Study of Post-war Arab Politics, 1948–1958* (London: I. B. Tauris, 1965), p. 28. The National Bloc was formed in 1927 with the singular aim of ending the French mandate and achieving the full independence of Syria. Its orientation was secular and its core leadership was largely Sunni, land owning and city/town dwelling, but its top ranks included members of the mercantile class as well.

182 Interview with Salwa Dajani, June 14, 2004.

183 See Khaled Azm, *Mudhakarat Khaled Azm* (Beirut: Dar Al Muttahidah Publishing, 2003), I, p. 248; Irslan, II, p. 683.

Front-page tribute in *al Hayat Newspaper* by Kamel Mrowa,
'An Example . . . in Saadallah al Jabri', June 25, 1947; front-
page tribute in *al Qabas Newspaper* by Naguib Rayyess, 'The
Man We Are Eulogising Today Wanted to Build a State', April
6, 1948.

184 Khieryyeh Qassmieyyeh, *The Vanguard/Al Raeel Al Arabi Al
Awwal. Hayyat wa Awraq Nabih and Adel Al Azmah* (London:
Riad El-Rayyes Books Ltd, 1991), p. 159; 'During the Reign
of Saadallah al Jabri's Cabinet', *al Sabah Newspaper*, April 9,
1939; Irslan, II, p. 683.

185 Hanna Batatu, *Syria's Peasantry, the Descendants of Its Lesser
Notables, and Their Politics* (New Jersey: Princeton University
Press, 1999), p. 40. See also Elizabeth Thompson, *Colonial
Citizens*, for an incisive study of women's issues during
mandated Syria. For more background on the dynamic of
feminism in early twentieth century Egypt and the wider Arab
world, see Leila Ahmad's *Women and Gender in Islam* (New
Haven: Yale University Press, 1992), pp. 169–88; and Ellen
Fleischmann's 'The Other Awakening', in *A Social History of
Women and Gender in The Middle East*. Ed. Margaret Meriwether & Judith Tucker (Colorado: Westview Press, 1999),
pp. 89–122. Of Syrian women's participation in national
demonstrations, Fleischmann says, 'In Syria, women organised
their own nationalist demonstration during the visit of the
King-Crane Commission to Damascus in 1919 . . . During the
1922 nationalist demonstrations in Syria, women marched at
the head of the crowd, ululating "at such a high pitch, bringing
the thousands of men behind them to an explosive roar" and
causing the French to balk at using force' (p. 111).

186 Philip Khoury, in *The French Mandate*, writes: 'The
government wanted to avoid economic changes in industry and
agriculture that would foster growth of an organised urban
proletariat and emancipation of the peasantry. The members
of the government were all landowners or members of big land
owning families and they were anxious to preserve the
dominant position of their class' (p. 604).

187 *Al Ayyam*, June 22, 1947. The same is mentioned in

Saadallah's 1936 diaries and Ahmad al Jundi's book (*In Memory of Saadallah al Jabri*: Talas Publishing, Damascus, 1948) on Saadallah's one-year memoriam.

188 Interview with Alia al-Jabri, October 18, 2004.

189 For details on the scandal see Seale, *The Struggle for Syria* (pp.42–46) and *Mudhakarat Khaled al Azm*, v. II, pp. 181–2.

190 President al Quwwatli (1891–1967), of the Quwwatlis of Damascus, was twice elected to the presidency of Syria (1943–1949 & 1955– 1958). He was one of Syria's most prominent nationalists during its struggle for independence, heading at one stage the National Bloc.

191 Geoffrey Furlonge, *Palestine Is My Country*, p. 152.

192 Seale, *The Struggle for Syria*, p. 61.

193 For details on the successive governments between 1949 and 1958, see Patrick Seales's *The Struggle for Syria* and Abdallah Khani's *Jihad Shukri Quwwatli fi Sabeel al-Istiqlal Wal Wihdah*, pp. 80–2.

194 For more details of the account, see Khaled Azm's *Mudhakarat Khaled Azm*, v. II, p. 307, and v. III, p. 106.

195 Khaled Azm, *Mudhakarat Khaled Azm*, v. III, p. 105.

196 Letter to Antonia Gaunt, October 25, 1977.

197 Ali al Jabri's 1980 diary, entry March 13.

198 For details about the cabinets in which Majddedine served, see Patrick Seale's *The Struggle for Syria*, pp. 77 & 258.

199 Lt Colonel Abdel Karim Nahlawi and Brigadier Mawaffak Assassa of the Air Force were the two main leaders of the coup.

200 For a detailed background of the Syrian regimes' profile, see Hanna Batatu's *Syria's Peasantry, the Descendants of its Lesser Rural Notables*, pp. 144–52.

201 Batatu, *Syria's Peasantry*, p. 32.

202 Ali al Jabri, 1971 diary. Entry: January 5.

203 Ahmad al-Jundi, *In Memory of Saadallah al-Jabri* (Damascus: Talas Publishing), p. 127. No date of publishing is indicated. This defence aside, it should be noted that Saadallah and Hananu's political collaboration was not without its competitive moments.

204 Yasser Tabbaa, *Constructions of Power and Piety in Medieval Aleppo* (Pennsylvania: Pennsylvania State University Press, 1992), p. 53.

205 Interview with Rick Watson, January 30, 2003.

206 Interview with Allan Walrond, February 1, 2004. This is mentioned as well in the *Palo Alto Times* or *San Jose Mercury* article on Ali's disappearance, which was written sometime in September 1964.

207 Correspondence with Sir Maurice Laing, March 2, 2004.

208 Lawrence Durrell, *Justine* (New York: Penguin Books Ltd, 1991), p. 82.

209 Correspondence with Michael Moore, January 19, 2005.

210 Correspondence with Beth Regardz, March 5, 2005.

211 Ibid.

212 Ali's Stanford University Transcript, 1961–4.

213 Correspondence with Ann Miller, March 12 & 14, 2005.

214 Susan Sontag, 'Notes on Camp', 1964, p. 1.

215 Correspondence with Beth Regardz, March 5, 2005.

216 The article appeared in either the *Palo Alto Times* or the *San Jose Mercury*, sometime in September 1964. A copy of the article was in Beth Regardz's box of Ali keepsakes.

217 Letter from Ali al Jabri to Beth Regardz, October 10, 1964.

218 Letter from Ali al Jabri to Beth Regardz, November 19, 1964.

219 Letter from Ali al Jabri to Diala Jabri, April 1975.

220 Interview with Diala Jabri, November 8, 2003.

221 Correspondence with Sara Waterson, January 23, 2004.

222 Interview with Antonia Gaunt, February 1, 2004.

223 Correspondence with Sara Waterson, January 23, 2004; Interview with Antonia Gaunt, January 31, 2004.

224 Interview with Diney Buirski, January 31, 2004.

225 Ibid.

226 Correspondence with Sara Waterson, January 23, 2004.

227 Interview with Frank Drake, February 1, 2004.

228 Correspondence with Sara Waterson, March 4, 2004.

229 Letter to Majddedine and Hala, May 27, 1966.

230 Edward Rothstein, 'The Travels and Adventures of Serendipity', rev. of *The Travels and Adventures of Serendipity* by Robert K. Merton and Elinor Barber, *New York Times*, January 31, 2004.

231 Correspondence with Sara Waterson, January 23, 2004.

232 Ibid.

233 Interview with Frank Drake, February 1, 2004.

234 Letter from Ali al Jabri to Hala and Diala al Jabri, August 1967.

235 Letter from Ali al Jabri to Saadieyh al Tall, November 29, 1969.

236 Interview with Alia al Jabri, October 18, 2004.

237 Interview with John Dollar, June 8, 2005.

238 Ibid.

239 Correspondence with Sara Waterson, January 23, 2004.

240 Letter from Ali al Jabri to Saadieyh al Tall, July 1, 1970.

241 Ali al Jabri 1981 Diary. Entry: December 29.

242 Ali al Jabri 1970 diary. Entry: August.

243 Letter from Ali al Jabri to Diala al Jabri, May 21, 1976.

244 Ali al Jabri 1971 diary. Entry: September.

245 Ibid. Julia most probably refers to Julia Hornak, Dr Hourani's stepdaughter, who became a close friend of Ali's.

246 Letter from Ali al Jabri to Diala al Jabri, June 13, 1975.

247 Ibid.

248 Letter from Ali al Jabri to Saadieyh al Tall, November 29, 1970.

249 Ali al Jabri January–June 1973 diary. Entry: April 16. It seems intended as a draft of a letter. Recipient not mentioned.

250 Letter from Ali al Jabri to Diala Jabri, May 21, 1976.

251 Letter from Ali al Jabri to Diala Jabri, April 1975.

252 Ali al Jabri December 1971–February 1972 diary.

253 Letter from Ali al Jabri to Hala al Jabri January 1, 1971.

254 Ibid.

255 Ibid.

256 Letter from Ali al Jabri to Diala al Jabri, April 1975.

257 Ibid.

258 Letter from Ali al Jabri to Diala al Jabri, June 13, 1975.

259 Letter from Ali al Jabri to Diala al Jabri, September 1973.

260 Ali al Jabri December 1971–February 1972 diary. Entry: January.

261 Letter from Ali al Jabri to Diala al Jabri, June 13, 1975.

262 Ibid.

263 Ibid.

264 Ibid.

265 Ibid.

266 Ali al Jabri September–November 1972 diary.

267 Ali al Jabri January–June 1973 diary. Entry: April.

268 This series hangs on the walls of Ronnie Cohen's apartment.

269 A sketch of King Ashurbanipal in the September 1971 diary.

270 Ali al Jabri April–July 1976 diary.

271 Letter from Ali al Jabri to Diala al Jabri, April 17, 1975.

272 Ali al Jabri September–November 1972 diary.

273 Interview with Allan Walrond, May 19, 2004.

274 Ali al Jabri January–June 1973 diary. Entry: April.

275 Interview with Antonia Gaunt, October 1, 2003.

276 Ali al Jabri December 1971–February 1972 diary.

277 Ali al Jabri July–September 1972 diary. Excerpt from a draft letter to the editor. Newspaper not mentioned.

278 Ali al Jabri September–November 1974 diary.

279 Ali al Jabri September–November 1972 diary.

280 Letter from Ali al Jabri to Diala al Jabri, June 9–July 20, 1976.

281 Ibid.

282 Interview with François Larche, April 11, 2004.

283 Letter from Ali al Jabri to Diala and Hala al Jabri, December 21, 1975.

284 Letter from Ali al Jabri to Diala al Jabri, May 12, 1976.

285 Interview with Antonia Gaunt, October 1, 2003.

286 Amal Ghandour, the author.

287 Letter from Ali al Jabri to Diala and Hala al Jabri, December 21, 1975.

288 Lawrence Durrell, *Justine*, p. 17.

289 André Raymond's 'Cairo', in *The Modern Middle East*, details the number of foreigners in the Egyptian Capital in the 1920s. By 1927, the foreign community reached 59,460, out of whom there were 11, 221 British, 18, 575 Italians and 20,115 Greeks. There were also around 34,103 Jews. The overall population of the city was a little over one million (pp. 319–20).

290 Ali al Jabri 1977 diary. Entry: February 11.

291 Ali's Cairo diaries, unlike his other diaries, do not dwell on the names of or life with friends. However, they do mention Peroncel Hugo at least twice. Interviews confirm that Ali and Peroncel Hugo became very good friends.

292 Ali al Jabri 1977 diary. Entry: January 18. This demonstration was part of the famous food riots that erupted when President Anwar Sadat attempted to increase the price of bread. Andre Raymond ('Cairo' in *The Modern Middle East*) describes the riots as 'the revenge of another Cairo which one could have passed through for years without knowing anything about it.' (p. 332).

293 Letter from Ali al Jabri to Antonia Gaunt, October 25, 1977.

294 Letter from Ali al Jabri to Antonia Gaunt, July–August, 1977.

295 Letter from Ali al Jabri to Antonia Gaunt, October 25, 1977.

296 Ali al Jabri 1977 Diary. Entry: sometime in September 1977.

297 Joel Gordon, *Nasser's Blessed Movement* (Cairo: American University Press, 1992), p. 42.

298 Ali al Jabri 1977 diary. Entry: February 23–4.

299 Ibid., entry: February 10.

300 Ali al Jabri 1977 diary. Entry: possibly February.

301 Ibid., entry: possibly February.

302 Ibid.

303 Letter from Ali al Jabri to Diala al Jabri, December 17, 1977.

304 An Egyptian cigarette brand.

305 Ali al Jabri 1977 diary. Entry: possibly October.

306 Ibid.

307 Ibid, entry: April 21.

308   See Khaled al Azm, *Mudhakarat*, v. II, p. 467.

309   Letter from Ali al Jabri to Antonia Gaunt, October 25, 1977.

310   Max Rodenbeck. *Cairo, the City Victorious* (New York: Vintage Books, 2000), p. 131. Khedive Ismail was ruler of Egypt from 1863 to 1879.

311   In his 'Egypt and Europe: from French Expedition to British Occupation', in *The Modern Middle East*, Roger Owen provides a succinct analysis of the circumstances that led to the British occupation of Egypt in 1882. He concludes that 'finally the emergence of a popular, national movement in 1881 and 1882 seemed sufficiently threatening to European interests to call for the occupation of Egypt by British troops' (p. 120). For more details, see pp. 113–19.

312   Rodenbeck, *Cairo*, p. 141. Roger Owen, 'Egypt from the French Expedition', p. 123.

313   Cited in Wilson, *LOA*, p. 100.

314   Navid Kermani, 'Silent Sirens', Commentary, *Times Literary Supplement*, October 1, 2004, p. 15.

315   Ibid., p. 15.

316   Ibid., p. 12.

317   Ibid., p. 15.

318   For a concise review of the events that preceded the 1967 war, see Avi Shlaim, in *The Iron Wall* (New York: W.W. Norton & Company, Inc, 2000), pp. 236–41. Shlaim argues that Nasser had no intention to go to war, but embarked on 'an exercise in brinkmanship that was to carry him over the brink' (p. 237).

319   Ghassan Tueni, 'Azmat al Hukum Ba'd al Nakssah', (Regime Crisis After the Relapse), file 2, *An-Nahar Newspaper*, November 12, 1967, p. 1. The lecture was given on August 1, 1967, at the American University of Beirut.

320   Quoted and paraphrased by Fuad Ajami in his *The Arab Predicament* (Cambridge: Cambridge University Press, 1992), pp. 110–11.

321   Although the 1952 land reforms undermined the landed aristocracy, limiting holdings to 200 feddans (one feddan is equal to 1.038 acres or 0.42 hectares), they benefited principally those

owning between 11 and 50 feddans, Egypt's middle peasantry. Moreover, subsequent land reforms lowered the ceiling to further benefit this stratum. John Waterbury, in *The Egypt of Nasser and Sadat* (Princeton: Princeton University Press, 1983), argues that the regime's ties to the middle peasantry should not be exaggerated, but agrees there was close collaboration between the two (p. 59). Significantly, Nasser was averse to any form of political activity organised independently of his regime. Requests for trade unions in the agricultural sector were rejected even after 1957 when the regime supposedly turned towards Socialism. There were no schemes for profit sharing in agricultural areas and the minimum wage was unenforceable (see Patrick C. O'Brien, *The Revolution in Egypt's Economic System* (England: Oxford University Press, 1966), p. 296).

322   In 1952, the Free Officers regime banned all political parties and outlawed strikes. In the 1950s and 1960s, three parties were successively introduced by the state as the political mouthpieces of all classes and embodiments of its ideological message: the Liberation Rally (1953–1957), the National Union (1958–1961), and the Arab Socialist Union (1962). The Nasser regime was hostile to all parties of the left and right that claimed an independent inspiration and legitimacy. One of the most important actions by the new regime soon after its takeover was the crushing of the Kafr al Dawar workers' strike and the arrest and execution of Mustafa Khamis, the leader of the Communist Party. Its moves against the Muslim Brotherhood were no less harsh. One such example was the long imprisonment of Sayyid Qutub, the Muslim Brotherhood's most powerful voice in the 1950s and 1960s, and his execution in 1966, along with six of his compatriots.

323   One of the most famous assassinations was that of Kamel Mrowa, publisher of *al Hayat Newspaper*, one of the region's leading newspapers, and staunch Nasser critic. The investigation file on the 1966 hit points to the Egyptian intelligence services.

324   Miles Copeland in *The Game of Nations* (New York: Simon and Schuster, 1969) states that, by 1967, Egyptian bureaucracy

had one million civil servants, 800,000 more than the maximum capacity of the state (p. 128).

325 Peter Woodward, *Nasser* (New York: Addison Wesley Longman Limited, 1997), p. 113.

326 Copeland, *The Game*, p. 268.

327 Asher Susser, *On Both Banks of the Jordan*, pp. 124 & 127. In compliance with the defence pact signed between Jordan and Egypt before the 1967 war, the Egyptian command was responsible for the overall military response. The Egyptian Major General Abd al-Munim Riyad, Chief of Staff of the United Arab Command, commanded the Jordanian front.

328 L. Rogan and Avi Shlaim, ed. *The War of Palestine, Rewriting the History of 1948* (Cambridge: Cambridge University Press, 2001), pp. 208–9. The afterword was written by Edward Said. The quotes are not sequential, but reversed.

329 Ibid., p. 210.

330 Roger Cohen, 'A Blood Bond Brings Two Allies Together Again', *The International Herald Tribune*, March 12, 2005, p. 2.

331 Ajami, *Predicament*, p. 110.

332 Ibid., p. 133.

333 Robert Mabro in his 'Alexandria 1860–1960' (Anthony Hirst and Michael Silk, Ed, *Alexandria Real and Imagined*, Hampshire: Ashgate Publishing, 2004) indicates that in the early twentieth century foreigners, including non-Egyptian locals 'of Ottoman origin', represented 26 percent of the population (p. 248).

334 Durrell, *Balthazar*, pp. 151–2.

335 Durrell, *Mountolive*, p. 147.

336 For Durrell, Arabs and Copts are two distinct sects. In *Balthazar*: 'The communities still live and communicate . . . Arabs and Copts and Syrians . . . ' (p. 151).

337 E. M. Forster, *Alexandria: A History and a Guide* (New York: Oxford University Press, fourth edition, 1986). Introduction by Lawrence Durrell, p. xvi. Interestingly, Durrell, during his stay in Alexandria in the 1940s, did not seem that enamoured with the city about which he later wrote with such rapture. In

'A Passage through Alexandria: the City in the Writing of Durrell and Forster' (*Alexandria Real and Imagined*) David Roessel introduces a Durrell palpably unimpressed and bored with the city. Roessel argues that Durrell's original intentions were for a novel about Greece, his true love, but fear of alienating friends in such a small setting pushed him towards the Alexandria he had left behind. This, Roessel concedes, does not mean that Durrell's opinion of Alexandria did not change for the better by the time he started writing Justine. (pp. 324–8).

338 Durrell, *Mountolive*, p. 147.

339 Perhaps one of the sharpest reviews was by Alfred Kazin, who wrote: 'What is wrong with this novel is that it does not carry anything forward . . . It is writing that exists merely to call attention to Mr Durrell's exceptional literary sensibility . . . You know that Mr Durrell will jog along, more in touch with his own delightful imagination than with any of the notorious stinks, festers, sores, and dungheaps of Egypt . . . Mr Durrell seems to me fundamentally a writer concerned with pleasing his own imagination, not with making deeper contact with the world through his imagination.' (Lawrence Durrell's Rosy-finger'd Egypt in *Contemporaries*. Boston: Little Brown, 1962), pp. 189 & 191.

340 Khaled Fahmy, 'Towards a Social History of Alexandria', Anthony Hirst and Michael Silk, Ed, *Alexandria Real and Imagined* (Hampshire: Ashgate Publishing, 2004), p. 305. After the 1956 Suez war, Nasser's effort to 'retake' Egypt went into overdrive. In Michael Haag's words: 'All remaining British and French citizens were expelled from Egypt; a third of Egypt's Jews, mostly those with foreign nationality, were driven into exile by police harassment and economic pressure; and the remainder of the foreign community dwindled as manufacturers and exporters were Egyptianised. In a climate of fear and anger the old cosmopolitan Alexandria was destroyed.' (*Alexandria, City of Memory*, New Haven: Yale University Press, 2004), p. 318.

341 Forster, *Alexandria*, p. xviii.

342 Ibid., p. xvi.

343 Keeley, *Cavafy's Alexandria*, p. 5.

344 Ibid., pp. 4–5.

345 Ali al Jabri 1977 Diary. Entry: September 1.

346 Keeley, *Cavafy's Alexandria*, p. 5.

347 Letter from Ali al Jabri to Antonia Gaunt, October 25, 1977.

348 Jean Pierre Peroncel Hugo, *Le Radeau de Mohamet* (Paris, Liu Commun, 1983) p. 204.

349 Ali al Jabri 1980 diary. Entry: January 22.

350 Ibid., entry: February 28.

351 He took a brief course at the Musée des Arts et Traditions Populaires.

352 Ali al Jabri 1982 diary. Entry: August 12.

353 Letter from Ali al Jabri to Antonia Gaunt, May 10, 1979.

354 Joseph Massad, *Colonial Effects,* p. 15.

355 Interviews with Rula Atallah Ghandour (November 28, 2004); Allan Walrond (February 1, 2004); Raghida Ghandour (May 13, 2005); François Larche (April 10, 2004).

356 *The Baath Newspaper,* March 14, 1980.

357 Ali al Jabri 1980 diary. Entry: March 13. The disturbances Ali was referring to are those between government forces and the Islamic brotherhood. For details, see Patrick Seale's *Assad* (London, I. B. Tauris, 1988) which mentions two hundred dead (pp. 323–32).

358 Letter from Diala al Jabri to Saadieyh al Tall, July 7, 1980.

359 Ihsan was referring to the longstanding feud in central Arabia between the Rashids of the Shammar tribe and the Al Sauds of the Anazeh. The Ottomans supported the Rashids while the British leaned towards the Al Sauds.

360 The letter is not dated, but since it was addressed to King Khaled, whose reign was between 1975 and 1982, it must have been written sometime between 1975 and 1979, since Ihsan himself passed away in 1980.

361 Ali al Jabri 1982 diary. Entry: May 21.

362 Interview with Raghida Ghandour, May 13, 2005. The same emotions were conveyed to Fadi Ghandour, Rula Atallah Ghandour and Hazem Malhas.

363 Unsent letter from Ali al Jabri to Antonia Gaunt, sometime in June 1978.

364 Saadieyh established the government-supported museum in 1971.

365 Ali al Jabri 1980 diary. Entry: April 27.

366 Ibid., entry: June 20.

367 Ibid., entry: July 7.

368 Ibid., entry: July 21.

369 Ali al Jabri 1981 diary. Entry: March 5.

370 Ibid., entry: March 18.

371 Ali al Jabri 1984 diary. Entry: February.

372 Ali al Jabri 1990 diary. Entry: September 18.

373 Ali al Jabri 1987 diary. Entry: July 14.

374 Ali al Jabri 1981 diary. Entry: November 22.

375 Interviews with Raghida Ghandour (May 13, 2005); Fadi Ghandour (December 10, 2004); Hazem Malhas (December 1, 2004); François Larche (April 10, 2004).

376 Correspondence with Diala al Jabri, September 10, 2005.

377 Interviews with Cecil Hourani (February 5, 2005); Diala al Jabri (August 29, 2004).

378 King Hussein died on February 7, 1999.

379 Ali al Jabri 1999 diary. Entry: January 28. In 1999, Queen Noor invited Ali and Jaafar Toukan, one of Jordan's most well established architects, to propose their visions of Hussein's mausoleum. For the project Ali did extensive research of the mausoleums of historical Muslim leaders and made a special trip to Jerusalem. Of Ali's final design, Toukan states: 'It was a design of beautiful perspectives, glimpses of spatial visions. However, he did not take into consideration the setting and ignored real considerations. The design reflected only his dreams; they showed a cluster of ideas, inspired by Jerusalem's Dome of the Rock and a few Islamic mausoleums, but not consolidated into a specific project.' To the Queen's request that space next to King Hussein be allowed for her, Ali responded that he 'could not see Your Majesty dead'. So he skipped that part of the assignment. Interview with Jaafar Toukan, January 19, 2005.

380 Ali al Jabri 1980 diary. Entry: June 19.

381 Ibid., entry: June 7.

382 Interview with Rula Atallah Ghandour, November 28, 2004.

383 The official permission for Ali's burial in Petra (a privilege already accorded to archaeologist Ken Russell, Ali's only neighbour on that hilltop) was obtained through the efforts of Prince Raad.

384 Interview with Fadi Ghandour, December 10, 2004.

385 Jack Kroll, 'Genet's Algerian Epic', *Newsweek Magazine*, December 12, 1971, p. 58.

386 Ali al Jabri 1984 diary. Entry: November.

387 Homs is one of Syria's main cities.

388 Edom covered the area between the southern shore of the Dead Sea and Northern Aqaba. Archaeologists place Edom in the eighth or ninth century BC; however, recent excavations suggest it may have existed as early as the eleventh century BC.

389 Ali al Jabri 1981 diary. Entry: April–May.

390 Ali al Jabri 1983 diary. Entry: October or November.

391 The time frame is very early 1980s.

392 1982–3.

393 The fifteenth-century Mausoleum is located in Balkh, Afghanistan.

394 Interviews with François Larche (April 10, 2004); Raghida Ghandour (May 13, 2005); Nawal al Abdullah Kattan (December 11, 2004); Suhail Bisharat (June 26, 2005).

395 Interview with Nuha Batchon, December 12, 2004. She owns the Gallery which held two exhibitions of Ali's works, the first in 1979 and the last in 2000.

396 Ali held six exhibitions between 1978 and 2002: 1978 (location unknown); 1979 at the Gallery; 1983 at The National Gallery; 1984 at the British Council; 1995 and 1998 at Darat al Funun; 2000 at the Gallery.

397 Pam Dougherty, Ali Jabri at the National Gallery, 'What Kind of Future Do We Leave Our children?', *The Jerusalem Star Newspaper*, June 16, 1983.

398 Salameh, Ne'matt, Gifts Left By Time: Ali Jabri at Darat Al Funun, *The Jordan Times Newspaper*, July 1, 1995.

399 Rami Sajdi, a friend, brought the jars and the incense, but the idea and its execution were Ali's.

400 Hans Morgenthaler, 'Peter Eisenman's Realist Architecture', The Stanford Presidential Lectures and Symposia in the Humanities and Arts, 1998, p. 1.

401 An excerpt from the last biography Ali wrote for the 2003 Disorientation Exhibition in Berlin.

402 Interview with Aysar Akrawi, January 22, 2005. Akrawi worked with Ali on several preservation projects. She became director of the Petra National Trust in 1994. The PNT, on whose board Ali sat, is an NGO concerned with conservationist projects in historical Petra, the Nabataean city in the south of Jordan.

403 Ali al Jabri 1982 diary. Entry: September 18.

404 Ali al Jabri 1982 diary. Entry: September 12.

405 Interview with François Larche, April 11, 2004.

406 Interview with Jaafar Toukan, January 19, 2004.

407 Interview with Aysar Akrawi, January 22, 2004.

408 Ibid.

409 Ali al Jabri 1988 diary. Entry: March 23.

410 Ibid., entry: April 7.

411 Interview with Tony Atallah, February 23, 2005.

412 Ali al Jabri 1983 diary. Entry: June 22.

413 From his last biography written for the Berlin Disorientation Exhibition, 2003.

414 'Interview: Ali al Jabri, The Pain of Painters With Causes', *Eastern Art Report*, October 1990, p. 20.

415 Interview with Raghida Ghandour, May 13, 2005.

416 Ali al Jabri 1984 diary. Entry: November 22–3.

417 Recounted by Rula Atallah Ghandour (November 28, 2004), who was present at the dinner. Story was confirmed by Fadi Ghandour and Hazem Malhas, who were also present.

418 Letter from Ali al Jabri to Antonia Gaunt, July–August, 1977.

419 Interview with François Larche, April 10, 2004.

420 'Interview: Ali al Jabri', *Eastern Art Report*, p. 31.

421 The late Issam al Said (1938–1988) was one of the most celebrated Iraqi painters.

422 Diala mentions that the painted tree is in the Bisharat's farm in Yadudeh, Jordan.

423 Yourcenar, *Memoirs of Hadrian*, p. 247.

424 Another title for Um Kalthoum, the Lady in Arabic.

425 *Sah al Nawm*, which literally means 'sleep has woken', is another way of saying good morning in colloquial Arabic. It is also often used, as in the series, as a pun to alert a 'sleeper' to an obvious fact.

Index

Location references for photographs and other illustrations are entered in *italics*.

Abbasids, 195
Abdul Hamid II, Sultan, 188
Abdullah II, King, 155
Abu El Futuh, 116, 119
Abu Mohammad, 10
Abu Taeyh, Audeh, 35
Adonis, 24
al-Ahad, 184
Ain Diwar, 63, 65
Ajami, Fuad, 132
Alami, Musa: Arab Revolt
    (1916), 184; glossary entry,
    181; al Quwwatli confides in,
    74; Saadieyh's first husband,
    25, 49, 58; Wasfi al Tall works
    for, 181–2
Alawites, 78, 188
Aleppo, 45–9; Ali recalls, 101;
    anti-Jewish riots, 173;
    description, 81–2; Hala and,
    24; Jabri family and, 28;
    Saladin and, 195; as separate
    state, 188; square named after
    Saadallah, 78, 82, 145
Alexandretta, 183–4
Alexandria: Ali at college, 48, 68;
    Ali's vision, 137; Cavafy and,
    18, 119, 185; more modern
    times, 136; in the Quartet,
    134–5

*Alexandria: A History and a
    Guide* (E. M. Forster), 34
Alexandrian Quartet (Lawrence
    Durrell), 86, 111, 133–5, 137
Alia, Princess, 165
Allenby, Field Marshal Edmund,
    184
Allied Supreme Council, 196
Amal Hayati (Umm Kalthoum),
    125
Aminah, 153
Amman: Ali arrives, 148, 150;
    Ali takes photographs, 157–8;
    Hala buried, 147; hills, 17;
    mother in, 25; a painter in, 21;
    parochial nature, 143;
    rectitude, 141; Saadieyh goes
    to, 61; strangeness, 18–19
Amman-Aqaba highway, 21
Andalusia, 29
Antonia: Ali draws heart
    shapes for, 19; gets to know
    Ali's other friends, 30;
    marriage to envisaged, 110;
    meets Sara, 94; memorable
    letter to, 169; mentioned, 99;
    recollects Ali, 93–4;
    Ridgmount Gardens, 106;
    Rumm Valley, 36; secrets
    kept from, 107

Aqaba: Ali yearns for, 148;
  described at night, 32;
  development scheme, 156;
  glossary entry, 182–3; heat, 8;
  Ihsan, 48; paintings, 20–1;
  photographs in, *7, 9*
Aqbal Al Leil (Um Kalthoum),
  178
Arab Development Society, 181
Arab League, 181, 182, 194
Arab Revolts, 34–7; Ali and the
  series of, 50; glossary entry,
  183–4; Ihsan, 48; 1918
  campaigns, 21
Arabs: ability to haggle, 56;
  Alexandrian Quartet and, 134;
  Ali encaptures, 139; Ali's
  feelings of loyalty, 13; Ali's
  frustration with, 108–9; Ali's
  position on fringe, 43; Ali's up
  to date knowledge, 107; art,
  169, 170; 'descent into
  irrelevance', 4; 'evil seeming to
  come from', 5; gesture of
  respect, 12; initiation into way
  of life, 113; Lawrence and, 43–
  4; malevolence of politics, 126;
  misdirection, 113; Nasser, 120,
  122, 130–1; nationalism, 52;
  1918 Revolt, 21; sense of
  betrayal, 122; stirrings within
  Ali, 97; world of as seen by Ali,
  11, 104
Arafat, Yasser, 5, 131, 194
Area A, 196–7
Area B, 197
Arendt, Hannah, 107
Army of Salvation, 182
Arsuf, Battle of, 196
Ashrafs, 28
Ashurbanipal, King, 106

Asmahan, 111
Assad, Hafez, 76, 78, 80, 131
Assyria, 106
Atallah, Tony, 166
Atassi, Hashim, 65, 75
Averroes, 195
Awdat al Wai (Tawfiq Hakim),
  128
Awwamah, 119
al Ayam, 68
Ayla, 195
Ayyubids, 183, 195, 196
Azm, Khaled, 75

Baaths, 78
Baghdad, 56, 61, 176, 184, 194
Baldwin IV, 196
Balfour Declaration, 184, 197
al Barazan, Husni, 191
Bardot, Brigitte, 88
Basmalah, 168
Basra, 184
Batatu, Hanna, 187
Baudelaire, Charles, 32
BBC, 152
Beardsley, Aubrey, 87
Beckett, Samuel, 147
Bedouin, 46
Beirut: Ali's interest in, 169, 173;
  Community School and
  University, 97;
Damascus and, 46; Greater
  Lebanon, 187
Bekaa Valley, 188
Bell, Gertrude, 52
Berlin, 21
Bilbeisi House, 163
Biltaji, Aqel, 20
bin Yehya, Ahmad, 76
'Black September', 5
Blackmur, R. P., 44

Bleak House (Charles Dickens), 81
Blue Area, 196
Bonwit Teller, 24
Borges, Jorge Luis, 18
Bosra, 194
Branch, William, 89
Bristol University, 93–6; Ali
 accepted by, 92; Ali leaves,
 98–9; London compared with,
 101; Saadieyh supports Ali, 12
British Mandate, 182, 187–8
British Museum, 170
Buñuel, Luis, 179
Burckhardt, J. L., 195

Cairo: Ali moves to, 14, 23, 110;
 City of the Dead, 31–2, 185;
 Lawrence and, 46, 124; 1970s,
 131–2; Wasfi murdered, 5
Cairo Conference, 193
California, 86–7
Caliphate, 189
Camp David, 132
Carchemish, 192
Castle of Otranto, The (Horace
 Walpole), 96
Cavafy, Constantine P.:
 Alexandria the myth, 137; Ali's
 diary entriess, 34; *The City*, 18;
 glossary entry, 184–5; kindred
 spirit, 119
Chapman, Thomas, 192
Churchill, Winston, 56, 187, 193
Citadel, The, Aleppo, 81
City, The (Constantine P. Cavafy),
 18
City of the Dead, Cairo, 31–2,
 120, *121*, 185
Clemenceau, Georges, 54
Coates, Mr, 89–92
Coates, Mrs, 89–92

Cold War, 190
Cole, USS, 176
Conrad of Montferrat, 196
Constantinople, 194 – *see also*
 Istanbul
Constructive Enterprise, 182
Copts, 134
Cornell, Joseph, 171
Creative Experiment, The (C. M.
 Bowra), 34
Cromer, Lord, 124
Curzon, George Nathaniel,
 Marquess, 185–6
Curzon Street, London, 13

Dahoum, 39, 41, 42
Damanhour, 30
Damascus: Aleppo and, 45, 188,
 195; Beirut and, 46; Hijaz rail-
 way, 193; Lawrence claims from
 Feisal, 56; McMahon and, 184;
 Turkish troops surrender, 186
Dante Alighieri, 195
Darat al Funun, 163
Darwish, Mahmoud, 172
Dawalibi, Marouf, 76
Day'it Tishrine (Duraid
 Lahham), 29, 191
de Pres, Terence, 107
*Decline and Fall of the Roman
 Empire* (Edward Gibbon), 154
Department of Publications, 182
al Din, Nur, 195
al Din Zengi, Imad, 195
Diney, 19, 93, 94, 99
*Discreet Charm of the Bourgeoisie,
 The* (Luis Buñuel), 179
'Disorientation', 21
'Diversity of Iraqis, The, the
 Incohesiveness of their Society
 and their Progress in the

Monarchical Period Towards a
Consolidated Political Structure'
(*Modern Middle East*), 187
Dollar, John, 98
Dome of the Rock, 35
Druze, 190
Durrell, Lawrence, 34, 134–5,
    137, 185 – *see also* Alexandrian
    Quartet

'Easter Hymn' (A. E. Housman), 1
Eastern Art Report, 169–70
Eban, Abba, 25
Egypt, 113–15, 120–38; Alex-
    andrian Quartet's depiction,
    135; Majddedine, 78; Nasser,
    120, 122, 125, 131, 135, 136;
    new order, 132; two Egypts,
    137–8
Eisenman, Peter, 163
Elizabeth II, Queen, 156
Ernst, Max, 171
Essa, 19, 30

Fadi, 19, 159
Fahd, Crown Prince, 145
Fairmount Hotel, San Francisco,
    89
Fairouz, 29, 186
Farouk, King, 66, 123, 124
Far'oun, 183
Fatimids, 195
Fattah, Ismail, 170
Fawzieh, Empress of Iran, 66–7
Feisal, ibn al Hussein I, King of
    Iraq, 53–7; Aqaba seized, 183;
    Arab
Revolts, 35–6; character, 55; end
    of reign, 116; glossary entry,
    186–7; Ihsan and, 75–6;
    Lawrence and, 35–6, 38, 50,

53, 192–3; mentioned, 41;
    photograph, *55*
Fez, 34
Fisk, Robert, 176
Forster, E. M., 185
Fort Kayet Bay, 136
France, 54–7; Saadallah on, 63;
    sphere of influence, 186; Syria,
    52, 184, 187–8
François, 19, 30, 161
Frank, 93, 96, 99
French Mandate, 48, 64–7, 186,
    187–8
French Mandate, The (P. Khoury),
    188
al Fustat, 185

Garcia Marquez, Gabriel, 74
Gattopadro, Il (Guiseppe Tomasi
    di Lampedusa), 63, 64
Gauguin, Paul, 32
Gaza, 176, 195
Genet, Jean, 32, 160
Geneva, 57, 62
George and Mary, 99
Ghor, 24 – *see also* Jordan Valley
Goya, Francisco de, 32, 88
Grateful Dead, 88
Greater Lebanon, 187

Haidar, Sharif Ali, 189
Hajj, 168
Hakim, Tawfiq, 128
Halabi, Jabir, 28
Halabi, Lisa – *see* Noor, Queen
Hama, 45, 184, 188, 197
Hananu, Ibrahim, 81
al Hariri, Rafik, 176
Hashemites: Ali in Amman, 150;
    Ali, Lawrence and, 33; Ali
    paints, 36, 52; Ali's love for,

155 158–9; Aouni branch, 188;
Aqaba, 183; dreams, 35, 52;
end of, 116; England forsakes,
56; Ihsan and, 53; Jabris,
Lawrence and, 50; kingdom
189, 190; Lawrence, 56; Wasfi
al Tall, 181, 182
Hassan (grandson of Prophet
Mohammad), 188
Hattin, Battle of, 195, 196
Hayward Gallery, 106
Hazem, 19, 30, 34
Hellenism, 184
Hijaz: Ihsan invited to, 146;
Ma'an, 193; Ottomans, 188–9;
railway, 184;
Saladin in, 195: Sharif Hussain,
56
Hittites, 46
Hogarth, D. G., 192
Holocaust, 107
Homs, 45, 184, 188, 197
Hourani, Akram, 70
Hourani, Albert, 92, 154
Hourani, Cecil, 154
House of World Cultures, Berlin,
21
Housman, A. E., 1
Hummuda, Yahya, 194
Hussein ibn Ali, Sharif, of Mecca,
54–6; glossary entry, 188–9;
Ottomans, 53; 1916 Revolt, 35;
Sir Henry McMahon and, 183–
4, 188–9
Hussein ibn Talal, King of
Jordan: death, 155–9; glossary
entry, 190; perplexed perhaps
by Ali, 37; PLO and, 5;
sympathetic character of, 159;
Wasfi al Tall and, 6, *9*, 182; as
young man, 35

Hussein, Saddam, 131

ibn al Ass, Amr, 185
ibn al Hussein, Abdullah, 35, 190
ibn al Hussein, Feisal – *see* Feisal
ibn al Hussein, King of Iraq
ibn Ali, Sharif Hussein – *see*
Hussain ibn Ali, Sharif, of
Mecca
Ibn Rushd, 195
ibn Saud, 55–6
ibn Talal, Hussein – *see* Hussein
ibn Talal, King of Jordan
Ibn Tulun mosque, 34, 163
I-Ching, 100, 101, 102, 168
'Influence of the Crusades on
European Military Architecture
to the End of the Twelfth
Century ' (T. E. Lawrence), 192
Intifada, 176
Iraq: Britain acquires, 196;
cruelty, 52; displacement crisis,
176; Feisal's kingdom, 50, 187;
Hashemites acquire, 56;
Kuwait invasion, 131
Irslan, Adel, 66–7
Irslan, Shakib, Prince, 57, 190–1
Islam: Ali tries, 168; Ali writes
about, 160; 'dust in the mouth',
120; 'empty vessel', 113; return
of old traditions, 136; a touch
of, 101
Ismail, Khedive, 124
Israel: Ali and, 97; birth of, 124;
King Hussein and, 5; 1967 war,
129; onslaught on Lebanon,
176; Palestinian conflicts, 107–
8; PLO recognises right to
exist, 194; Sadat, 132; Trans
Jordan in the days before, 25
Istanbul, 28, 53, 194

Jabal al Druze, 188

al Jabri, Alai'ddine (uncle), 8

al Jabri, Ali:

CHARACTER: altruistic
passions, 160; complexities,
30; confused desires; 99, 100;
contradictions, 158; delicacy,
4; immaturity, 99; lack of
articulacy with officialdom,
164; lack of cynicism, 172;
lifestyle desired, 105; nagging
nature, 19; practicality, lack
of, 4; romanticisms, 113; self-
absorption and its fading,
160; self-image, 167;
sexuality, 42, 119–20; a
stranger wherever he went,
43; thin-skinned nature, 15,
164

FAMILY – *see also* entries for
individual family members:
Aunt Saadieyh, 1–17, 147–
55; Ali shouted and cursed at
by, 10–11; Ali writes to, 97–
8; control over Ali, 142;
essence of relationship with,
8; her expectations of Ali, 12–
13; legacy to Ali, 1–2, 12,
155; mentioned, 57;
supported by, 99; turbulence
of relationship, 143–4, 148,
169; yin and yang, 14;
brother: dies in infancy, 25;
families: opinions on, 102,
104; *father* (Majddedine), 83,
86, 89, 92–3; *grandfather*
(Ihsan), 116, 118–19; *mother*
(Hala): accused by, 15; her
disappointment with, 92–3,
97; extracts from letters, 83,
101–2; praise from, 16;

resemblance to, 30; *sister*
(Diala): accused by, 15;
letters, 107

MISCELLANEOUS: arrested and
detained, 80–1; black
influences, 106–7;
conservation as a vocation,
160; dancing, 30, 93; death,
21–3, 171, 178; drinking, 19;
exile, use of word, 16–17,
114; hashish, love for, 96;
history, idea of, 167;
interview, 169–70; Islam,
101, 160, 168; library, 166;
physical appearance, 19, 30,
140–1; reminiscences of, 30;
stuck in rut, 17; tourism,
ideas for, 164, 165; voice, 29

PAINTING: ability at, 4; Aleppo,
absence of, 82; Arab art and,
169, 170; beauty, 162;
destroys, 92; discovered after
death, 119; exhibitions, 162–
3; Hashemites, 36, 52; hatred
of selling, 166; Jordan's
history, 161; Mamluks, 136;
many faces in, 171; Nasser,
126–7, 129–30; nature of,
17–18; Stanford University
class, 87, 88; Umm
Kalthoum, 111–12, 178

PEOPLE AND PLACES:
Alexandria, 137; Arabs – *see*
Arabs; Bristol University,
93–6, *95*, 98–9; Durrell, 137;
Hashemites, 155, 158–9;
Jordan, 18, 139–43, 147,
169; King Hussein, 155–9;
Lawrence, 32–46; Nasser,
123; Stanford University, 83,
86–9; Wasfi al Tall, 8

PHOTOGRAPHS OF: Aqsa
Mosque Jerusalem, early
1960s, *3*; author and, *140*;
City of the Dead, *121*; London
1970s, *103*; mid-1950s with
father, *71*; passport, *84–5*;
Petra, *23*; rifles, *162*; Rugby
School, *72–3*; six years old,
69; skiing, *69*; working, *33*; as
young child, *27*

al Jabri, Alia (cousin), 26

al Jabri, Diala (sister): Ali's
paintings, 92; blames Ali and
Saadieyh, 15; a Christian falls
in love with, 168; epilogue, 172–
9; finds Ali dead, 22; hearsay
according to, 60; Ihsan's death,
145; in Kuwait, 15; letters, 16,
107, 175; mentioned, 2; told
stories by Hala, 58; a tortured
soul, 14; university, 14; voice,
29; Wasfi's house, 151, *151*;
Wasfi's love for, 8; with Ali and
Wasfi, *9*

al Jabri, Hala (mother), 58–62;
Ali at Stanford, 89; Ali feels
for, 14; Ali resembles, 30; Ali
sent to Austria, 92; America,
60–1, 172; blames others and
blamed herself, 15; character,
60; death, 147; describes Ali
flatteringly, 16; Ihsan's death,
145; illusion of serenity, 57; a
liberated woman, 24; mentions
possibility of suicide, 58; as
mother to Ali, 2; a painting
based on, 92; Palestine, 62;
photographs, *27, 59*; pride in
Saadallah, 67; university
degree, 49; as a young woman,
25

al Jabri, Ihsan (grandfather): Ali
stays with, 116, 118–19; Cairo,
110 – *see*
also Nile apartment; complains
about Ali, 116, 118; complains
about Hala, 60; death, 76, 78,
143–5; Feisal and, *55*, 75–6;
Geneva, 57, 62; Gertrude Bell
on, 52; Hala and, 58; Hashemites and, 53; lack of dignity,
75; Nile apartment, 31, 108,
115 – *see also* Cairo; Ottoman
connections and switch, 48–9,
116; Permanent European
Delegation, 191; photographs:
with Feisal, *55*, with leopard,
77, with Nasser, *117*, with
Saadallah, *51*, with Saadieyh,
59

al Jabri, Kamal (grandfather), 49

al Jabri, Majddedine (father): Ali
at Stanford and, 83, 86, 89; Ali
not enough of a 'man', 93;
death, 8, 97, 151; Kuwait, 173–
4; mentioned, 4, 61; 1940s, 24;
partners, 15; photographs, *51,
71, 79*; protects Jews, 173;
public office, 48, 49, 70, 78, 82;
slaps Ali, 92

al Jabri, Nafe' (great
grandfather), 49

al Jabri, Nawal (cousin), 81

al Jabri, Saadallah (great uncle),
64–8: Aleppo square named
after, 78, 82, 145; Arab
inclinations, 53; death, 75;
diary entry on Hala, 60–1;
mentioned, 80; photograph, *51*;
political career, 48; prison, 62;
quoted, 63; speaks up in court,
81

al Jabri, Saadieyh – *see* Al Tall,
    Saadieyh al Jabri
al Jabri, Subheiyeh, 57
al Jabri family, 48–50; Ali promises
    to remember, 13, 14; Ali
summarises, 48; bad blood, 8, 16;
    chronicles of, 28–9; drama of
    encapsulated, 144; family tree,
    26, 28; Hashemites and, 53–4;
    just 'dust in the mouth', 17;
    memories, 154; opinions on
    Nasser, 122; pain and sadness,
    2, 4; wielding levers of power,
    52
Jamil, 6
Jericho, 25
Jerusalem: Abdullah ibn al
    Hussein assassinated, 190;
    Arab Office, 181;
Arab quarter, 58; Hala's pre-
    natal treatment, 25; Palestine
    and, 156; Saadieyh moves from,
    61; Saladin's assault, 195–6;
    Sykes-Picot Agreement, 197
Jesus Christ, 25
Jesus College, Oxford, 192
John, 19, 30, 93, 99
Jordan – *see also* Trans Jordan:
    Ali's mixed feelings for, 18,
    139–43, 147,
169; Ali's paintings, 161;
    'degenerative urbanism', 21;
    modern state ushered in, 35,
    160–1; nature of, 16–17; prime
    minister assassinated, 5;
    Transjordan becomes, 190
Jordan Museum of Popular
    Traditions, 148
Jordan Valley, 42, 63 – *see also*
    Ghor
Joshua, Prophet, 148

Jouvenel, Bertrand de, 52
Junner, Sara, 192

Kaa'ba, 35
Kalthoum, Umm: Ali initiated,
    177–8; Ali's painting, 169;
    compared to Nasser, 125;
    compared to other singers,
    111–12; mentioned, 175
Karnak, 34
Kassak Ya Watan (Duraid
    Lahham), 191
Kate, 93, 94
Keeley, Edmund, 136, 137
Kermani, Navid, 125–6
Khalaf, Salah, 6
Khaldieh, 144, 145
Khalid, King, 145
Knights Templar, 196
al Kouddouss, Ihsan Abd, 133
Kroll, Jack, 160
Kuwait: Ali in, 97; Diala and
    Hala in, 15; Iraqi invasion, 131;
    Majddedine moves to, 49, 78;
    memories of, 173–4

Ladbroke Grove, 30
Lahham, Duraid, 29, 191
Laing, Sir Maurice, 86
Lancaster, Burt, 64
Las Meninas (Diego Velasquez),
    92
Lawrence, T. E, 32–50; Aleppo,
    45–7; Ali and, 37; Cairo, 124;
    Feisel and, 50, 53; French and,
    55; glossary entry, 192–3;
    hidden character of, 38–9;
    Ma'an, 20; mentioned, 29;
    peace in Middle East, 56;
    perspective on Arab world, 43–
    4; speculations on sexuality, 41

Lawrence of Arabia and his World
  (Richard Perceval Graves), 34
League of Nations, 187, 191
Lebanon, 176, 184, 186–7, 196
Leigh Woods, 30, 94
Lempicka, Tamara de, 111
Lloyd George, David, 54
London Designers Collection, 109
Lulwa, Sheikha, 173

Ma'an, 19, 20, 193
al Maghout, Mohammad, 191
Majlis Mabou'than, 49
Mamluks, 47, 136, 183, 196
Massad, Joseph, 142
Maysaloun, Battle of, 187
McMahon, Sir Henry, 183–4, 189
McMahon Pledge, 183–4
Mecca, 52, 193
Medina, 193
Mehmet V, 48, 116, 145
Merzbau, 18
Mint, The (T. E. Lawrence), 34,
  193
Mohammad, Ayesha, 10
Mohammad, Prophet, 28, 188
Mongols, 47
Montgisard, Battle of, 196
Morganthaler, Hans, 163
Mosul, 54, 197
Mother McCree's Uptown Jug
  Champions, 88
Muhsin, 11
Mukheibeh, 170
Mukhabarrat, 157
Muqaddissi, 182
Murad IV, 194
Murad, Leila, 112
Mysterious Mother (Horace
  Walpole), 96

Nabataeans: Aqaba, 183; gods,
  35; incense jars, 163; Petra, 20,
  194
Nasser, Gamal Abdel, 120–32;
  achievements, 127, 128;
  Alexandrian Quartet and, 135;
  Ali on, 123; Aqaba, 20;
  disillusionment after, 178; early
  ambitions, 115; effect on
  Egypt, 120–32, 136; emergence
  of, 190; excuses himself, 128–9;
  Ihsan's sycophancy, 49, 76,
  146; king of his own hill, 16;
  oratory, 125–6; Palestine, 125;
  photograph, *117*; power handed
  to, 75; reputation, 131; Umm
  Kalthoum and, 111, 112; view
  of Egypt's past, 111; Wasfi al
  Tall's hostility, 182
National Gallery, Jordan, 18
National Portrait Gallery, 34
Nawal, 19, 170
Noor, Queen, 37, 156
Nuha, 19

Osman I, 194
O'Toole, Peter, 38
Ottomans: Ali describing
  Saadieyh, 8; Allenby's
  campaign, 184; Aqaba under,
  183; Arabs and, 29, 187;
  Caliphate, 189; Feisal
  coordinates campaign against
  with Allies, 186; glossary entry,
  194; Ihsan and, 48–9, 53, 116;
  deserts; al Jabri family origins,
  28; San Remo Conference, 196;
  Shakib Irslan and, 190–1

Palestine: Ali's sympathy, 107–8;
  Arab regimes and, 130; Army

of Salvation, 182; Balfour
Declaration, 184; Black
September, 5–6; Britain
acquires, 196; Egypt and, 122,
124; Feisal, 53; Hala promises,
62; Musa Alami and, 181;
Nasser, 125; 1948 refugees,
190; 1967, 156; orange groves,
29; 60 years old?, 178; to be
torn apart, 57; Trans Jordan
and, 25; Zionists, 54, 186
Palestine Liberation Organisation
(PLO), 5, 6, 181, 194
Paris, 141, 147, 150
Paris Peace Conference, 186,
189, 192, 196
Pasa, Cemal, 49
Perencel-Hugo, Jean Pierre, 114,
139
Permanent European Delegation,
191
Persephone, 11
Petit Prince, Le (Antoine de St
Exupery), 172
Petra: Ali and *23*; Ali's grave, 23,
50, 180; glossary entry, 194–5;
horse hospital, 166; love for, 19;
Nabataean stones, 20
Pharos, 136
Picot, François-Georges, 196

Qasr-al-Abd, 161
al Quwwatli, Shukri, 74, 75

Radi, Nuha, 170
Raghida, 19, 30, 147, 170
al Rafiq, Aoun, 188
Ram's Head Theatrical Society, 88
Raynald of Chatillon, 196
Red Sea, 21
Regardz, Beth, 26, 91

'Remembering the First Century'
(Adonis), 24
Richard I, King, 196
Rick, 106
Rida, Rashid, 53
Ridgmount Gardens, *103*, 106
Robert College, Istanbul, 49
Roberts, David, 34
Ronnie, 19, 106
Rugby School, *72–3*, 89
Rula, 19, 158
Russ (dog), 25

Sa Narji'ou Yawman (Fayrooz),
29
Sabaeans, 193
al Sabah, Sheikh Fahd, 49, *79*,
173, 174
Sadat, Anwar, 126, 132, 136
Safavids, 194
Sagan, Françoise, 133
Sahh al Nawm, 191
Said, Edward, 34, 44, 130, 131
al Said, Issam, 170
Saladin, 26, 47, 195–6
Salah, Fadwa, 6
Salt, 148
San Remo Conference, 196
Sartre, Jean-Paul, 160
al Saud, Abd al Aziz, 146, 189
Saudi Arabia, 56, 189
Sayyegh, George, 17
Schwitters, Kurt, 18
Seale, Partick, 67
Seljuk Turks, 47, 195
Seven Pillars of Wisdom, The
(T. E. Lawrence), 33, 34, 36,
39–42, 193
Seville Exhibition 1992, 166
Sèvres, Treaty of, 194
Shahid, Serene Hussein, 58, 60

Sharafat, 58, 60
al Sharif, Omar, 38
Sheraton Hotel, Cairo, 5
Shiites, 195
Shirkuh, 195
Shmeisani, 30
Shukeiri, Ahmad, 194
Silent Sirens (Navid Kermani),
   125
Simone, Nina, 10
Siwwi, Adel, 170
Sontag, Susan, 88
Sparta, 102
St Exupery, Antoine de, 172
Stanford University, 26, 83, 86–9
Storrs, Sir Ronald, 54
Struggle for Syria, The (Patrick
   Seale), 67
Suez Canal, 183, 184
Sunnis, 74, 195
Sweileh, 151–2, *151*
Switzerland, 68
Sykes, Mark, 196
Sykes-Picot agreement:
   England's reluctance to alter,
   193; French and British, 186;
   glossary entry, 196–7; loose
   ends left, 54; McMahon Pledge
   and, 184
Syria, 74–7; Ayyubids, 196; Class
   A mandates, 196; crossroads,
   68; Feisal attempts to form
   government, 186–7; France, 52,
   184, 187–8; French Mandate,
   64–5; Lawrence, Feisal and, 50;
   Lawrence visits, 192; Nasser,
   115; 1949, 70; 1950s, 78;
   Saladin conquers, 195; *Seven
   Pillars of Wisdom*, 41
Syrian National Congress, 186
Syro-Palestinian Congress, 191

Talal, King, 35
al Tall, Saadieyh al Jabri (aunt)
   – *see also* al Jabri, Ali, 1–17,
   147–55; Ali staying with Ihsan
   and, 116, 118; Aqaba 1960s, *7*;
   Aqsa Mosque Jerusalem, early
   1960s, *3*; character of, 150;
   control over Ali, 142;
   correspondence with Diala, 16;
   death, 141; dementia, 2, 154;
   essence of relationship with Ali,
   8; expectations of Ali, 12–13;
   full of life, 177; houses in
   Palestine, 25; Ihsan's death,
   145; illusion of serenity, 57–9;
   leaves Palestine, 61; legacy to
   Ali, 1–2, 12, 155; letters from
   Ali, 98–9; loneliness, 150;
   marriage, 49, 182; photograph,
   59; physical appearance, 2;
   pride in Saadallah, 67; shouts
   at and curses Ali, 10–11;
   supports Ali, 99; turbulence of
   relationship with Ali, 143–4,
   148, 169; yin and yang with
   Ali, 14
al Tall, Wasfi, 5–13, 151–5; Ali's
   death and, 23; assassinated, 5–
   6, 143, 151, 178; glossary
   entry, 181–2; Hashemite
   credentials, 182; magnificence
   of house, 151–5, *151*;
   Mausoleum, *149*; photographs,
   7, 9; Saadieyh marries, 49;
   Saadieyh's love for, 61;
   strength of, 177
Tapline, 70
al Tawsheh, Ghawwar, 191
Tikrit, 195
Tlas, Mustafa, 81
Tobiads, 161

Trans Jordan – *see also* Jordan:
  British acquire, 187, 196;
  Feisal and, 53; Hashemites, 56,
  190; Ma'an, 193; semi-British
  protectorate, 25; supply lines
  from Aqaba, 183
Tueni, Ghassan, 128
Turks – *see* Ottomans
Tyre, 196

Ulemmas, 28
United Arab Republic, 49, 76,
  102, 116
United Nations, 176
Urabi, Colonel, 124

Vassar College, New York, 25,
  49, 60
Velasquez, Diego, 88, 92
Victoria College, Alexandria, 68,
  123, 155
Vol de Nuit (Antoine de Saint
  Exupery), 172

Wadi Rumm, 35, 36, 37–8, 166
Wahhabis, 55

Wajdi, Anwar, 112
Walpole, Horace, 96
Waterson, Sara, 93, 94, 96, 98
Weizman, Ezer, 197
Weizmann, Chaim, 57, 197
Wexner Center for the Visual
  Arts, 163
Widad, 19
Wilde, Oscar, 106
Wilson, Jeremy, 34, 41
Wind Among the Reeds, The
  (W. B. Yeats), 170–1
Wolley, Leonard, 192
World Jewish Organisation, 197

Yeats, W. B., 170
Yemen, 49, 76, 116
Young Turks, 183, 189
Yourcenar, Marguerite, 34, 185

Zaghloul, Saad Pasha, 124
al-Zahir Ghazi, Al Malik, 47, 81
Zaidis, 188–9
Zaim, Husni, 74–5
Zengids, 195
Zionists, 54, 186, 190, 197